Studia
Linguistica
Universitatis
Iagellonicae
Cracoviensis

128
(2011)

Studia
Linguistica
Universitatis
Iagellonicae
Cracoviensis

Jagiellonian University Press

REVIEWERS
Elżbieta Chrzanowska-Kluczewska (Jagiellonian University, Cracow)
Danuta Gabryś-Barker (University of Silesia, Katowice)
Elżbieta Mańczak-Wohlfeld (Jagiellonian University, Cracow)
Marek Stachowski (Jagiellonian University, Cracow)
Elżbieta Tabakowska (Jagiellonian University, Cracow)
Ewa Willim (Jagiellonian University, Cracow)

COVER DESIGNER
Paweł Bigos

TECHNICAL EDITOR
Mirosław Ruszkiewicz

PROOFREADER
Kamil Stachowski

TYPESETTER
Kamil Stachowski

The publication of this journal was financed by the Faculty of Philology
of the Jagiellonian University.

The editor declares the paper version to be the original one.

ISBN 978-83-233-3255-8
ISSN 1897-1059

www.wuj.pl

Wydawnictwo Uniwersytetu Jagiellońskiego
Redakcja: ul. Michałowskiego 9/2, 31-126 Kraków
tel. 12-631-18-81, tel./fax 12-631-18-83
Dystrybucja: tel. 12-631-01-97, tel./fax 12-631-01-98
tel. kom. 506-006-674, e-mail: sprzedaz@wuj.pl
Konto: PEKAO SA, nr 80 1240 4722 1111 0000 4856 3325

CONTENTS

Studia Linguistica Universitatis Iagellonicae Cracoviensis
128 (2011)

MARTA DĄBROWSKA
Jagiellonian University, Cracow

LANGUAGE ECONOMY IN SHORT TEXT MESSAGES

Keywords: short text message, language economy, shortening strategies, contrastive study

Abstract

The purpose of this paper is to investigate some of the formal characteristics of the genre of the short text message, with a special focus on the concept of language economy, which typically underlies the use of this mode of communication. The subject of analysis are text messages in two languages, English and Polish, which are compared in terms of the methods of text shortening used by the two language systems. The elements studied include word clippings, vowel deletion, word-letter substitution, word-number substitution, spelling simplification, and pronoun deletion. The aim is to establish the preferred options in the two languages and identify reasons for such choices.

Used mainly in private communication, short text message language is an infrequent subject of study (cf. Thurlow and Brown 2003, Baron 2008). When analysing Computer Mediated Communication (CMC), a new channel of communication – and for some even a new genre (cf. e.g. Crystal 2001) – researchers focus more on the language of electronic media in general, especially the language used in Instant Messaging, chatrooms or discussion lists, etc. (cf. Baron 2008). One of the most extensive studies devoted to short text message language and its numerous aspects to date is the book *Txtng. The Gr8 Db8* written by Crystal (2008), which has served as the basis of my analysis. Interesting observations concerning the form and use of text messages, especially in the American and Japanese context, are to be found in Baron (2008). A brief analysis concerning the purpose as well as the formal characteristics of text messages is also provided by Biber and Conrad (2009). All refer to a paper by Thurlow (2003), one of the earliest studies on the subject, which offers useful information concerning the reasons for texting and the forms of text messages in British English. Besides, worth mentioning are also works by

Ling (2005, 2007) on the use of text messages and predictive texting in Norwegian, as well as the analysis of text adaptations in short text messages found in Swedish by Hård af Segerstad (2002).

Texting may involve numerous linguistic phenomena. One of them are borrowings from one language into another, as e.g. borrowings from English into Polish (cf. Dąbrowska 2004), another the question of linguistic inventiveness (cf. Thurlow and Brown 2003, Crystal 2008) or the influence of texting and the CMC on the communicative patterns of youth and the decline of literacy (cf. Baron 2008). Moreover, its analysis may contribute to the discussion concerning specific registers (cf. Biber and Conrad 2009). Finally, as my paper will demonstrate, the analysis of text messages may provide interesting data concerning language economy. As Crystal (2008: 65) says, the keyboard was originally created not for texting, but for calculating, therefore communicating by means of messages written with the help of the keypad is not the most natural thing. Sending a text message costs money, so the longer the message, the more expensive it will be. Additionally, most mobile phones have a limited number of characters per text, usually around 160 (cf. Thurlow and Brown 2003). However, as Thurlow (2003) claims, the average length of text messages in British English is only around 65 characters, and up to 46 in Norwegian (cf. Ling 2007). The primary consideration accounting for the limited length of text messages must therefore be that it is an uncomfortable and time-consuming activity (cf. Crystal 2008, Dąbrowska 2010). For this reason text message users have developed a number of abbreviation strategies. Linguistic shortening is not a new phenomenon in the context of the English language, it was, for instance, often observed and even commented upon publicly (in negative terms), e.g. in the period of the Restoration, as was the case with, for instance, Jonathan Swift (cf. Baugh and Cable 2002: 259–260, Crystal 2008: 51–52). To date, linguists have primarily analysed the shortening of text messages in the English medium (Thurlow and Brown 2003, Ling and Baron 2007, Baron 2008, Crystal 2008, Biber and Conrad 2009). There are also some data available in other languages, viz. in German (Döring 2002), Swedish (Hård af Segerstad 2002), and Norwegian (Ling 2005), however, their limited number and sometimes rather scanty characteristics may lead to the assumption that the same type of shortenings are to be observed in any language. As the following analysis will prove, however, identical strategies cannot be shared by all languages in which messages are composed, or may be shared to a different degree (cf. Crystal 2008). The purpose of this paper is thus to examine text messages written in English and in Polish in terms of the shortening strategies used, provide their classification and frequency, and find possible answers as to why certain choices are typically made or avoided in the two respective languages.

The following analysis was based on 100 examples of messages with at least one shortened element in them – 52 in English and 48 in Polish. Altogether 94 individual examples of various abbreviations were found in the Polish text messages, and as many as 184 in those written in English. In the case of the Polish messages they were all written by native speakers of Polish, friends, family, and colleagues (which immediately implies a certain degree of solidarity and informality, of which the shortening is a manifestation), aged between 25 and 60, whereas the messages written in English were generated by users of English as a first language (Great Britain, the USA), English as a second language (India, Kenya), and English as a foreign language (Poland, Ukraine, Romania). The discrepancy between the number of examples of shortening in each of the two languages, despite an almost identical number of sample messages, shows immediately that there is a much greater preference (as well as possibly linguistic means) to economise on the length of text messages in English rather than in Polish. It must be noted that while the English messages (65 of which were analysed in total) came from the period between Jan–May 2010 (i.e. 5 months only), it was necessary to examine the Polish messages over a period of 11 months (July 2009 – May 2010), which meant scanning as many as 230 messages, in order to find a more or less matching number of abbreviated texts. It is already at this point that we can see a difference between the two languages in terms of the options they offer as well as their users' strategies.

This paper is divided into a number of sections, each focusing on particular categories of shortenings appearing in the English and then in the Polish messages, respectively. An initial comparison of categories identified in the two groups indicates differences between them, and the detailed analysis attempts to establish reasons for the choices made. Additionally, after presentation of the classification some comments are offered on the subject of ethnic as well as gender preferences for the given types of abbreviations.

Text messages in English

Clippings and contractions

The most natural option for making words shorter is to clip or contract them, typically by cutting off the ending or the second part of the word, and more seldom also the beginning, or a middle part of it. English words of foreign origin tend to be longer than native Germanic vocabulary, and are the most likely candidates for clippings. This method can also be used with some parts of speech characterised by additional endings like adjectives and adverbs. The examples of clippings and contractions (17 of them) found in the material are represented by the following:

1. Some work *tomo* and then back to pune [tomorrow]
2. Looks like there is a long delay in your *pol* cell [Polish]
3. Now in a *resto* [restaurant]
4. Wrt dwn hotel *add* [address]
5. Hope all well *wi* [with] u
6. xtra thx za *vege* [vegetarian]
7. will leave the other at the station if *poss* [possible]
8. Yes, all well, hotel right *opp* [opposite] museum
9. Yes, correct. In *govt* [government] schools it wud be the 2nd or 3rd *lang* [language]
10. tickets are *approx* [approximately] £65
11. Before you book *pl* [please] give me the price

12. **Pl** [please] be safe **sis** [sister]
13. Don't know **exact** [exactly], but yr nephew **comp** [computer] expert will. If not **comp** [computer] guys/shop by church
14. until **v** [very] late on Sunday **eve** [evening]

The above material contains examples of other types as well, but it can be seen that this group of abbreviations is still quite sizeable with 17 examples out of 184 altogether. As stated above, the words clipped and contracted would mainly include longer words of foreign origin, and thus among the words found here are examples such as *address, approximately, computer, exactly, government, language, opposite, please, restaurant, vegetarian*, with just a minimal number of Germanic vocabulary, such as *evening, sister, tomorrow*, and *with*. It can thus be seen that the trimming of the syllable or syllables significantly shortens the words and no doubt saves the sender the problem of possible mistakes with a complicated spelling, and, most importantly, contributes to the speed of message typing. The above examples appear to be quite typical words with high frequencies of use in the language, therefore their predominantly clipped form should not on the whole cause difficulties with their proper interpretation. In the case of a few, e.g. *add* and *resto* it is the context that will help the addressee decide what they refer to (cf. Crystal 2008). The presence of forms like *tomo* can be understandable on account of their length, whereas elements like *pl* and *v* may be explained by their high frequency. The word *sis*, on the other hand, is in fact more of a term of endearment as a form of address, rather than just a shortening, similar to other forms which are often subjected to the strategy of a clipping, e.g. *bro, ma, pa*, etc. This strategy is surely the simplest and least risky of all.

Vowel omission

The strategy of deleting sounds and notably vowels from long words results in forms which may be more difficult to decipher. It is therefore found with items of vocabulary which are more predictable due to their high frequency of use in language. As these collected examples (38 in all) show, vowel omission concerns mainly auxiliaries / function words and some set phrases:

1. I got your **msg** [message] and 7 is fine.
2. Looks like there is a long delay in your pol cell **msgs** [messages]
3. So u'll reach by 9 **thn** [then]. **Wrt dwn** [write down] hotel add
4. I m **vry** [very] sory
5. can u met me **nw** [now] bqz after one hour I **hve** [have] 2 go out of Delhi
6. I **m** [am] in **trffic** [traffic]
7. We **r** [are] at lunch still **nd** [and] **wl** [will] end late
8. **Wl** [will] cal
9. Ya I **hv** [have] to know exact no by 4.30 as cook **cming** [coming]
10. **pls** [please] text me
11. so sorry u **cdn't** [couldn't] b with us

12. ***xtra*** [extra] ***thx*** [thanks] za vege
13. certainly ***wl*** [will] ***b*** [be] ***n*** [in] ***tch*** [touch] … ***Hpy*** [happy] ***jrny*** [journey] u take ***Cr*** [care]
14. I look ***fwd*** [forward] to seeing ur photo
15. OK 16.30 więc c u ***tmrw*** [tomorrow]
16. Mobile ***dischargd*** [discharged]
17. ***gd*** [good] ***mng.*** [morning]

With 46 items, this is certainly a considerably larger group than the previous one. The strategy itself is not new, either – it has long been observed (cf. Crystal 2008: 26–27) that it is relatively easy to decipher a message built out of consonants only, as they are the main message carriers, whereas it is in fact impossible to do so if we remove all the consonants and retain only vowels (Arabic or Hebrew words are spelled only with consonants). It can be seen that indeed the most popular items here are either words typically associated with the text message medium, as e.g. *message*, or simple functional vocabulary such as auxiliaries *will*, *have*, the linking word *and*, adverbs like *tomorrow* and *now*, and also such popular words as *forward* and *morning*. The remaining vocabulary most often comprises short words, as *are*, *be*, *back*, *down*, *extra*, *from*, *good*, *how*, *in*, *touch*, *very*, *write*, etc., where in most cases only one vowel has to be deleted, and therefore the message remains clear (it has to be added at this point that due to their length examples like *r*, *b*, *m* can be classified as members of the vowel omission as well as the word-letter substitution category discussed below). With more complex and lesser-used words only one vowel gets deleted, viz. *dischargd*, *cming* or *trffic*. It can be concluded, therefore, that this strategy has its limitations; on the other hand, however, it may be fairly safely applied in the case of the English language, which tends to contain a large percentage of short, often monosyllabic words.

Word-letter substitution

This strategy appears to be related mainly to the above-mentioned fact, i.e. that the English language contains a large percentage of monosyllabic words. This makes it fairly easy to find words which sound like individual letters of the English alphabet, and at the same time makes it impossible for many other languages which use longer words and are additionally inflected (i.e. receive various endings), to utilise this strategy. The list of examples (51) below shows, though, that the words which typically get substituted this way are fairly limited in number:

1. will certainly pray 4 ***u*** [you]
2. When ***u*** [you] come it wud be ideal if ***u*** [you] came at least two days before the conference
3. ***U*** [you] must come!
4. This ***s*** [is] my swiss mobile. Let me know if ***u*** [you] get this text alright
5. These 'cannot be displayed' msgs frm ***u*** [you] shud ***b*** [be] sum icons.
6. Ok wish u [you] happy flight. Hope ***c*** [see] ***u*** [you] sun.

7. can *u* [you] meet me nw bqz after one hour I hve 2 go out of Delhi. Re *u* [you] in *d* [the] hotel I *m* [am] near of Sunny. I sent *u* [you] sms this morning hve *u* [you] got?
8. We *r* [are] at lunch still nd wl end late. Wl cal in *d* [the] evening
9. we *r* [are] going out at friends place for lunch…
10. so sorry *u* [you] cdn't *b* [be] with us. But it seems *u* [you] had a lot on.
11. Go 4 help, they *r* [are] nice
12. OK 16.30 więc *c* [see] *u* [you] tmrw
13. *c* [see] *u* [you] tonite
14. *Cu* [see you] in Geneva
15. *R* [are] *u* [you] back in delhi? How was *d* [the] trip?

It can be seen that with as many as 51 examples of this strategy the variety of options is in fact very small, as it comprises only 7 different elements. The most frequent one, which seems to have become almost an officially acknowledged marker of the electronic code is the second person pronoun *u*. Indeed, not everyone uses it, and at times some inconsistencies can be seen, as in "its still preferable for *u* to come to X on 15th evening, but up to *u* when *u* can come. Before *you* book pl give me the price;" however, many text message senders have accepted it so much that they have also begun forming the possessive *ur* or even the future form *u'll*. One of the most widely used markers of the short text message code is the sequence of word-letter substitutions *c u* (sometimes also spelt as one word) – the element was recorded 5 times among the analysed examples. Some bolder text message users also risk less typical word-letter substitutions in a sentence, and not in such set phrases as *c u*, i.e. words like *b* 'be', *r* 'are', *m* 'am', and *d* 'the'. The use of *s* for 'is' may in fact be just a misprint, but it may also be used as a shortening, although based, similarly as *m* and *d*, only on partial homophony (paronomasia). The use of *d* for 'the', although not matching the sound of the word in Standard English exactly, is an example of a regional pronunciation of the sound, here illustrating the Indian pronunciation of the word (cf. Crystal 2008).

Word-number substitution (logograms)

One of strategies typically enumerated in publications concerning the use of English in electronic media, and one that no doubt adds a special flavour to electronic language, is that of substituting a whole word with a single numeral. Besides the use of the word-letter substitutions discussed above, word-number substitutions are mainly responsible for the fact that electronic communication is treated as a unique form of written language. This strategy was not, however, all too frequently used in the collected samples (7 examples):

1. Hi X, just *2* [to] let you know im thinking of you
2. will certainly pray *4* [for] u. hope *2* [to] be in XXX
3. I hve *2* [to] go out of Delhi
4. which time u hve flight *2*mrw [tomorrow]

5. Go **4** [for] help, they r nice
6. hope u all had a fantastic new year and your hangovers were not **2** [too] bad.
    Iv had a couple of days off **2** [to] rest

The examples show us clearly that the number of options here is limited. The most frequently used figures are naturally *2* for the infinitival marker *to*, an Old English preposition *to* in *tomorrow* or possibly the adverb *too*; and the numeral *4* for the preposition *for*. One other option which may be found in the electronic language, though it did not appear here, is the figure *8*, typically found in the word *great – gr8*. Thus, as imaginative as the strategy is, it is not very helpful or very widespread.

Non-standard spelling

A strategy involving the modification of the spelling of words is yet another one quite often used by message senders. Unlike in other languages, e.g. Polish, where orthographic norms are to a large extent mandatory, and text message users do not as a rule flout them for the sake of shortening a message, the English language has a long tradition of spelling simplification reforms (e.g. Mulcaster or Hart in the 16th c., Webster in the 18th c. or Pitman and Ellis in the 19th c. – cf. Baugh and Cable 2002), and the fact that someone spells a word differently, thereby making the word shorter and less complicated, does not necessarily mean the person is not well educated (cf. Crystal 2008). The category is represented by 22 examples in all:

1. it **wud** [would] be ideal if u came at least two days before
2. msgs frm u **shud** [should] b **sum** [some] icons.
3. **thanx** [thanks] for call
4. wish u hapy flight. Hope c u **sun** [soon]
5. **gud** [good] morning can u met me nw bqz after one hour I hve 2 go out of Delhi
6. Much **luv** [love]
7. **Gud** [good] morning X I m in trffic I wil there 10:00 am
8. Hi X **gud** [good] evening … U **tel** [tell] me ur flight time
9. can they **tel** [tell] u by 4pm pls
10. **wil** [will] be bk by 4.30pm
11. In govt schools it **wud** [would] be the 2nd or 3rd lang
12. c u **tonite** [tonight]
13. I m vry **sory** [sorry]
14. don't **wory** [worry] u **wil** [will] reach airport on time
15. So **sory** [sorry] but we have to refuse. Wl **cal** [call] in d evening

The 22 elements may broadly be divided into a group with simplification of vowels (the more typical one) and a group with simplification of consonants. Among the words manifesting changes of vowels, the most frequent ones are *would, good, should, soon, some* and *love*. Such forms appear to be more risky inventions than modifications of the consonantal type, which basically involve only a consonant deletion or the simplification of geminated spellings, as in *will, tell, call, sorry, happy*. They may occasionally be more complex and make use of a substitution of two or three letters by one with an equivalent sound, e.g. *tonight – tonite* or *thanks – thanx*. These two are used in electronic communication so often that they have largely become conventionalised.

Deletion of pronouns and auxiliaries

Analysis of the collected examples demonstrates that strategies of shortening and simplifying text messages go beyond the level of spelling, to which all the above categories, except for the first one (clippings and contractions) belong. The remaining two types appear to also involve the level of grammar. This strategy, which is likewise quite characteristic of the casual as well as the intimate style levels, and also of slang reflected in writing, is that of pronoun deletion when in the position of the subject, typically the first person singular (cf. Joos 1959), as otherwise some confusion as to the referent might result, and occasionally of an auxiliary dropping in complex verb forms as well. This group consists of 19 examples:

1. *Looks* [it looks] like there is a long delay in your pol cell msgs. *Hope* [I hope] you reached safe and happy
2. *slept* [I slept] just enough. *Could* [I could] not charge cell till now
3. *Wish* [I wish] u hapy flight. *Hope* [I hope] c u sun.
4. *Wl* [I will] cal u in d evening
5. *Am* [I am] afraid I didn't see ur msg until v late on Sunday eve. *Hope* [I hope] all well wi u.
6. *will* [I will] send an e-mail tomorrow
7. *Have* [have you a] time to meet?
8. *will* [I will] leave the other at the station if poss
9. *Am* [I am] staying here tonight
10. *Going* [I am going] there in a bit
11. *Sounds* [it sounds] like u r having the adventure of a life time
12. *Back* [I am back] from Wales
13. Just *landed* [I have landed]

This fairly numerous group mainly involves the deletion of the personal pronoun *I*, as in *I will, I am, I could, I wish, I slept, I hope* or *it* in forms like *it sounds, it looks*, thereby making the above examples subjectless sentences, unacceptable in formal Standard English. Occasionally, the chunks deleted can be a combination of a pronoun and an auxiliary, where, for instance, there is a reference to some past activity just completed, i.e. *I have*, as in *I have just landed* or a structure with the copula *be*, e.g. *I am back* or *be* as an auxiliary verb, as in *I am going*. There is also an example of a grammatically simplified question *Have you a time to meet*, where the subject *you* is deleted. It must be noted that this method allows for quite a considerable saving of text space, and has been widely accepted in informal language, hence its visible popularity.

Apostrophe deletion

Yet another option of saving time and space while texting (although admittedly not to be compared in terms of space saving to the one above) which also involves the field of grammar is the deletion of the apostrophe, mainly in the contraction of pronouns and auxiliary verbs, and occasionally in genitive formations with nouns. Indeed, the space saved this way is minimal, therefore it may rather be seen as getting rid of a redundant feature of spelling. The incorrect spelling with the apostrophe omission in a form like *it's* can potentially be misleading. However, the context should mostly help disambiguate the meaning (cf. Thurlow and Brown 2003). This strategy is illustrated by 8 examples:

1. Hi X, just 2 let you know *im* [I'm] thinking of you
2. Oh my god X *iv* [I've] just seen the news
3. *Its* [it's] there!
4. Hi X *its* [it's] Y
5. *its* [it's] terrible
6. *its* [it's] still preferable for u to come to Sheffield
7. Hi guys *im* [I'm] back in the land of the living
8. Hi X my *friend* [friend's] name is Y

This group is certainly not very sizable. The most frequent instance is the omission of the apostrophe in the contraction of *it's* (4 examples), the others are *I'm* and *I've* (with an additional simplification of spelling) as well as one example of the nominal genitive, i.e. *friend's name*, in which case the entire genitive suffix *'s* is deleted. The presence of this type of shortening has to be acknowledged, yet its popularity seems to be surprisingly low in comparison with the results found by Baron (2008).

Text messages in Polish

Clippings and contractions

When the above plethora of options used by senders of texts in English is compared to the examples recorded in Polish, a striking difference is immediately seen. Among the analysed examples it is in fact possible to identify a maximum two types of strategies, and the first of them – the use of clippings and contractions – by far outnumbers the other. As many as 84 elements out of 94 belong to this category, which is a much greater number than that of the corresponding group of English messages, leaving the remaining strategy of the two above-mentioned ones almost unnoticeable (10 examples). With so many items it is much harder to identify typical examples within this group, as it comprises a great variety of individual words. However, on closer examination it is possible to subdivide this large number into certain subgroups which are enumerated below.

- conventional clippings and contractions (44 examples)
  1. Więc we *czw*[artek] o 13.30 *niem*[iecki]-*ang*[ielski]. – 'So on Thurs at 1.30 German-English'
  2. X ile pytań z *hist*[orii] *j*[ęzyka] *ang*[ielskiego] na *egz*[amin] chcesz sformułować? – ' X, how many questions in the history of the English language do you want to formulate for the exam?'
  3. Może znajdziesz przed wyjazdem czas na kawę np. we *wt*[orek] lub *śr*[odę]? – 'Do you think you will find some time for a coffee before your trip, e.g. on Tues or Wed?'
  4. Ja jestem gotów na spotk. w *pon*[niedziałek] lub we *wt*[orek] – 'I'm ready to meet on Mon or Tue'
  5. Ale dziś X jest pierwszy raz w X a w *niedz*[ielę] mają jakieś szkolenie – 'But it is X's first time there today, and they have some training on Sun'
  6. Jakoś się nie czuję bojowo przed tym *egz*[aminem]… w *pon*.[niedziałek] mam poprawki – 'Somehow I'm not feeling the daring spirit before this exam… I have re-sits on Mon'
  7. Ja jutro nie dam rady, w *czw*[artek] rano zdaję *j*[ęzyk] *ang*[ielski] – 'I can't tomorrow, I have my English exam on Thurs'
  8. Ja w *czw*.[artek] wieczorem jadę do *Wa*[rsza]*wy* – 'I'm going to Warsaw on Thurs evening'
  9. My po 3 *tyg*.[odniach] zwiedzania mamy dość. – 'After three weeks of sightseeing we are exhausted'
  10. Dzięki za *info*[rmację] – 'Thanks for the information'
  11. *Spoko*[jnie], czyli do jutra – 'Relax, till tomorrow then'
  12. *Pozdro*[wienia] × 2 – 'greetings'
  13. *Pozdr*[owienia]/[awiam] × 12 – 'greetings/I'm sending you my greetings'

Although the Polish language does not favour clippings and contractions as much as English does, there are some shortenings which have functioned in the language for many years on account of their frequency of use, especially in the educational context (e.g. they can be found in various documents). These examples will include firstly the shortened names of the days of the week, typically clipped to the 2–3 first letters, which are here represented by: *pon, wt, śr, czw, niedz – poniedziałek, wtorek, środa, czwartek, niedziela* (there is also *pt*, but it will be classified elsewhere), as well as the word *tyg*. (*tydzień* – in locative singular *tygodniu*) – the week itself. The other typical examples are names of school subjects such as *hist* (*historia*) and names of languages, here illustrated by (*j.*) *ang* (*angielski*) and (*j.*)*niem*. (*niemiecki*). Moreover, there are other items of vocabulary linked with education, as *egz* (*egzamin*) and *odp* (*odpowiedź*). Other than these, one can also include some items of informal language or slang here, typically heard in the language of youth, namely *info* (*informacja*) and *spoko* (*spokojnie*). To this group also belong the names of two cities *Wawa* (*Warszawa*) (the middle syllable missing) and *Krak* (*Kraków*), both of which have long been in use in informal language. Last but certainly not least, a new convention which has developed specifically in connection with the SMS language of users of Polish is a leave-taking formula (besides another option to be mentioned in a different category), viz. *pozdr(o)*, which may either come from the plural noun *pozdrowienia* or the verb in the 1st person singular *pozdrawiam*. As the examples of conventionalised abbreviations tend to be widely recognised, they do not seem to be a frequent source of ambiguity.

- innovative clippings and contractions (40 examples)
  1. Do *zoba*[czenia] × 3 – 'see you'
  2. *Ew*[entualnie], jeśli Ci bardziej pasuje – 'possibly, if it suits you better'
  3. Myślę, że *ewent*[ualnie] drugi tydzień listopada – 'I think that possibly the second week of November'
  4. *Dzie*[kuję]! Ja *pozdr*[awiam] Cię z *zimn*[ego] X, choć te -8 *st*[opni] w *por*[ównaniu] z -25 w *Kra*[kowie] jest ciepłem. *Str*[asznie] jednak marznę i *zazdr*[oszczę] Ci ciepełka! *Trz*[y]*m*[aj] się dzielnie i rob *zdj*[ęcia]. *C*[ałuję]. X – 'Thank you! I'm sending you my greetings from a cold X, although these -8 degrees in comparison with -25 in Cracow is warm. But I'm really freezing and I envy you the warmth! Hold on bravely and take photos. Kisses, X'
  5. Spoko, program od dawna mam *zainst*[alowany]. Jeszcze raz dzięki za *impr*[ez]*ę* i miłego weekendu ☺ – 'No problem, I've had this programme installed for a long time. Once again thanks for the party and have a nice weekend'
  6. Sorry ze dopiero teraz *odp*[owiadam]. Miałam straszne *ostat*[nie] 2 dni... Niestety w pt jestem w pracy od rana do *wiecz*[ora]. – 'Sorry that I'm replying only now. The last two days were terrible. Unfortunately, on Fri I'm at work from morning till evening'
  7. Wstępnie umówiliśmy się nie na najbliższy, a *nast*[ępny] tydzień – 'we have tentatively agreed to meet not this, but next week'
  8. *Serd*[ecznie] dziękuję. Pozdr – 'Heartfelt thanks. Greetings'
  9. przeglądałam te *tłumacz*[enia] – ale pomysłowi! – 'I've looked through those translations – they are really inventive'
  10. X potrzebuje to zabrać 7 *wrze*[śnia] więc chyba po twoim powrocie ok. – 'X needs to take it on 7 Sept, so it should be OK after you've returned'
  11. Cały sierpień ja zajmuję się *kaw*[iarnią], więc jestem. Dzięki za pozdr z X. – 'I am looking after the coffee-shop for the whole of August, so I'm here. Thanks for your greetings from X'

The examples found in this subgroup, i.e. 40 items, contain forms which have a very low frequency in text messages or are complete innovations of a given individual user. Such examples are usually not very numerous in relation to the total length of the message – typically up to four items per message, although there might be some individual cases of users who made use of many more in one text, e.g. "*Dzie*[kuję]! Ja *pozdr*[awiam] Cię z *zimn*[nego] X, choć te -8 st w *por*[ównaniu] z -25 w *Kra*[kowie] jest ciepłem. *Str*[asznie] jednak marznę i *zazdr*[oszczę] Ci

ciepełka! *Trz*[y]*m*[aj] się dzielnie i rob *zdj*[ęcia]. *C*[ałuję]. X." Some other exm
amples include, e.g., „Dopiero teraz doładowałem *kom*[órkę]. Ja jestem gotów
na *spotk*[anie]. w *pon*[niedziałek] lub we *wt*[orek]" or „Sorry że dopiero teraz
odp[owiadam]. Miałam straszne *ostat*[nie]. 2 dni... Niestety w *p*[ią]*t*[ek] jestem
w pracy od rana do *wiecz*[ora]." Altogether, my analysis has shown that a vast
majority of abbreviated words in this section would typically lose the last two syllables and keep only the first one, e.g. *dol*[inie], *dzie*[kuję], *kom*[órkę], *nast*[ępny],
pozdr[awiam], *str*[asznie], *serd*[ecznie], *spotk*[anie], *wiecz*[ora], *zazdr*[oszczę],
zimn[ego], *zdj*[ęcia], *zoba*[czenia], possibly on a subconscious assumption that one
third of the word is already enough for someone to recognize it (cf. the concept of
word redundancy in C-Tests developed in Germany at http://www.c-test.de). It has
to be acknowledged, however, that most of these examples do not terminate at a
syllable boundary, but mostly before a vowel, having attached the consonants of
the syllable which follows to the preceding part which is kept (viz. *pozdr*[awiam]
vs. the correct division into syllables *po-zdra-wiam*), or retaining just the first
few consonants of the entire word (viz. *odp*[owiadam], *str*[asznie], *zdj*[ęcia], etc.).
This might, therefore, confirm the earlier conclusion that consonants are more
essential than vowels to carry the meaning of words.

Vowel/sound omission

As mentioned above, the second and final group of abbreviations found in the Polish
material, characterised by a deletion of sounds (particularly vowels) and an additional
clipping, consists of only 10 elements:

1. Lot biuro i hotel ***bdb*** [bardzo dobre] – 'The flight, the office and the hotel were
   very good'
2. ***Pzdr*** × 6 [Pozdrawiam/Pozdrowienia] – 'Greetings'
3. ***Trzm*** [trzymaj] się dzielnie i rob zdj – 'Hold on bravely and take photos'
4. Niestety w ***pt*** [piątek] jestem w pracy od rana do wiecz. – 'Unfortunately, on Fri
   I'm at work from morning till evening'
5. Przekaż p. X żeby pilnie zapisała się na semin ***mgr*** [magisterskie] w usosie. –
   'Tell Miss X that she should urgently enroll for the MA seminar in USOS'

This very limited number shows that texters seem to dislike to use forms which
consist of consonants (sometimes only some consonants of the original word) alone.
Out of these the only one really well-accepted among message senders is the form
pzdr [pozdrawiam / pozdrowienia], which was found in 6 messages out of 10, and
thus it can already be recognised as a new convention. The abbreviation *pt* (*piątek*)
has also been long recognised outside the electronic context, likewise the forms
bdb (*bardzo dobre*), which is a typical way of writing the "very good" mark in the
school system, and *mgr*, which is a frequent abbreviation referring to the MA studies / work / student. The only innovation which does not seem to be as yet generally
shared is the form *trzm* [trzymaj się], a combination of both a clipping and a vowel
omission. It can therefore be concluded that Polish users do not favour this form of

shortening, most likely because Polish words tend to be polysyllabic, and therefore such abbreviations may cause ambiguity.

Having enumerated categories of shortenings it is still worth examining some additional sociolinguistic aspects of the abbreviated messages. Two important points have already been mentioned above, viz. 1) the fact that the use of shortenings is recorded twice as frequently in English as it is in Polish (and that it took twice as long to find a comparable number of messages with abbreviations in Polish as it did in English), and 2) the fact that a much greater variety of strategies of shortening messages was used by the authors of the English texts than by those writing in Polish. Additionally, concerning the English messages, which, as mentioned above, were generated by people of various nationalities, it is worth examining whether there might be any tendencies for a higher frequency of abbreviations for any particular group. A closer investigation actually proves that it is the Indian users who show special preference for this kind of strategy – among the 52 English messages collected as many as 26 were generated by Indian texters. The second largest group, which consisted of 16 messages, was that written by British senders. Finally, 5 English messages were produced by Polish users of English; the remaining ones were a miscellaneous group.

One more sociolinguistic variable worth examining is that of gender of the texters. Among the users of English 31 abbreviated messages out of 52 were written by male senders, with the remaining 21 created by female senders. In the case of the Polish language 20 out of 48 shortened messages altogether were written by female senders, which leaves us with 28 messages generated by male respondents. Although it is hard to generalise on the basis of this limited number of messages, the above results might indicate a slightly greater tendency to observe the standard rules of language use on the part of females, which means that it would be more typical of males to make use of shortening (and thus non-standard) strategies in text messages (cf. Baron's (2008) findings concerning gender in Instant Messaging).

Concluding remarks

- The above analysis has proved that both English and Polish make use of abbreviation strategies in short text messages, however, the two languages utilise different options.
- The English language offers many more possibilities of shortening than does Polish, due to which texters in Polish use abbreviations half as often as persons sending text messages in English.
- The strategy common to both languages is that of clipping, which in Polish may be further subdivided into conventional and innovative examples. The primary reason for the selection of this option appears to be the greater average length of Polish words, which, additionally, get further extended as the result of attaching inflectional endings. This feature of the Polish language is probably also the main reason why the Polish users are not able to use other strategies, such as

word-number or word-letter substitutions, since the form of particular words is not fixed, but changes depending on their position and function in the sentence.

- The use of clippings is one of the less popular options found among the shortenings in English messages. The strategies used most frequently are word-letter substitutions and vowel omissions. However, since the former uses a limited number of items, although of high frequency (as *u, r, b*, etc.), it is the vowel omission strategy that offers users the greatest advantages. This option, found also in a handful of Polish examples, does not easily apply to Polish due to a greater length of words and their changeable endings. This, in turn, can cause a greater ambiguity in recognising the actual word, hence the need to combine it with a clipping.

- Two further strategies used in English, this time with fewer examples, are the non-standard spellings and the pronoun / auxiliary omission. The former appears to be more risky than the vowel omission, as here the variety of spellings may be much more dependent on the individual sender, whereas the vowel omission should as a rule produce the same result every time. The spelling of English words cannot in many cases be predicted. What is more, simplifying the spelling is not as profitable in terms of time- and space-saving as vowel omission is.

- As far as the omission of a pronoun or an auxiliary is concerned, the gain may not be very considerable as the omitted pronoun is typically the first person singular *I*, and occasionally the third person singular *it*, and thus both are short words. A greater advantage can be observed when the sentence is in the present perfect or present continuous tense, or else in a passive construction, where beside the pronoun the auxiliary is also omitted. This strategy is not of much use in Polish. Unlike English, Polish typically uses sentences with the understood subject if it is not expressed by a noun, and thus the gain in time and space is none. Regarding the apostrophe deletion, least preferred by English senders, this strategy has no application in Polish, as the Polish language does not make use of the apostrophe at all.

In summary, although the need to shorten text messages appears to be fairly universal, its frequency will vary from language to language. Also, the variety of possible strategies will depend on the features of each language, with the number of options more limited in the case of highly inflected languages than in the case of more analytic languages, such as, e.g., English. It may be concluded that the more analytic the language is, the more varied shortening strategies can be applied.

References

Baron N. 2008. *Always on. Language in an online and mobile world*. Oxford.
Baugh A.C., Cable T. 2002. *A history of the English language*. [ed. V]. Upper Saddle River, New Jersey.
Biber D., Conrad S. 2009. *Register, genre and style*. Cambridge.
Crystal D. 2001. *Language and the Internet*. Cambridge.

Crystal D. 2008. *Txtng. The Gr8 Db8.* Oxford.

Dąbrowska M. 2004. English impact on the electronic media communication. – Duszak A., Okulska U. (eds.) *Speaking from the margin: global English from a European perspective.* Frankfurt am Main: 261–274.

Dąbrowska M. 2010. Functions of code-switching in electronic communication. – Jodłowiec M., Leśniewska J. (eds.) *Ambiguity and the search for meaning: English and American studies at the beginning of the 21st century.* [vol. 2 *Language and culture*]. Kraków: 91–106.

Döring N. 2002. 'Kurzm. wird gesendet' – Abkürzungen und Akronyme in der SMS-Kommunikation. – *Muttersprache. Vierteljahresschrift für deutsche Sprache* 112 (2): 97–114.

Hård af Segerstad Y. 2002. *Use and adaptation of written language to the conditions of computer-mediated communication.* Göteborg.

Joos M. 1959. *The five clocks.* Bloomington.

Ling R. 2005. The sociolinguistics of SMS: An analysis of SMS use by a random sample of Norwegians. – Ling R., Pedersen P. (eds.) *Mobile communications: Re-negotiation of the social sphere.* London: 335–349.

Ling R., Baron N. 2007. Text messaging and IM: A linguistic comparison of American college data. – *Journal of Language and Social Psychology* 26 (3): 291–298.

Internet sources

C-Test [Der Sprachtest]. Available at http://www.c-test.de/deutsch/index.php

Ling R. 2007. The length of text messages and use of predictive texting: Who uses it and how much do they have to say. – *AU TESOL working papers* no. 4. Washington, D.C. Available at http://www.richardling.com/papers/2007_Text_prediction_paper.pdf.

Thurlow C., with Brown A. 2003. Generation Txt? The sociolinguistics of young people's text-messaging. – *Discourse Analysis Online.* Available at http://extra.shu.ac.uk/daol/articles/v1/n1/a3/thurlow2002003.html.

Studia Linguistica Universitatis Iagellonicae Cracoviensis
128 (2011)

MARCIN JAROSZEK
Jagiellonian University, Cracow

FACTORS DETERMINING THE DEVELOPMENT OF MODALITY IN ADVANCED L2 SPEECH – A LONGITUDINAL STUDY

Keywords: modality, language transfer, discourse, foreign language learning

Abstract

The article discusses the results of a longitudinal study of how modality, as an aspect of spoken discourse competence of selected thirteen advanced students of English, developed throughout their three-year English as a Foreign Language tertiary education. The study investigated possible factors determining the development of three aspects of modality: (1) epistemic modality, (2) specific modality, that is those modality expressions that are both characteristic of natural English discourse or are underrepresented in L2 discourse, and (3) modality diversity. The analysis was carried out in relation to a number of variables, including two reference levels, one represented in English native discourse and the other observed in teacher talk in actual Practical English classes, language type exposure, as registered by the subjects of the study on a weekly basis.

Introduction

Nearly two decades since Poland's opening to the innovative English as a Foreign Language (EFL) methodologies, the English language has become widely popularized in the country and the number of those speaking it has grown remarkably. Some have only learned to pidginize English, some use it accurately and fluently for professional purposes. It could seem then that these advanced users of English should demonstrate high levels of communicative competence, the development of which is the main objective of most teaching methods widely applied in EFL classrooms. However, day-to-day observation often contradicts this claim. Many advanced EFL learners' L2 (second language) production is rife with awkward utterances, unnatural wording or artificial responses in one-on-one communicative encounters.

The reasons might be aplenty. One may be EFL teachers' possible perception of communicative competence as comprising grammar competence and sociolinguistic competence only, often overshadowing the speaker's capability of constructing textually coherent and cohesive stretches of speech. This negligent approach to discourse competence might account for why many advanced learners' L2 production is stigmatized with grammatically appropriate, yet somewhat unnatural collocations or sentence wording. L2 discourse is not merely a term restricted to any interactional act. In fact, its meaning and structure often exceed the interactional frame of communication. Whether discourse is clear, coherent and, above all, rich in natural discourse mechanisms often underlies the learner's success or failure in L2 communication, unless the aim is to merely pidginize the language.

Communication is then not just a mechanical, raw transfer of information from the speakers to their recipients. Nor is it a disorderly exchange of turns or a meaningless, indefinite interactive tug of war. Communication, realized through discourse construction, is a spontaneous allocation of power and an unpredictable, yet logical flow of ideas. It is, or rather should be, structured poetry, with its stanzas placed by the speaker in a specific order, verses interacting with one another, and meaning inferable from the very specific context of this social act. To master this competence is quite an undertaking for a second language (L2) learner. Although successfully utilized in their first language, L2 discourse construction requires that the learner demonstrates specific knowledge of linguistic instruments, understanding of L2 cultural codes and the skills to combine these elements into an individual utterance, unique for the discourse maker, yet still not exceeding the bounds of the social communicative rigor.

Do advanced L2 learners have the capabilities to construct a natural discourse? What domains of discourse construction pose lesser difficulty to a Polish advanced user of the English language? What is the place of discourse competence development in English Language Teaching (ELT) and do EFL teachers realize the significance of discourse competence and, if so, do they actually develop it in their classrooms? And finally how does advanced students' discourse develop in the long term and what factors might stimulate or impede the process? These are the questions which certainly need answering in modern Applied Linguistics, questions which this article will attempt to address in relation to a narrow patch of English discourse construction – modality.

1 Modality in discourse construction

Basically, modality can be defined as the expression of the speaker's opinion about belief, likelihood, truth and obligation, or "attitude, obviously ascribable to the source of the text, and explicit or implicit in the linguistic stance taken by the speaker/writer" (Fowler 1998: 85). Modality, however, seems to be a more complex phenomenon and its definition can, and should be extended e.g. onto the speaker's culture, personality or temporary mood. As proposed by Givón (1993: 169)

> the propositional modality associated with a clause may be likened to a shell that encases it but does not tamper with the kernel inside. The propositional frame of clauses. ... as well as the actual lexical items that fill the various slots in the frame, remain largely unaffected by the modality wrapped around it. Rather, the modality codes the speaker's attitude toward the proposition.

Studies distinguish a number of modality types, such as discourse-oriented modality, epistemic and root modality as well as boulomaic, deontic or perception modality (Adolphs 2007: 257). This discussion, for the sake of clarity, will discuss epistemic, deontic and boulomaic modality as this trichotomy will be analysed in the empirical portion of the research.

Givón (1993: 169) defines epistemic modality as encompassing "judgements of truth, probability, certainty or belief" (for example *he might go*), and deontic modality as involving "evaluative judgements of desirability, preference, intent, ability, obligation or manipulation" (i.e. *he must go*). Palmer (1986: 51) specifies the realm of epistemic modality as comprising "at least four ways in which a speaker may indicate that he is not presenting what he is saying as a fact, but rather:

  (i) that he is speculating about it
  (ii) that he is presenting it as a deduction
  (iii) that he has been told about it
  (iv) that it is a matter only of appearance, based on the evidence of (possibly fallible) senses.

The first example represents what is often referred to as judgements. The three remaining types reflect the evidentiality of speech. As Palmer (1986: 51) asserts, the binding force of these four aspects is "the indication by the speaker of his [lack of] commitment to the truth of the proposition being expressed".

The interpretation of deontic modality is a complex undertaking, as its classic definition restricts it to obligation only (Adolphs 2007: 257), and its meaning has been sometimes extended to desirability (cf. Givón 1993: 169). But if desirability is indeed interpreted as a domain of deontic modality, it will encroach upon the territory traditionally reserved for boulomaic modality, which realizes "wish", "want", "love" and "hate" worlds of the discourse creator (Chrzanowska-Kluczewska 2009: 163). Wish, hate, love and desirability represent neither evidentiality of discourse nor the speaker's commitment to truth. They, however, encompass the speaker's emotional stance on the communicated ideas. Therefore, both modality types will be discussed in the empirical portion of this research under one heading of *deontic modality*, in the extended meaning, juxtaposed with *epistemic modality*.

Although linguistically, modality – whether epistemic, deontic or boulomaic – is traditionally realized through the use of modal auxiliaries, modality devices include more than just common *can, might* or *should*. It can also be realized through a number of lexical verbs (e.g. *seem*) and modal adverbs (e.g. *inevitably*) (Adolphs 2007: 258), modal adjectives (e.g. *likely*) as well as whole modal formulas. These devices allow the speaker to soften their stance on or their attitude to the expressed opinion (McCarthy 1991: 85). The following extracts illustrate this phenomenon:

Extract 1

> We ***certainly do*** know that violence is a problem, and when we measure things like adolescent depression, which ***often*** follows from the experience of violence, ranging from psychological to physical, that is ***quite*** extreme and ***appears*** to be growing.
>
> (Justice Talking: School Violence – Air Date: 1/22/07)

Extract 2

> MARILYN LAWRENCE: ***I think*** people have the right to understand in a historical documentary that the language is only going to be used when it ***might*** be deemed appropriate. But when we think it's deemed appropriate, we ***should*** have the conversations with our children about how people talk that way or don't talk that way or shouldn't talk that way instead of banning it from others.
>
> KELLY TURNER: What's the difference between "Saving Private Ryan" and airing, you know, an unedited version of you know "Die Hard" or another movie that has the same amount of profanity? ***I guess*** I don't ***really*** see a difference. Just based on the content of the film, ***I'm not sure*** that ***would*** make it okay to say those things.
>
> (Justice Talking: The FCC Crackdown on Indecency – Air Date: 5/22/06)

As seen from the above samples, modality can be realized through adverbs such as *certainly, quite* or *really,* modal auxiliaries, e.g. *might, would* as well as verbs, such as *appear* or set expressions e.g. *I'm not sure.* Unchallenging as it might be to single out modality devices, determining whether they realize epistemic or deontic modality poses a serious difficulty. For example, the adverbial *really,* as it seems, can be an indication of the speaker's commitment to truth, which would suggest epistemic modality, yet it could also be, and often is, used emphatically as boulomaic modality.

It should also be noted that modality does not only represent "a private relationship between a rational self and the world (...) and can be seen as part of the process of texturing self-identity (...) inflected by the process of social relation" (Fairclough 2003: 117). It is then not only the speaker that constructs the meaning. The variation in meaning is often located "in the nature of the source and availability of the recipient role" (Hoekstra 2004: 24). It is then the mood or the stance of the speaker in the continual interaction with the interlocutor's reception of discursive arguments in which modality also materializes its function.

Since this project deals with modality as one of many discourse domains, no distinction will be made, as suggested by Halliday and Matthiessen (2004: 147), between modalization and modulation. Such a dichotomy could, and no doubt should, be subject to analysis in a separate study.

It is daily classroom observation that indicates that the cultural use of modality is "notoriously difficult for foreign learners to master" (Brazil 1995: 116) and that although EFL teachers do instruct their students on the use of modality, they may fail, for many reasons, to expose the students to a wider spectrum of modalizing devices which could exceed the frame of just modal verbs. The reasons might vary from the routine treatment which the pragmatic force and cultural use of modals receive in the EFL classroom (Lee 2007: 484), to the diversity of functions realized by modality markers, depending on the context and co-text of discourse (Adolphs 2007: 267), to the under-representation of modality-related vocabulary other than modal verbs in teaching materials (Holmes 1988, cited in McCarthy 1991: 85), which suggests that L2 instruction may not fully reflect natural English discourse. This claim is confirmed by Kasper's (1979) finding that early L2 production is characterized by *modality reduction* and it is in more advanced speech that learners begin to "make linguistic selections of sufficient delicacy" (Ellis 1992: 177). How natural these linguistic choices are, should, however, be further investigated.

2 Method

The main portion of the research is a longitudinal study of how modality, as an aspect of spoken discourse competence of selected advanced learners of English, developed over the period of three years and what factors might have affected this process. The study investigates the modality devices selected in the survey study and implements the data collection procedures which include a combination of deductive and heuristic tools, such as structured diaries for quantitative interpretation, and tapescript analysis for qualitative analysis. The specific methods are described in this section.

2.1 Research focus and research questions

The objective of the study was to investigate how advanced students' L2 modality developed over a specific period of language instruction. It was necessary then to longitudinally identify which modality devices were applied by advanced students of English as a foreign language and, if so, with what frequency these devices were actually used, as well as which factors might have determined the use of these mechanisms in the course of the study. The area of investigation was narrowed down to spoken production only.

With advanced learners under investigation, it could seem obvious that they will demonstrate high levels of communicative competence, and consequently a natural and abundant repertoire of modality devices. After all, the development of communicative competence is the main objective of most teaching methods widely applied in EFL classrooms. It is, however, day-to-day observation that even advanced students' L2 production is far from natural English speaking conventions. Communicative competence is often perceived, also by EFL teachers, as comprising grammar competence and sociolinguistic competence only. What seems to be dismissed is the development of discourse competence, which could account for why many advanced L2 learners are grammatically accurate, yet somewhat unnatural in the use of specific discourse devices.

Therefore, it seems relevant and interesting to investigate what position discourse competence development takes in ELT, in this research in relation to L2 modality. How advanced students' modality develops in the long term can also be an interesting endeavour. Such is a study of variables that might have a positive or negative effect on this development. The factors could include teacher talk, students' personality or exposure to authentic English. The main research question is then:

> What are possible factors that determine the development of L2 modality in advanced learners of English?

Specifically, the research questions are as follows:

> Does L2 modality develop?
> What modality aspects develop?
> What is the process of this development?
> Do advance L2 learners achieve native-like levels of modality use?
> What affects the development of L2 modality?
> Is teacher modality use similar to natural modality use?
> Do teachers promote the natural use of modality?

2.2 Sample and research instruments

Since the research questions refer in large part to the process of modality development, a longitudinal study will be conducted. The following sections will present the subjects and the research methodology implemented in the course of the study.

2.2.1 Subjects

The subjects initially included eighteen students of English at an English language teacher training college selected from three groups of freshmen. The number of students was a conscious choice, as it was anticipated that some of the students might, for various reasons, quit their education, thus naturally becoming excluded from the study. Eventually, thirteen students' modality development was analysed. There was an even number of students representing a high English proficiency and those representing a low proficiency selected in each group. The selection criterion was the entrance examination results. The subjects were
selected on the basis of document analysis after entrance examinations in July and September 2004. Both spoken and written test results were analysed. All the selected students gave consent to their participation in the study, had the magnitude of their required commitment in the course of the study explained to them, and were instructed on the procedures of data collection. They were, however, not informed as to the objective of the research, since it would have most likely affected their language performance, thus distorting the results.

2.2.2 Reference subjects

The teachers, whose discourse was subject to analysis, were fully qualified profession-als with extensive experience and expertise in teaching English-oriented subjects to university students. A total of twelve teachers included four men and eight women, six with PhD and six with MA degrees. The age range was from thirty to fifty-two, with the average of forty-one.

The English native college student, whose discourse was also subject to analysis, was a twenty-four-year-old female studying in the same college on a regular basis. She was a relatively extroverted type, extremely diligent and self-motivated.

2.2.3 Research instruments

The study commenced in October 2004 and was completed in May 2007, spanning a total of three academic years of the subjects' college education. The development of the subjects' spoken modality was measured periodically with the use of the tools described below. In addition, a number of instruments were used in an attempt to determine what factors affected this process. This section stipulates the data gathering tools.

Student Diary. The aim of the diary was to identify what type of English the subjects were exposed to over the period of three years. The students were obligated to fill in a weekly diary form which was designed to record the type of their L2 exposure. In the first part the subjects were to specify the amount of time they spent in con-tact with a given type of English. The second part of the diary included the types of classroom interaction in college courses throughout the week. The diary clearly stated that the students were to specify the proportions of the interaction types as used in the classes with respect to student talking time. When absent from college, the students were to fill in the first part of the diary only. The subjects were instructed on how to interpret the terms used in the diary form. The diaries were collected on a weekly basis. Since some subjects happened to occasionally fail to hand in their forms, the results needed to be statistically calculated.

Student Interviews (English). The development of the subjects' modality was meas-ured longitudinally over a period of three years. Their modality was measured on the basis of spoken performance samples seven times throughout the study: in No-vember 2004, February 2005, June 2005, October 2005, June 2006, October 2006 and May 2007. For each recording, the subjects took part in two approximately ten-minute discussions in groups of three. One discussion was designed to trigger the subjects' informal output, the other the formal one. The samples were tapescribed and examined for the use of modality devices.

Native Speaker Interview. In May 2007, the spoken production of a native speaker of English was recorded according to the same procedures as the regular student interviews. She participated in two approximately ten-minute discussions in a group of three (the remaining two students were non-native speakers of English). She was a student at the same college as the research subjects, hence she served as a reliable reference point in the study. The aim of this interview was to help compare the subjects' L2 modality with that of their peer. It is realized that interviewing one person only is by no means representative, yet it does offer some reference for further analysis.

Teacher Talk Analysis. As indicated in the pilot study, much of the reported classroom interaction involved a lock-step procedure. It can be concluded that it is also teacher talk that might have been one of the major factors affecting the students' modality development. It seemed reasonable then to analyse the modality devices applied by the teachers of the research subjects throughout a three-year college program. Each teacher's one forty-five-minute lesson unit was tapescribed and analysed. This helped investigate possible relationships between teacher discourse and the students' modality development.

Weekly diaries. The student questionnaires were returned on a regular, weekly basis. In the first year of the study the return rate was 100%. In the second and third year, the return rate decreased in individual cases. The subjects were asked not to hand in the questionnaires that could contain unreliable data, if they were to fill them in after a considerable period of time from the reported week. To retain the representative proportions for L2 exposure types measurement the following equation was used:

$$ExT = TN \times \frac{35}{Nq}$$

where ExT represents the proportionate L2 exposure, TN represents a total of exposure hours as reported in the returned questionnaires, Nq represents the number of returned questionnaires and 35 represents the constant number of weeks in one year of L2 exposure

Recordings. Student interviews. The students were interviewed seven times throughout the study, three times in year 1, twice in year 2 and twice in year 3, mostly in groups of three, occasionally in groups of four in well-insulated rooms without the presence of the researcher. But in recording 1, the student communication was video-recorded to help the interpretation of possible inaudible utterances for more reliable tapescription. A total of approximately 420 minutes of students' L2 interaction was recorded and tapescribed. The recorded material spans the period of 31 months of the subjects' discourse competence development.

Teacher talk. A total of twelve teachers were recorded in regular college classes. They were not informed as to the precise time of the recording to enhance the reliability of the sample. A total of approximately 540 minutes of classroom communication was tapescribed and put to analysis, out of which approximately 180 minutes of teacher talk was analysed.

2.2.4 Statistical calculations

Since most of the data will be presented numerically, it was necessary to calculate the following intensity ratio, which would reflect the actual modality intensity levels:

$$MIR = \frac{n}{L}$$

where *MIR* represents the modality intensity ratio, *n* represents the number of occurrences found and *L* represents the length of language output, as realized in transcribed text signs.

The ratio calculation helps sustain the proportions of speech stretches and the number of devices used. The length of speech, therefore, had no effect on the calculation result of modality intensity. A similar procedure was used in the calculation of other intensity discourse types, unless otherwise stated.

There will be an attempt to relate the student level of modality with the teacher levels, which will be an average calculation of the teachers' language output in actual classes (referred to as teacher reference), and with a native speaker's level, calculated from the language output of an individual native speaker female student recorded in the same communicative settings, referred to as native reference. To examine the reliability of the native reference levels, two other samples of native speaker's language output are provided. They are not taken as reference points, though.

It should also be realized that the number of thirteen students is by no means a large statistical sample. The results of this study, therefore, should not be generalized to a larger population.

2.3 Procedures

It was realized that before the actual measurement of L2 modality development was undertaken in the main stage of the study, the research objectives might need to be revisited, the area of actual investigation narrowed down and designed data collection tools improved in *preparatory stages of the research*. Therefore, the first phase – *a survey study* – was aimed at identifying L2 spoken modality devices applied by advanced learners of English and at selecting these mechanisms that would be further investigated due to e.g. their frequency or intensity of occurrence in performance samples, or other features of interest to this project. This will be further discussed in Subchapter 3.2. The second stage – *a pilot study* – was conducted to examine the designed data collection procedures and to suggest possible procedural alterations to be implemented in the main study.

The third stage – *the main study* – took a longitudinal form, hence its three-year duration. Its structure is presented in the table below.

Procedure	Aim	
Six students in each of the three groups will be investigated (three "weak" students, and three "strong" ones).		
1. Documentation analysis (exam results – spoken and written)	to select the subject representing a variety of proficiency levels	INITIAL PROCE-DURES

2. Initial classroom observation	to determine their cooperativeness and confirm exam-based selection of the subjects	INITIAL PROCEDURES
3. Polish interview	to communicate the aims of the research to the subjects and to train them in data collection procedures	
4. English interview (formal and informal)	to analyse the subjects' L2 modality	REGULAR PROCEDURES
5. Diary analysis – on a weekly basis	to examine the subjects exposure to L2 and its effect of the development of their discourse competence	
6. Native speaker interview	to determine a native reference for contrastive analysis	ADDITIONAL PROCEDURES
7. Teacher talk analysis	to examine teacher talk for the use of discourse mechanisms and its effect on student discourse competence	

3 Results

Since the potential repertoire of modality devices is rich, its analysis offers numerous opportunities for interpretation. The following section will attempt to present and discuss the development of overall modality intensity as well as deontic, epistemic and specific types of modality with reference to possible factors that might have affected their use.

3.1 Overall modality

The students' overall modality did not statistically alter over the period of three years. As illustrated in Figure 1, although some changes in their modalization of speech are observed, (e.g. S1 from 0.009243 in the first measurement to 0.005892, or S9 from 0.006319703 to 0.008641), the average development trend indicates the intensity of the subjects' overall modality did not change. Individual deviations from the trend level should be attributed to incidental malperformance on the part of the students, rather than to any particular factors determining modality intensity in their discourse. Modality as such is a vast area of language use and it is only after an in-depth analysis that the changes in its development become evident.

Student	Recording 1	Recording 2	Recording 3	Recording 4	Recording 5	Recording 6	Recording 7
S1	0.009243	0.005636	0.011737	0.015221	0.006484	0.005509	0.005892
S2	0.005236	0.004443	0.01053	0.007271	0.008531	0.006548	0.008165

S3	0.009004	0.007259	0.004236	0.010169	0.008282	0.012446	0.007422
S4	0.011318	0.005854	0.006446	0.006386	0.005411	0.005521	0.009988
S5	0.006824	0.005952	0.007628	0.008737	0.005884	0.007117	0.010844
S6	0.015536	0.004467	0.008472	0.011978	0.009552	0.013723	0.011293
S7	0.007084	0.003842	0.005757	0.002932	0.007488	0.008224	0.009025
S8	0.010943	0.010593	0.015422	0.011687	0.016393	0.01148	0.017047
S9	0.00632	0.010548	0.006737	0.005261	0.004547	0.004575	0.008641
S10	0.007246	0.005425	0.011892	0.012813	0.014974	0.006239	0.007849
S11	0.011194	0.013405	0.010474	0.005888	0.008069	0.011473	0.00891
S12	0.006533	0.010652	0.009192	0.006169	0.00738	0	0.011797
S13	0.013633	0.011269	0.009552	0.010218	0.003371	0.005512	0.01087
Av	0.00924	0.007642	0.009083	0.008825	0.008182	0.007567	0.009826
NR	**0.008146**						
TR	**0.0073**						

Figure 1. Individual overall modality development

What can be concluded from the overall intensity of the subjects' modality is that it is higher, if only slightly (0.008624), than the teacher reference level (0.0073) and the native reference level (0.008146). The reason might be the approximately three-fold overrepresentation of *maybe* in their discourse 0.000654, as compared with 0.000163 in the native reference and 0.000231 in the teacher reference as well as *should* 0.000795, as compared with 0.000489 in the native reference and 0.000228 in the teacher reference.

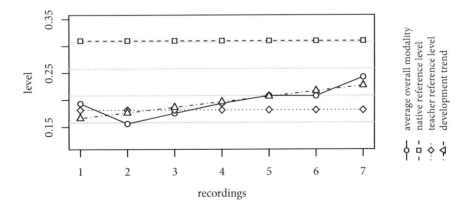

Figure 2. Average overall modality development

The lowest modality among the teachers is not surprising. The factual nature of teaching, particularly in lectures, promotes a more directive speaking style. Notwithstanding new methodological trends, teachers still remain authorities as a source of knowledge, or at least attempt to maintain this position, hence they modalize their speech to a lesser extent, particularly in lectures where the dominant teaching mode is lockstep and much of the teaching is knowledge transfer. As illustrated in Figure 4, the highest overall intensity is observed in workshops (Use of English 3 (workshops), with the modality intensity ratio of 0.0105, and British Studies (workshops), with the modality intensity ratio of 0.0243). The lowest modality intensity ratio was found in TEFL 2 (lecture), with the ratio of 0.0026, and US history (lecture), with the ratio of 0.0030.

Modality type	College student	Native 2	Native 3
Overall modality	0.008145976	0.006977778	0.009449

Figure 3. Native reference overall modality

Although it is the type of class that appears to determine the level of modality intensity used by the teachers, modality can also be dependent upon individual teachers' idiocratic discourse features. Teacher modality in reading 3 workshops, for instance, was comparably low (0.0058) in this form of classes, which corresponds with a low intensity ratio in this teacher's British Literature lecture (0.0033). Similarly, teacher modality in phonetic workshops was comparably high (0.0111) in this form of classes, which corresponds with a relatively high intensity ratio in this teacher's lecture in linguistics (0.0064).

	Teachers	Overall modality		Teachers	Overall modality
T1	linguistics + grammar	0.0064	T10	TEFL 2 – lecture	0.0026
T2	TEFL 1	0.0078	T11	use of English 2	0.0105
T3	listening 1	0.0055	T12	American literature	0.0038
T4	grammar & writing 1	0.0070	T13	U.S. history	0.0030
T5	voice emission	0.0049	T14	reading 3	0.0058
T6	intro to lit	0.0045	T15	use of English 3	0.0070
T7	Br. & U.S. studies	0.0243	T16	speaking 3	0.0132
T8	phonetics	0.0111	T17	integrated skills 3	0.0041
T9	British lit	0.0033	**AVERAGE**		**0.0073**

Figure 4. Teacher overall modality

3.2 Specific modality

Although overall modality change was insignificant, alteration of modality development was observed in the area of selected modality devices referred to in this discussion as specific modality. The devices classified as belonging to specific modality types were the ones that were either underrepresented in the discourse of the survey study subjects or non-existent in their speech. It was assumed that if a given device was frequently used or overrepresented in the students' discourse, it could considerably distort the picture of statistical changes in the use of less frequently applied devices by counter-balancing the possible increase or decrease in the use of the other. Therefore, the devices selected for specific modality analysis are as follows:

I guess	*I suppose*	*in a way*	*a bit*
definitely	*fully*	*I would risk*	*able to*
seem	*I must say*	*somehow*	*at all*
supposed	*obvious*	*basically*	*let's say*
perhaps	*appear*	*against/for*	*consider*
probably	*likely*	*certainly*	*indeed*
got to	*I would say*	*kind of*	*entirely*
possible	*I'm afraid*	*simply*	*I feel*
bound to	*the fact is*	*quite*	*supposedly*
modal + have	*allowed*	*pretty*	*no way*
may	*as for me*	*so*	*sadly*
presume	*do/does*	*extremely*	*in actuality*
I believe	*honestly*	*for sure*	*I heard*
personally	*possibly*	*such*	*unfortunately*
completely	*deeply*	*that*	*would*
really	*rather*	*I'm in favour of*	
generally	*admit*	*I stand*	
I'm sure	*actually*	*totally*	

Devices rejected for specific modality analysis:

think	*in my opinion*	*in fact*	*I understand*
I don't know	*must*	*my opinion is*	*could*
maybe	*need*	*to be to*	*I mean*
will	*of course*	*that's my opinion*	*I'm certain*
can	*have to*	*I know*	
should	*agree*	*as far as I know*	

In eight subjects the development of specific modality was significant. Those subjects whose specific modality decreased were Student 1 (from a native-like 0.003466 in recording to 0.000842 in recording 7), whose final performance, however, distorts his average native-like results throughout the study (0.003418), student 11, whose final low performance could also be incidental, as in recording 6, her specific modality ranked highest among the modalities of all the subjects. Student 4 preserved the stable relatively high (0.002569) levels of specific modality throughout her college education.

Stu-dent	Record-ing 1	Recordr-ing 2	Record-ing 3	Record-ing 4	Record-ing 5	Record-ing 6	Record-ing 7
S1	0.003466	0.00161	0.003689	0.004613	0.00389	0.00324	0.000842
S2	0.001309	0.001616	0.002038	0.002105	0.001651	0.004365	0.002722
S3	0.000819	0.000558	0.000565	0.001695	0.002761	0.004631	0.003024
S4	0.003638	0.002927	0.00046	0.003831	0.001476	0.003155	0.002497
S5	0.000819	0.000558	0.000565	0.001695	0.002761	0.004631	0.003024
S6	0.000634	0.001117	0	0.002318	0.002183	0.004334	0.003279
S7	0.000272	0.00048	0.000822	0.000326	0.001123	0.001234	0.001444
S8	0.000189	0	0.001714	0.003811	0.007733	0.003827	0.006478
S9	0.000929	0.001346	0.000898	0.001435	0.00065	0.00183	0.001964
S10	0	0.001808	0.001622	0.002441	0.006551	0.002674	0.002512
S11	0.003731	0.004021	0.001232	0.001963	0.00269	0.005048	0.002096
S12	0.001225	0.000666	0.000968	0.001122	0.004428	0	0.00121
S13	0.000317	0.001252	0.001102	0.003314	0	0.002362	0.002836
av	0.001334	0.001382	0.001206	0.002359	0.002915	0.003179	0.00261
NR				0.0037			
TR				0.0029			

Figure 5. Specific modality development

The overall analysis of specific modality use shows a steady and significant development, from a low 0.001334 in the first recording through a mediocre 0.002359 in recording 5 to 0.00261 in recording 7 at the end of the study, as illustrated in Figure 6. It must be noted, however, that specific modality levels increased steadily right from recording 1 and reached the highest level (0.003179) in recording 6, exceeding the teacher reference level towards the native reference level of 0.003747. The average lower result in recording 7 is caused by the afore-mentioned individual lower levels of the three subjects, or by the influence of teacher discourse.

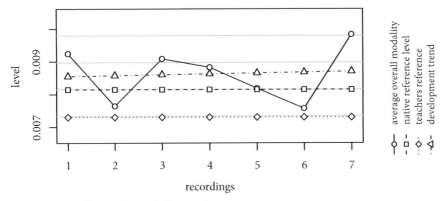

Figure 6. Overall specific modality development

Unlike overall modality results, no relation between the observed specific modality levels and the type of class was observed. Some workshops showed the teacher's specific modality at a lower level (e.g. TEFL 1 with the ratio at 0.0022; voice emission with the ratio at 0.0007) than lectures did (e.g. American literature with the ratio at 0.0035; U.S. history with the ratio at 0.0026), which suggests that it is the teachers' individual modality that determines their levels, and not educational settings.

	Teachers	Specific modality		Teachers	Specific modality
T1	linguistics + grammar	0.0026	**T10**	TEFL 2 – lecture	0.0018
T2	TEFL 1	0.0022	**T11**	use of English 2	0.0039
T3	listening 1	0.0035	**T12**	American literature	0.0035
T4	grammar & writing 1	0.0024	**T13**	U.S. history	0.0026
T5	voice emission	0.0007	**T14**	reading 3	0.0015
T6	intro to lit	0.0016	**T15**	use of English 3	0.0047
T7	Br. & U.S. studies	0.0102	**T16**	speaking 3	0.0015
T8	phonetics	0.0040	**T17**	integrated skills 3	0.0020
T9	British lit	0.0013	**AVERAGE**		**0.0029**

Figure 7. Teacher specific modality

The use of specific modality by the native reference showed a high level of 0.003747, which indicates discourse in many classes was inauthentic. It also suggests the students might have been developing their use of specific modality as a result of exposure to authentic English.

3.3 Epistemic and deontic modality

Epistemic modality, which encompasses judgments of truth, likelihood, certainty or belief, fails to show a regular development in individual cases. Although Student 4 reduced her modality from the ratio of 0.006467 in recording 1 to a stable level of 0.004994 in the final recording, similar to both native and teacher reference levels, and Student 11 from 0.007996 in recording 1 to 0.004717 in the final recording, a claim that students tailor their levels of epistemic modality to expository models (teacher and native output) would be an overstatement. It seems that higher or lower levels of epistemic modality depended on individual choices of the subjects, rather than on external factors.

S1	0.00491	0.002415	0.007713	0.009225	0.003026	0.002268	0.003367
S2	0.003927	0.001212	0.007133	0.004401	0.006604	0.003274	0.005988
S3	0.004366	0.0067	0.002824	0.00678	0.004486	0.005499	0.003024
S4	0.006467	0.003902	0.00046	0.002554	0.002951	0.004732	0.004994
S5	0.004342	0.003968	0.004958	0.007149	0.0045	0.003114	0.007072
S6	0.008878	0.000558	0.006495	0.006955	0.006277	0.007945	0.006922
S7	0.003815	0.002882	0.004523	0.001629	0.006365	0.004523	0.005776
S8	0.00717	0.005726	0.007197	0.005589	0.00897	0.005527	0.010228
S9	0.003903	0.006957	0.003369	0.003826	0.002598	0.00366	0.006284
S10	0.002415	0.002712	0.005946	0.009762	0.007487	0.003565	0.005338
S11	0.007996	0.010724	0.007394	0.004907	0.003765	0.003671	0.004717
S12	0.005308	0.005992	0.004354	0.004487	0.00369	0	0.00605
S13	0.006341	0.00626	0.005511	0.008009	0.003371	0.003937	0.005198
av	**0.005372**	**0.004616**	**0.005221**	**0.00579**	**0.00493**	**0.00431**	**0.005766**
NR				0.004888			
TR				0.0044			
L1R				0.00549			

Figure 8. Individual epistemic modality development

As indicated in Figure 9, average epistemic modality development shows virtually no dynamics, its overall development trend remaining at approximately 0.00515. Still, it should be noted that the students' epistemic modality was higher than both the native reference level (0.0049) and the teacher reference level (0.0044).

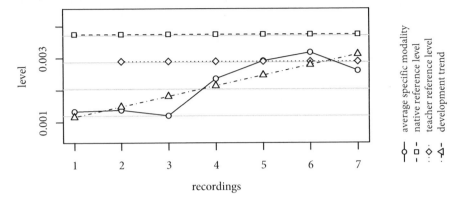

Figure 9. Epistemic modality development

The teachers' epistemic modality seems in large part to be dependent on the types of class. Workshops, as illustrated in Figure 11, promote epistemic modality (e.g. T11 with ratio at 0.0088; T16 with ratio at 0.0088, T7 with ratio at 0.0122). Lectures, in turn, seem to have an opposite effect. Epistemic modality in all lectures showed significantly low intensity levels, as compared with the average ratio of 0.0044 (e.g. T9 with ratio at 0.0015; T10 with ratio at 0.0022; T12 with ratio at 0.0015). A possible explanation could be, as claimed in the case of overall modality, an authoritarian teaching style in the lockstep mode, dominant in lectures, as well as a traditional role of the teacher as a source of knowledge in this educational setting.

Modality type	College student	Native 2	Native 3
Episthemic modality	0.004887586	0.003822222	0.004709
Deontic modality	0.002606712	0.002266667	0.002752
Ratio	1.875	1.68627451	1.711111

Figure 10. Native reference deontic and epistemic modality levels

The students' higher epistemic modality can be attributed to the use of *of course* over-represented in Student 6 (0.002024), Student 10 (0.002635), or Student 11 (0.005195), compared with the zero native reference level and the teacher reference level of 0.000272. Interestingly, the students did not use the natural *apparently* or *obviously* (0.000017). Instead, they resorted to the common *of course* (0.000167), which has the same modal value, although it is not interchangeable with the afore-mentioned modal adverbs.

	Teachers	Epistemic modality		Teachers	Epistemic modality
T1	linguistics + grammar	0.0028	**T10**	TEFL 2 – lecture	0.0022
T2	TEFL 1	0.0037	**T11**	use of English 2	0.0088

T3	listening 1	0.0035	T12	American literature	0.0015
T4	grammar & writing 1	0.0030	T13	U.S. history	0.0019
T5	voice emission	0.0033	T14	reading 3	0.0045
T6	intro to lit	0.0016	T15	use of English 3	0.0052
T7	Br. & U.S. studies	0.0122	T16	speaking 3	0.0088
T8	phonetics	0.0080	T17	integrated skills 3	0.0027
T9	British lit	0.0015	**AVERAGE**		**0.0044**

Figure 11. Teachers' epistemic modality

Like epistemic modality, deontic modality, which encompasses discoursal affection materializing in evaluative judgments of desirability, preference, intent, ability, or obligation, shows radically different levels in individual cases from recording to recording. Yet, since the overall average trend shows a fixed developmental tendency, individual deviations should be treated as idiosyncrasies, rather than as results of external factors (to be discussed at a later point).

S1	0.003755	0.002013	0.003353	0.00369	0.002593	0.00324	0.000842
S2	0.000654	0.002019	0.002038	0.002296	0.001376	0.00291	0.002177
S3	0.002183	0.000558	0.000847	0.002119	0.002415	0.005499	0.003299
S4	0.004446	0.000488	0.003223	0.003831	0.002459	0.000789	0.002081
S5	0.001241	0.000794	0.001144	0.000397	0.001038	0.003559	0.001886
S6	0.004439	0.002792	0.001412	0.003478	0.002456	0.005778	0.002914
S7	0.001635	0	0	0.000651	0.001123	0.001645	0.002166
S8	0.001132	0.002577	0.005141	0.005335	0.005568	0.003827	0.005455
S9	0.00223	0.002469	0.002695	0.001435	0.001299	0.000915	0.001964
S10	0.003106	0.000904	0.002703	0.003051	0.006551	0.002674	0.001884
S11	0.002132	0.002681	0.002465	0.000981	0.004303	0.005048	0.002096
S12	0.000817	0.003329	0.001935	0.001683	0.00369	0	0.004537
S13	0.004439	0.002087	0.002204	0.001381	0	0.001575	0.003781
av	**0.002478**	**0.001747**	**0.002243**	**0.002333**	**0.002683**	**0.003122**	**0.002699**
NR				0.002607			
TR				0.0018			
L1R				0.0057			

Figure 12. Individual deontic modality development

Although the overall results do not show radical changes in the average development, they do indicate a rising development trend. It is only in recording 2 that average deontic modality decreases to the teacher reference level (0.001747, as contrasted with the teacher reference level of 0.0018) and rises thereafter stabilizing around the native reference level (0.002699; native reference level of 0.002607). It could be concluded that, although initially affected by the teachers' low deontic modality, the students later exceeded the native reference level under the gradually increasing influence of authentic English they were exposed to in each year of education and teacher talk radically decreasing in year 3.

L2 exposure	Year 1	Year 2	Year 3
Authentic English	49 482 min.	107 503 min.	82 699 min.
Teacher talk	83 621 min.	118 735 min.	64 449 min.

Figure 13. Overall L2 exposure

A higher level of the students' deontic modality over teachers' deontic modality results from the overrepresentation of selected modality devices in the students' discourse. The three flagrantly overrepresented forms are *should* with the students' ratio of 0.000795, as compared with the teachers' ratio of 0.000228 and the native ratio of 0.000489, *have to* with the students' ratio of 0.000331, as compared with the teachers' ratio of 0.000178 and the higher native ratio of 0.000652, as well as deontic *really* with the students' ratio of 0.000437 increasing towards the end of the study, as compared with the teachers' ratio of 0.000231 and the native ratio of 0.000326.

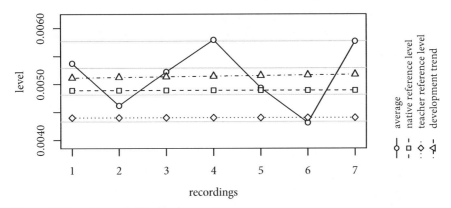

Figure 14. Deontic modality development

It seems that whereas the students might have overused *should* or *have to* as a means of persuasion or the deontic *really* as a means of compensation for the lack of other deontic devices, the teachers might have focused more directly on concrete information, which could slightly lower the deontic modality of their discourse. It is also possible that the students' communicative contexts were more conducive to the use of deontic modality devices, as their task in one of two activities in each recording was to argue a point, find a solution or convince their partners. In this respect, the teachers may have been more focused on the transfer of knowledge, especially in longer stretches of speech.

Teachers		Epistemic modality		Teachers		Epistemic modality
T1	linguistics + grammar	0.0010	T10	TEFL 2 – lecture		0.0004
T2	TEFL 1	0.0030	T11	use of English 2		0.0022
T3	listening 1	0.0020	T12	American literature		0.0023
T4	grammar & writing 1	0.0036	T13	U.S. history		0.0012
T5	voice emission	0.0009	T14	reading 3		0.0006
T6	intro to lit	0.0025	T15	use of English 3		0.0012
T7	Br. & U.S. studies	0.0058	T16	speaking 3		0.0000
T8	phonetics	0.0022	T17	integrated skills 3		0.0007
T9	British lit	0.0010	**AVERAGE**			**0.0018**

Figure 15. Teacher deontic modality

Yet it would be an overstatement to claim that it is lectures where the teachers' deontic modality decreases and workshops where it increases. As illustrated in Figure 15, it is an individual characteristic rather than one attributed to the type of class that determines the level of teachers' modal intensity levels. For example, the deontic modality level in T9 lecture (British literature), with a low ratio of 0.0010, is still higher than in the same teacher's T14 workshops in reading comprehension (0.0006). (Figure 16 on p. 49.)

A possible explanation could be a correlation between the students' reported anxiety in classes and the teachers' deontic modality. As shown in Figure 18, after the rejection of T6 and T17, which distorted the results, the correlation is significant (-.535 with p = .040).

	Deontic modality	Reported anxiety		Deontic modality	Reported anxiety
T1	0.001	2.5	T10	0.0004	7.5
T2	0.003	0	T11	0.0022	1.5
T3	0.002	0	T12	0.0023	0
T4	0.0036	2.5	T13	0.0012	0
T5	0.0009	5	T14	0.0006	10
T6	0.0025	10	T15	0.0012	0

	Deontic modality	Reported anxiety			Deontic modality	Reported anxiety
T7	0.0058	1.5		T16	0	9
T8	0.0022	2.5		T17	0.0007	0
T9	0.001	10				

Figure 17. Teacher deontic modality vs. students reported anxiety level

	T deontic modality	Reported anxiety
T deontic modality	1 p = —	-0.535 p = .040
Reported anxiety	-0.535 p = .040	1 p = —

Figure 18. Correlation between students' anxiety and teachers' deontic modality with T6 and T17 rejected

This suggests that either the lack of deontic modality on the part of teachers' discourse increases classroom anxiety, or classroom anxiety negatively affects their use of deontic modal devices. Although never certain, the former relation seems more plausible.

An attempt was also made to correlate the students' deontic with their epistemic modality. The variables included student gender, initial modality levels, and final modality levels. However, results in most cases show little correlation. As illustrated in the correlation table (Figure 19), the only significant correlation was found between final deontic modality and final epistemic modality (.5704, with p=,042).

	Gender	Year 1 epistemic modality	Year 1 deontic modality	Year 3 epistemic modality	Year 3 deontic modality
Gender	1 p = —	0.3313 p = .269	0.1677 p = .584	0.4746 p = .101	0.0689 p = .823
Year 1 epistemic modality	0.3313 p = .269	1 p = —	0.3159 p = .293	0.1367 p = .656	0.4878 p = .091
Year 1 deontic modality	0.1677 p = .584	0.3159 p = .293	1 p = —	0.0585 p = .849	0.1151 p = .708
Year 3 epistemic modality	0.4746 p = .101	0.1367 p = .656	0.0585 p = .849	1 p = —	**0.5704** **p = .042**
Year 3 deontic modality	0.0689 p = .823	0.4878 p = .091	0.1151 p = .708	**0.5704** **p = .042**	1 p = —

Figure 19. Deontic vs. epistemic modality correlation

These findings could indicate that those who modalize their discourse to clarify their stance on the reliability of the conveyed information also show more affection in discourse construction. It could also be said that those who show more deontic affection in their discourse tend to assume a limited stance on the truthfulness of the conveyed information. Yet, since no such correlation was found in relation to initial modality levels, this claim seems to have somewhat weak grounds.

As shown in the ongoing discussion, it is not the intensity of the use of modality devices that distinguishes Polish users of English from native speakers of English. Although slightly diverting from the native reference model in the final measurements, the difference was not jarring. This somewhat surprising finding challenges a common belief that Polish users of English modalize their L2 speech radically less frequently than native speakers of English do in their L1. It seems then that it is not so much the modality intensity levels in the subjects' speech that make a difference as the diversity and distribution of modality devices throughout their discourse.

3.4 Modality diversity

Unlike in the previous calculations, where a simple linear relation ratio was used to proportionally illustrate modality levels, in the case of modality diversity a more complicated ratio had to be applied. It would be naïve to expect that, having a virtually infinite number of modality devices, a ten-minute stretch of speech will include twenty different devices whereas a hundred-minute one will display proportionally more devices, which in this case would mean two hundred. Therefore, the following equation was used for modality diversity calculation:

$$Md = \frac{n}{\sqrt{L}}$$

where Md represents modality diversity, n represents the number of modality devices used and L represents the length of language output

As shown in Figure 20, six cases show a steady increase in the number of modality devices, particularly S5 from the ratio at 0.193729237 to a high 0.3691294, S7 from a low 0.115548685 to an average 0.2280034. It is interesting to note that whereas in the initial measurement the students' modality diversity ranged from a low 0.1155 to 0.2814, in the final measurement their levels stabilized at 0.2424. It seems that not only did the students' modality diversity increase but it tended to approach a specific level, higher than the teacher reference level of 0.1814, although lower than the native reference level of 0.31.

The average modality diversity development shows a clear regularity, similar to the other trends described in the earlier sections of the discussion. In the second measurement the ratio decreases below the teacher reference level and increases thereafter, exceeding the teacher reference level in the fourth measurement and approaching the native reference level in the final recording with the ratio at 0.2424, as compared with the native reference level of 0.31.

Student	recording 1	recording 2	recording 3	recording 4	recording 5	recording 6	recording 7
S1	0.220942783	0.198626524	0.274686578	0.279198907	0.249918941	0.090006121	0.1740777
S2	0.198983016	0.100483484	0.221162934	0.235160415	0.248827741	0.305163518	0.2309715
S3	0.181700321	0.094517494	0.134439542	0.247016091	0.222911285	0.238179297	0.2321115
S4	0.281467456	0.132517831	0.107285269	0.178685422	0.199606105	0.140413989	0.2651957
S5	0.193729237	0.139443338	0.136704149	0.219212251	0.186048524	0.253094724	0.3691294
S6	0.201744792	0.145180176	0.16787322	0.255541369	0.214766045	0.228044587	0.2290393
S7	0.115548685	0.131495499	0.141943743	0.126336503	0.174142817	0.223054454	0.2280034
S8	0.164832677	0.118440095	0.16660954	0.239091267	0.316569925	0.185576872	0.2769716
S9	0.177236112	0.149805379	0.179827	0.131212205	0.162195076	0.192494103	0.2180035
S10	0.167183464	0.150346195	0.185996222	0.172905403	0.281216689	0.149270359	0.212631
S11	0.212232523	0.258890187	0.173755588	0.125306298	0.185545443	0.299915852	0.2289343
S12	0.202071752	0.206421543	0.197957642	0.142093947	0.190164039	0.223606798	0.2260955
S13	0.195867257	0.204294462	0.191670793	0.166182672	0.071106819	0.16836406	0.2608696
average	0.193349	0.156189	0.175378	0.193688	0.207925	0.207476	0.242464
NT	0.310000	0.310000	0.310000	0.310000	0.310000	0.310000	0.310000
TR	0.18146192	0.18146192	0.1814619	0.1814619	0.1814619	0.18146192	0.181462

Figure 20. Modality diversity development

Again, the shift from the teacher reference level towards the native reference level can be attributed to the circumstance that whereas in the first year of the research the students' exposure to teacher talk outweighed their exposure to authentic English by nearly two to one, the ratio was approximately one to one in the second year and one to two in the third year of the study. It seems that exposure to language type as such had a decisive effect on the increasing repertoire of modality devices employed by the students.

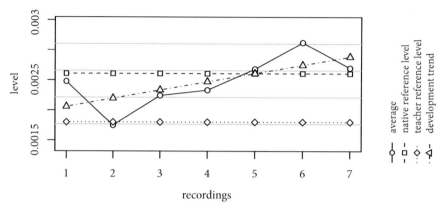

Figure 21. Modality devices distribution development

	Teachers	Distribution		Teachers	Distribution
T1	linguistics + grammar	0.144561	**T10**	TEFL 2 – lecture	0.1278946
T2	TEFL 1	0.249461	**T11**	use of English 2	0.2816715
T3	listening 1	0.1562515	**T12**	American literature	0.1741213
T4	grammar & writing 1	0.1984269	**T13**	U.S. history	0.1681792
T5	voice emission	0.1479478	**T14**	reading 3	0.1915725
T6	intro to lit	0.1343433	**T15**	use of English 3	0.2089996
T7	Br. & U.S. studies	0.278325	**T16**	speaking 3	0.153393
T8	phonetics	0.2461449	**T17**	integrated skills 3	0.06382
T9	British lit	0.1597395	**AVERAGE**		**0.181462**

Figure 22. Teacher modality diversity

The use of modality devices in teacher discourse is not a regular one. The diversity levels cannot be linked to class types. Whether someone uses a wider or a narrower range of modality devices is attributable to individual discourse quality, rather than to the nature of the subject taught.

Conclusions

As the analysis indicates, it is often not so much the intensity of modality that distinguishes L2 learner speaking conventions from a natural conversational style as the qualitative features of language spoken output. Whereas the students did not deviate much from the native reference level of modality, they did use fewer modality devices, although it must be noted that significant progress was made in the course of the study.

This finding indicates that L2 learners, even advanced ones, may in fact have a poor repertoire of modality resources (predominant use of deontic *should* and epistemic *maybe* in this study), or may still rely on their L1 devices. Both possibilities have apparent teaching implications. At beginner or intermediate levels, such a finding traditionally does not call for immediate action. This teaching tranquility may result from the optimism that at this stage of their linguistic interlanguage development the learners need not demonstrate familiarity with a wider range of modality devices, which they must have been introduced to, and which they should fully internalize further in the course of their L2 learning.

The results of this study debunk the naïveté of such an approach and suggest that the diverse and natural use of modality devices should be promoted from the very beginning of language instruction. The subjects of this study did make progress in this respect, yet in addition to formal instruction they were exposed to a variety of input through content-based instruction, teaching subject matter and informal contact with natural English. Regular learners rarely enjoy such L2 exposure.

A similar distribution was found in the use of specific modality devices as well as deontic modality mechanisms throughout the study. In all cases it was mainly the teacher factor that seems to have stimulated the development in the first year, and the authentic L2 factor that promoted the development in the third year. This finding can be attributed to the ratio of teacher talk contact hours to authentic English contact hours, changing from two-to-one in the first year to one-to-two in the second year. This observation suggests that although teacher talk does have an effect on the learners' discourse construction, exposure to large amounts of authentic English, whether through interactive face-to-face contact or passive reception of input has a stronger impact on the development of natural deontic and specific modality use.

On the other hand, the results indicate that teacher talk may indeed have an effect on learners' modality, yet not continually a positive one. For instance, the linear analysis shows an eventually restricting effect of teacher talk on the development of specific modality. As for other modality aspects, teacher talk had at most a reinforcing value. This finding, however, should not be interpreted as a mere criticism of the teachers' discourse competence. A foreign language classroom has its apparent limitations, and for various reasons, including educational ones, teacher talk is, and sometimes must be artificially formalized, focused mainly on knowledge transfer or factual teaching and, consequently, deficient in communicative devices, thus departing from natural, standard discoursal conventions.

In addition, it has also been found that teachers' deontic modality may be directly linked to anxiety experienced by L2 learners. The analysis shows that the higher deontic modality on the part of the teacher, the lower anxiety levels on the part of the students. This finding has an apparent teaching implication if anxiety is regarded as a detriment to L2 learning.

Although this research has shown a number of developmental patterns in discourse construction with respect to modality and identified possible factors determining it, there are areas which require further investigation. Future research could focus on identifying other factors that most likely determine L2 modality development. Possible factors include personalities, IDs, or learning styles of the speaker. It is also commendable to correlate discourse construction with the speakers' age, yet in such a case the procedures would be more than challenging. Selecting an appropriate age group of advanced learners for a longitudinal study could prove impossible, since most university learners are of relatively the same age.

In addition, future research should explore the development of discourse domains other than those included in this investigation, such as use of back-channeling devices or references, as well as discourse marking. However, what could be more relevant and what this research sets solid grounds for is a qualitative analysis of the development of individual aspects of L2 modality contrasted with their L1 counterparts. Future research could contrastively analyse what specific linguistic devices are employed by individual discourse makers to realize deontic modality or other modality types in their mother tongue and the target language, respectively. Such a qualitative procedure would help distinguish subtle differences and track the transfer of many individual linguistic and paralinguistic phenomena from L1 to L2.

References

Adolphs S. 2007. Definitely maybe: Modality clusters and politeness in spoken discourse. – Skandera P. (ed.) *Phraseology and culture in English*. Berlin: 257–272.

Brazil D. 1995. *A grammar of speech*. Oxford.

Chrzanowska-Kluczewska E. 2009. Possible worlds – text worlds – discourse worlds in a dialogic context. – Chrzanowska-Kluczewska E., Gołda-Derejczyk A. (eds.) *The contextuality of language and culture*. Bielsko-Biała: 157–171.

Ellis R. 1992. *Understanding second language acquisition*. Oxford.

Fairclough N. 2003. *Analysing discourse: textual analysis for social research*. London.

Fowler R. 1998. *Language in the news: Discourse and ideology in the press*. London.

Givón T. 1993. *English grammar: A function-based introduction*. [vol. I]. Amsterdam, Philadelphia.

Halliday M.A.K. and Matthiessen C. 2004. *An introduction to functional grammar*. London.

Hoekstra T. 2004. *Arguments and structure: Studies on the architecture of the sentence*. New York.

Kasper G. 1979. Communication strategies: Modality reduction. – *Interlanguage Studies Bulletin* 2: 99–111.

Lee P. 2007. Formulaic language in cultural perspective. – Skandera P. (ed.) *Phraseology and culture in English*. Berlin: 471–496.

McCarthy M. 1991. *Discourse analysis for language teachers*. Cambridge.

Palmer F.R. 1986. *Mood and modality*. Cambridge.

year 1

	TOTAL	Games	Lockstep	Groupwork	Pairwork	Non-authentic listening	Authentic listening	Other informal correspondence	Writing informal emails	Chatting on the net	English interaction with non-NS	English interaction with NS	Original English films/programs:
S1	16142		8054	286	429	520	1658	305	425	215	0	35	4215
S2	12449		5910	440	478	380	764	0	37	100	40	35	4265
S3	15532		3830	200	580	275	1274	863	395	3740	125	0	4250
S4	12447		5125	2000	800	557	1455	30	20	0	265	360	1835
S5	14785		8895	570	485	185	1565	0	165	0	70	0	2850
S6	14960		7195	1980	885	315	1990	0	0	120	420	60	1995
S7	9250		6485	165	325	220	995	0	0	0	805	55	200
S8	11965		7695	322	480	305	1763	60	0	0	0	0	1340
S9	16959		8996	355	388	390	1480	0	115	50	3435	555	1195
S10	15332		7645	262	515	360	1590	50	135	35	825	320	3595
S11	9210		4252	155	345	220	653	150	180	650	1260	15	1330
S12	10399		4469	985	670	300	950	15	285	90	145	60	2430
S13	8235		5070	355	230	100	800	50	25	55	0	120	1430

year 2

	TOTAL	Games	Lockstep	Groupwork	Pairwork	Non-authentic listening	Authentic listening	Other informal correspondence	Writing informal emails	Chatting on the net	English interaction with non-NS	English interaction with NS	Original English films/programs:
S1	15125		9988	383	499	472	1012	170	255	289	34	85	1939
S2	18873		5692	2030	1068	669	712	0	30	50	0	2	8620
S3	32263	7675	2957	637	1946	402	965	874	777	5052	1749	680	8549
S4	17022		5796	3082	1264	616	1396	0	27	0	225	130	4486
S5	23282		12366	1043	621	371	1707	0	0	0	0	1425	5748
S6	22443		11175	4666	1212	449	1471	32	96	170	21	0	3151
S7	18941		12440	815	803	450	976	0	0	0	3268	94	94
S8	16130		12089	630	783	359	1413	0	25	0	164	0	667
S9	22080		11738	471	570	670	1093	32	0	0	4930	133	2444
S10	22484		14770	536	498	466	1098	0	128	74	962	159	3793
S11	9811		3357	665	1806	679	1366	113	762	460	0	604	0
S12	121472		6154	2377	1251	237	1019	2505	3973	2666	54062	41911	5315
S13	17951		10213	1475	2500	275	1350	0	146	97	0	0	1895

year 3

	TOTAL	Games	Lockstep	Groupwork	Pairwork	Non-authentic listening	Authentic listening	Other informal correspondence	Writing informal emails	Chatting on the net	English interaction with non-NS	English interaction with NS	Original English films/programs:
S1	17322		6613	421	570	883	245	117	292	379	306	438	7060
S2	18767		1684	854	811	261	509	0	183	0	342	274	13849
S3	53236	6848	3033	467	1008	783	143	913	4566	6666	6574	11459	10775
S4	15692		3886	2659	1052	650	269	0	68	0	2888	272	3948
S5	0		0	0	0	0	0	0	0	0	0	0	0
S6	15691		3834	3889	1660	502	257	26	0	26	371	62	5065
S7	17541		6211	185	406	477	9	0	0	0	5683	247	4324
S8	15063		7306	772	850	628	251	0	16	0	4891	0	350
S9	25801		5522	378	531	881	276	0	48	0	6090	8435	3640
S10	22031		10019	857	632	1098	118	0	159	95	1321	4009	3723
S11	11333		3243	739	1125	761	311	2863	2183	0	0	0	107
S12	24709		4113	3052	2043	500	200	0	583	350	12291	0	1575
S13	12294		8987	1117	1225	444	219	0	20	0	0	0	283

TOTAL EXPOSURE

	TOTAL	Games	Lockstep	Groupwork	Pairwork	Non-authentic listening	Authentic listening	Other informal correspondence	Writing informal emails	Chatting on the net	English interaction with non-NS	English interaction with NS	Original English films/programs:
S1	48590	0	24655	1090	1498	1874	2915	592	972	883	340	558	13213
S2	50089	0	13287	3324	2358	1310	1985	0	250	150	382	311	26734
S3	101031	14523	9821	1303	3535	1460	2382	2650	5738	15457	8448	12139	23574
S4	45161	0	14807	7741	3116	1823	3120	30	115	0	3378	762	10269
S5	38067	0	21261	1613	1106	556	3272	0	165	0	70	1425	8598
S6	53094	0	22204	10534	3757	1266	3719	58	96	316	812	122	10210
S7	45731	0	25135	1165	1534	1147	1980	0	0	0	9755	397	4618
S8	43159	0	27090	1724	2113	1292	3427	60	42	0	5054	0	2358
S9	64840	0	26256	1204	1489	1941	2849	32	163	50	14455	9123	7279
S10	59847	0	32433	1655	1645	1924	2806	50	422	205	3107	4489	11111
S11	30354	0	10851	1560	3276	1660	2329	3127	3125	1110	1260	619	1437
S12	156580	0	14737	6415	3964	1037	2169	2520	4841	3106	66498	41971	9320
S13	38480	0	24270	2947	3955	819	2369	50	191	152	0	120	3608

Figure 16. Individual L2 exposure

Studia Linguistica Universitatis Iagellonicae Cracoviensis
128 (2011)

MICHAEL KNÜPPEL
University Library, Kassel

W. BANG'S NOTE ON MF 18, 25 FF.

Keywords: Willy Bang, Edward Schröder, German studies, archive materials, history of linguistics

Abstract

The following short article deals with an unpublished comment W. Bang wrote on a passage from "Des Minnesangs Frühling". Bang was sending this short note for a journal edited by E. Schröder who used it for his own comment of the same passage but without referring to Bang.

On various occasions – for example, in the discussion of W. Bang's "Études Aztèques I."[1] and in the introduction to Bang's correspondence with H. Winkler, an Ural-Altaic philologist[2] – I have remarked on the versatility of this unusual scholar. While nowadays Bang is known mainly as a Turcologist – or rather, as one of the founders of modern Turcology – as well as for his contributions to both English and Iranian studies, few are aware of his role as researcher and teacher in the field of German studies. Bang's surviving letters are evidence of a frequent and comprehensive exchange with many leading scholars of his time, among them E. Schröder.[3] Parts of Schröder's literary estate are preserved in the manuscript collection at the *Staats- und Universitätsbibliothek* at Göttingen,[4] including a letter and three

---

[1] Van Tongerloo, Knüppel 2010; the text discusses the article "Études Aztèques I." by "Wl. Baligny," an acronym of Bang's name (Baligny 1890).

[2] Knüppel, Van Tongerloo 2009.

[3] The German Medievalist Edward Schröder (*18th May, 1858, Witzenhausen, †9th Feb., 1942, Göttingen) was appointed as professor ordinarius at the Georg-August-Universität, Göttingen, in 1902.

[4] Schröder's literary estate is catalogued as "Cod. Ms. E. Schröder" in the manuscript collection, the "miscellany" quoted and discussed here has the call number "Cod. Ms. E. Schröder 1423".

postcards by Bang as well as a "manuscript" Bang sent to Schröder. The latter is actually a very short note, a single sheet of paper comprising only a few lines and carrying no information on when or where Bang wrote it. It was originally written as "miscellany" for the *Zeitschrift für deutsches Altertum und deutsche Literatur* but for reasons unknown, it remained unpublished. One may assume that like many of Bang's other writings it was simply not followed through in the turbulent years after Bang's hurried departure from Belgium at the start of World War I.[5] The text of the miscellany reads as follows:

> *Zu MF.[6] 18, 25 ff.*
>
> *Die Stelle lautet bei Vogt, 1911, S 14:*
>
> *Ich hörte wīlent sagen ein mære,*
> *das ist mīn aller bester trōst,*
> *wie minne ein sælikeit ware*
> *und des anderen schaden nie erkôs.[7]*
>
> *Der letzte Vers fehlt in C̲, lautet vn anherschat nie erkōs in B̲, dessen Quelle wohl and'herschaft d. h. ander hērschaft las.*
>
> *Über die genaue Bedeutung von hērschaft liesse sich streiten; ich denke an „Herr-lichkeit" und interpretire die Stelle: wer von der Minne befallen ist, kennt nichts höhere, vor ihr hat von je her alle andere Lust und Freude zurückgestanden.*
>
> *W. Bang.[8]*

In a not much more extensive miscellany of eleven lines, Schröder himself would later comment upon the selfsame passage and read parts of line 28 like Bang before – "*an hêrschaft nie verkôs*"[9] – without, of course, referring to Bang.

The note discussed here is an example of Bang's lesser known work within the field of German studies. While his writings on oriental languages and literatures are as well-known as his contributions to English studies – e.g. his *Materialien zur*

---

5   After the outbreak of the war, Bang led a somewhat unsettled life before he moved to Berlin, where he was offered a professorship at the *Ungarisches Institut* at Berlin university in 1920. In those days, it had a minor "department" of Turkish Studies, which Bang chaired from then on. The miscellany seems to have been written before, since the correspondence between Bang and Schröder preserved in the manuscript collection (Cod. Ms. E. Schröder 35) dates to the years 1910 to 1918.

6   MF. = "Des Minnesangs Frühling" (cf. Lachmann, Haupt, Vogt 1911).

7   Cf. Vogt: "Ich hôrte wīlent sagen ein mære, daz ist mîn aller bester trôst, wie minn ein sælic arbeit wære und unversuochten nie erkôs" and n. 27: "K.] sælekeit L." and n. 28: "K.] Unde harn-schar H.".

8   On MF. 18, 25 ff. In Vogt, 1911: 14, the passage reads: *Ich hôrte wīlent sagen ein mære, das ist mīn aller bester trōst, wie minne ein sælikeit ware und des anderen schaden nie erkôs.* The last line is missing in C̲, it reads vn anherschat nie erkōs B̲, the source may have read and'herschaft, i.e., ander hērschaft. The exact meaning of hērschaft is open to dispute; I think of "glory" and in-terpret this passage as: He who is seized with courtly love knows nothing higher, since time immemorial, it has taken precedence over all other desires and pleasures. W. Bang.

9   Schröder 1932: 123.

Kunde des älteren englischen Dramas – his comparatively few articles on German language and literature have fallen into oblivion. But it was in this field that the exceptional scholar proved to be especially creative: He wrote poems in German dialect which likewise are mostly forgotten today. Among the material Bang had probably compiled himself but left behind when leaving Leuven, were two pages of his poems, likely to have been privately printed to be distributed among friends and colleagues.[10] Both those largely unknown samples of his poetry, conveying his interest in German dialects, and his comment on "Des Minnesangs Frühling" presented in this article demonstrate once more Bang's versatility. At the same time, they raise our awareness of the numerous aspects of his work which are still unexplored and of the surprises which the nowadays scattered, surviving letters from a once vast correspondence may still hold.

Works cited

Baligny Wl. [= Bang Willy]. 1890. Études Aztèques I. – *Le Muséon* IX (5). Nov. 1890: 513–514.

Knüppel M., Van Tongerloo A. 2009. Die Briefe von H. Winkler an W. Bang-Kaup. – *UAJb* N.F. 23: 70–105.

Lachmann K., Haupt M., Vogt F. 1911. *Des Minnesangs Frühling*. Mit Bezeichnung der Abweichungen von Lachmann und Haupt und unter Beifügung ihrer Anmerkungen. Leipzig.

Schröder E. 1932. MFR. 18, 27. 28 (Burggraf v. Rietenburg). – *Zeitschrift für deutsches Altertum und Literatur* 69: 123–124.

Van Tongerloo A., Knüppel M. 2010. Zu den „Aztekischen Studien" Willy Bangs. – *Indiana* 27: 229–236.

─────────────────

[10] A copy can be found in the appendix.

507

Sälber sueche!

Süeszi Beerli sett ig ässe,
Wo mer d'Mueter sueche tuet? —
Sälber sueche, sälber finde,
Denn so sind sie guet!

Rychi Meitli sett i liebe,
Wo mer d'Mueter sueche tuet!
Sälber sueche, sälber finde
Denn so sind sie guet!

's Härzhüsli.

Im chlynste Hüsli, wo-n-ig weisz,
Dört bi-n-i lang scho z'Huus:
's Härzhüsli vo mim Schätzeli, —
Und bchönn mi doch nit us.

's het Fänsterli und het Türe drinn,
Es weisz kei Mönch wie vill,
Und finde doch kei Usgang meh,
Cha sueche, wie-n-ig will!

Holde Täuschung.

Am Obe chumm ig 's Wägli uf,
I gseh scho Huus und Garte,
Und wüszt mi Schatz, wär zue-n-em chunnt,
Es tät mi gwüsz erwarte!

Was lachet zu de Bäume-n-us
I rot und wysze Farbe?
I weisz nit, blüeiht es Meitli so
Oder d'Rose-n-und Ille-n-im Garte!

Gsätzli vom Chilbichnab.

I.

Und e steialti Jumpfre-n
Und e bluetjunge Chnab —
E Distelfink und e Nachtchuz —
Und e Hochzyt und es Grab —
Und es Schätzeli, wo Nei seit,
Wenn mes frogt um e Schmutz:
Paszt ebig nit zäme,
Isch ebig nüt Nutz!

II.

Und e Bueb ohni Meitli,
Und e Herr ohni Gäld,
Und e Garte ohni Meie,
Und e Buur ohni Fäld,
Und e Schatz ohni Liebi
Gilt nüt uf der Wält:
Drum freut mi mys Schätzeli,
Drum freut mi my Schatz,
Si Liebi lauft über,
Het im Härz nümme Platz.

D'Liebi.

Ha d'Mueter gfrogt, was d'Liebi syg?
Het gseit, sie well mer's säge :
Es syg e wohri Höllestrof
Und fasch gar nit z'erträge.

Ha d'Mueter gfrogt, was d'Liebi syg?
Het gseit, es hitzigs Fieber,
Und wenn's die gföhrligst Chranket wär,
Sie wett se währli lieber.

Ha d'Mueter gfrogt, was d'Liebi syg?
's syg öppis für zum Ploge,
Aber wenn sie nomols jung chönnt sy,
Sie wett's no einisch woge !

Es tönt e Glogge. —

Es tönt e Glogge-n-übers Land.
Was tuet sie ächtert singe ?
Es truurigs Lied ? Es heiters Lied ?
Wär cha mer d'Antwort bringe ?

Es tönt e Glogge-n-über 's Land. —
Der Nachtwind tuets verträge.
Gang frog e-n-jedre, wie's em tönt ? —
's wird keine 's glychlig säge. —

Studia Linguistica Universitatis Iagellonicae Cracoviensis
128 (2011)

JANINA LABOCHA
Jagiellonian University, Cracow

THE OBJECT OF STUDY OF TEXT LINGUISTICS (TEXTOLOGY)

Keywords: text, utterance, discourse, text linguistics, textology, text autonomy, discourse analysis, text as a process

Abstract

Contemporary text linguistics once again faces the necessity to ask itself a question about the object of its study. The reason for it is the existence of new definitions of text in which text is understood as a process and not as a product, as well as the developing studies of discourse and its social, political, cultural, and ideological determinants. In the present article I attempt to defend the traditional understanding of text as a product, not at the same time negating the necessity of studying communicative and pragmatic processes of discourse determinants. In order to achieve this I use three concepts which, when treated as different aspects of the same phenomenon, may help to grasp the complex object of text linguistics, which is text treated holistically as an integral phenomenon generated in the process of language communication embedded in a broad cultural context. These three concepts which I treat as a unity, and at the same time as three aspects of defining the object of text linguistics are: text, utterance, and discourse.

Since the 1970s, i.e. the time when text linguistics began to develop as a separate branch of linguistics, it has been possible to observe the widening of the scope of investigation of this discipline. This has recently been a subject of discussion of various Polish researchers, some of their views are, therefore, worth recalling. Jerzy Bartmiński (2005: 47) sees modern textology as a common ground for linguists and literary researchers, which opens a prospect for the integration of the whole philological discipline. In his other works (Bartmiński 1998 as well as Bartmiński, Niebrzegowska-Bartmińska 2009: 12–13) the scholar also advocates a broad scope of textology, indicating that it encompasses all the detailed aspects of text. It may therefore be divided into a number of branches: theoretical textology (text theory), descriptive textology, and applied textology (practical). The first branch focuses on studying suprasentential units, which are able to function independently in the process of communication. The aim of the second branch – descriptive textology – is to study the structure, semantics, and pragmatics of concrete texts, and carry out their analysis and interpretation with the help of methods of linguistics and literary studies. The third branch, i.e. applied textology, covers practical operations on texts, their transformations, development, summarising, etc. Here Bartmiński also places editorship and text taxonomy. Bartmiński discusses the name of the discipline as well. As an advocate of the term 'textology' he points out that the name 'text linguistics' separates linguistic studies from the literary or anthropological studies of text (Bartmiński 1998: 19–20). It appears to me, however, that both of these terms may be treated synonymously (Labocha 2008), since, as the history and practice of the studies of this discipline have demonstrated, the linguistic aspect cannot in many cases be separated from the references to the theory of literature, poetics, folk studies, cultural studies, etc. Both terms – text linguistics and textology – imply a broader context than only the strictly linguistics one, i.e. they indicate the interdisciplinary approach to the subject.

Teresa Dobrzyńska (2005: 89) draws attention to the fact that in the recent years the opposition between text understood as a product of communication and text conceived of as a process in the interaction between the sender and the recipient has been sharpened, the process approach drawing attention of the majority of scholars. At this point I would like to add that at present many scholars approach the definition of text understood as a product critically (Duszak 1998: 21; Witosz 2009: 60). Dobrzyńska also points out the fuzzy character of such oppositions and concepts as text, utterance, discourse, as well as the terminological dilemmas connected with it. She also takes note of new tendencies in textology which broaden the scope of the subject matter of this discipline. These are changes connected with the appearance of the concept of the subject and all its human features in the humanities at the cost of the objective interpretations, which separate the product from its creator. In textology this manifests itself through the new understandings of text which consist in the attempts to grasp the strategy of formulating utterances and the schemata developed in a given culture. In the investigation of text this constitutes a shift towards discursive, interactive, pragmatically conditioned and culturally determined phenomena, which means moving into the realms of other disciplines and, at the same time, including many new phenomena in the area of textological studies (Dobrzyńska 2005: 89–92). Anna Duszak (2002: 29–30) states openly the existence of a new paradigm of linguistic thinking, competitive to text linguistics, the latter finding itself at present on the defensive position. The roots of these changes lie in the revaluation which took place in linguistics in the 1980s under the influence of the development of cognitivism. They involved, among others, the rejection of the modular approach towards language, focusing on the mutual infiltration of linguistic and paralinguistic knowledge, and stressing the dynamic aspect of linguistic communication, i.e. processes (strategies and operations) and not artefacts, i.e. concrete textual products. The conception of text accepted under the influence of these changes stresses the functionality, interactivity and intertextuality, and it becomes discourse analysis, a new version of text linguistics, because discourse creates, transforms, and expresses relations between man vs. culture and society (Duszak 2002: 31–35). The scholar views the new study of text and discourse as a link between linguistics and the other humanities and social studies. In another work of hers (Duszak 2010) she assumes the point of view of a discipline called critical discourse analysis (CDA), which combines the linguistic analysis of text with the social analysis of the context, i.e. the language external determinants of communication and social life. She investigates the social structure, power relations, systems of values, including ideologies, etc. on the basis of the discursive expression which these processes and social problems find particularly in public social relations. The object of these studies are detailed analyses of written texts, spoken interactions and mediated ones which take into consideration the relations between texts and discourses, communicative styles, the stylistic-rhetorical level of utterance as well as discursive methods and styles of constructing social identity.

Presenting her opinion about the modifications of the methodological foundations of text linguistics which marked the process of conceptualising the object of its studies from text to discourse Bożena Witosz states that

> when passing through various methodological 'turns' text linguistics formulated an integrated conception of text – the new proposals did not destroy the earlier findings, and already the first definitions of text which appeared on the Polish grounds announced and, more strictly speaking, determined the direction of further changes (Witosz 2007: 5). [Eng. transl. B. Witosz.]

I share the scholar's point of view, similarly as the opinion that, being under a strong influence of the Prague school of structuralism, Polish textology under the guidance of Maria Renata Mayenowa and her team has developed its firm theoretical foundations (Labocha 2008: 96–102). However, I have a different view than Bożena Witosz as regards the relationship between the concept of discourse and the concept of text. Witosz recognises the dichotomy between describing discourse as a process and text as a product as false, and stresses the fact that the features connected with discourse, i.e. its interactive, processual, and broadly understood situational character, can easily be shifted onto spoken and written texts. The interactive character of the written text is achieved in the process of its construction and interpretation, whereas the sender and the recipient get into interaction not only with text, but through text also with each other. I believe that it is precisely due to this that it appears necessary to introduce, side by side with the concept of text understood as a product of a certain semantic and syntactic structure corresponding to its generic characteristic and pragmatic function, also the concept of utterance which I define as an interactive event embedded in a broadly understood situational context. I treat text and utterance as two different aspects, or better still, two various interpretations of the same cultural phenomenon – of viewing it statically as a product, but at the same dynamically as a process (an interactive event). I perceive utterance as the externalisation of the sending and receiving strategy and as a tool of text interpretation or, viewing it differently, as a pragmalinguistic category of text. However, in my opinion the complete description must be supplemented by a third aspect of the cultural phenomenon, which is constituted by text. This is the concept of discourse understood as a norm of the linguistic (or more broadly – communicative) activity in a specific language and cultural community (discourse community, cf. Duszak 1998: 251–260). Discourse as a cultural norm is a factor which regulates individual and social communicative behaviour, including the forms of linguistic activities of a given community. Thanks to these norms and the rules of linguistic and extralinguistic activity corresponding to them we can communicate more easily and effectively, interact with others, and express ourselves in a certain manner and on a given subject. The realisations (actualisations) of these norms and rules are utterances and texts, which we can describe as actualisations of discourse or actualised discourses. The term *discourse* when used only in the singular number is understood as a cultural norm which regulates linguistic (communicative) behaviour, whereas the term *discourse* when used also in the plural number, i.e. in the form *discourses*, may be understood according to the conception presented by me as an expression synonymous with the term *utterance*. Thus, to sum up, text, utterance, and discourse are various perceptions of the same phenomenon which can be fully described in terms of three aspects, i.e. as a product, event, and norm (Labocha 2008: 73–79; 181–185). Witosz (2009) leans towards the newest conceptualisations which assume the multidimensional, cognitive model of text. She defies the understanding of text as an autonomous product and does not see the need to introduce the concept of utterance to the theory. She perceives text as a phenomenon which is not entitled to semantic autonomy resulting from its deconstextualisation and depersonalisation because it is impossible to think about text as a unit of human communication outside the situational and subjective context. As Witosz (2009: 60) writes (with which I fully concur):

> In order for some semiotic structure to be investigated as text at all, it must first be noticed by someone, recognised and interpreted, and thus introduced into a certain communicative context (text itself also bears traces of the reception situation foreseen by the author). [Eng. transl. B. Witosz.]

At this point a certain misunderstanding needs to be clarified. When writing about text autonomy, about the fact that it is a product of the process of communication, I have never assumed that its decontextualisation, separating it from the act of communication, means depriving it of its subjectivity and references to the situation, on the contrary, I have strongly stressed the existence of the pragmalinguistic layer in text which refers the latter to the sending- receiving strategy. It may for instance be evidenced by the following quote from my article "Odbiorca w tekście i wypowiedzi" ("The recipient in text and utterance") (Labocha 1996: 60):

> Internal interactivity, i.e. the discursive character of the text, constitutes one of important conditions of its sense. Its lack, e.g. in rough transcripts of speech utterances makes it difficult or even impossible to understand a text. The internal interactivity of text is thus an important criterion of its coherence. [Eng. transl. B. Witosz.]

A possible answer to the question as to what constitutes the object of text linguistics is that these are speech utterances and written texts which differ not only in terms of the form of their realisation and reception, but predominantly in the way they exist in the universe of linguistic and social communication. Unlike utterance, which in the spoken contact is always formed against the communicative situation, develops linearly in time and is live in the sender–recipient interaction, the written text is formed as a result of often strenuous activities which consist in the use of suitable compositional, stylistic, and linguistic strategies, in agreement with the requirements of the produced genre and the recipient's expectations connected with it. This is always the case when we work on a written text intended for a recipient who will be able to read that text at peace, reflect on its content, also on the content which demands the reconstruction of meanings expressed implicitly and the detection of various traces of the presence of subjective relations and other signals referring the text to the communicative situation of sending or receiving. In other words, at times we track in the written text traces of an utterance included in it, as the most important feature of utterance is its being anchored in the communicative situation. Sometimes, however, we produce a text in writing which is not meant for a quiet "reading to oneself," but which is to be delivered to a certain audience either in the form of "reading aloud" or else in the form of a speech without an overt presence of a piece of paper with the afore-prepared text. Such a text which is to come into existence as a speech utterance in a communicative situation must include distinct signals of the anticipated communicative situation, and thus it should possess, apart from its subject matter, a well-structured pragmalinguistic component which is responsible for the interactive strategy of the utterance on which the effectiveness of the rhetorical behaviour depends. It is rhetorically least advisable to reproduce the prepared text from memory. Between the reproduction and the complete improvisation, which, after all, if it is also to maintain a certain standard, requires earlier consideration, there exists a full range of methods of delivering an afore-prepared text, and this depends on a better or worse retention of the text prepared for delivery in one's head (Labocha 2002, 2006). I call written texts which are intended for delivery recorded texts (Labocha 2004). As a subject of text linguistic research they are linked with an extensive set of issues in the field of rhetorical education and social communication. On the other hand, this question can also be studied as one of the important problems of folklore studies and dialectology, whose subject matter are primarily spoken texts, but analysed and described on the basis of transcripts based on earlier recordings of speech utterances. To sum up, recorded texts are on the one hand texts written with an intention of being delivered, on the other, speech utterances of a certain degree of autonomy (acquiring independence of the communicative situation) recorded with the help of an audio (or video) recording and transferred onto paper or other carrier with the help of graphic signs (various kinds of transcriptions). Their language, style, composition, and generic features are very strongly subordinated to the influence of social factors (sociolinguistic parameters, such as mutual relationships of gender, age, education, profession, social status, etc.).

The recognition of semantic autonomy as a basic condition for treating a speech utterance or its part as text does not mean its absolute decontextualisation. In agreement with what has been discussed above, each text contains more or less visible traces of utterances, i.e. of a natural communicative process along with its components, which Krystyna Pisarkowa (1978) called the pragmatic background of utterance and described it as a structure consisting of the physical component (tools for and conditions of transmission, the number of participants of the speech act, place, time), the social component (social parameters of the interlocutors, e.g. age, gender, origin, education, profession, social rank as well as the types of relations between them) and the substance-related component (topics, their generic membership and characteristics, e.g. autobiography, family, professional and social life, services, etc.). To these components Pisarkowa added the inherent factor, i.e. the structure of the text itself, for which the direct background is the sender's intention and the function of the speech act, the sender's intention and the degree of importance of the act (according to the sender), the sender's intention and the degree of the act openness, as well as its purpose (for an official, public or only unofficial situation). However, a primary element of the inherent factor is the language substance, which varies depending on whether we deal with a written or a spoken text.

The autonomy of the written text results form the very act of its formation. As Janusz Lalewicz (1975: 53) wrote, the utterance is semantically independent of the context if its interpretation does not require the knowledge of this context. It needs to be stressed that here we are concerned with the interpretation and text understanding transmitted by an utterance, and not the lack of any traces of the context (understood as a communicative situation) in this text. The speech utterance, especially one which appears in an official situation, in a careful variety of speech, is adapted by the sender for a possible repetition as a result of endeavours to free it from any relations with the consituation, and at the same time to its exceeding the temporary limitations of space and time (Pisarek 1994: 17). Of course, autonomous text, written or recorded (primarily spoken) enters into a "dialogue" with other texts, i.e. into intertextual relations. The recorded text gets detached from the situation of its origin and opens itself to an infinite number of readings and interpretations, that is, it gains autonomy, contrary to utterance, which is always immersed in the communicative situation, and its extraction from it makes it semantically incomplete. It is only due to suitable editorial activities that it is possible for a part of an utterance which qualifies for decontextualisation to gain semantic autonomy as a recorded text (an edited part of a speech utterance which, due to its having created its own text world has been able to get detached from the communicative situation), e.g. a gossip, self-presentation, an account of some event.[1]

---

[1] Critical comments concerning such a conception were put forward by Bożena Witosz (2009: 60). I wish to add, however, that the understanding of text I have postulated should be considered in juxtaposition with the two remaining concepts: of utterance and discourse (Labocha 2008). What is crucial for me is that in isolation from them it is not possible to speak about meeting the definitional requirements of text in the process of language communication.

Text autonomy has a scalar character, its degree depends on various intratextual and extratextual factors, the author's and the editor's moves, the presence of metatext and paratext in it (Genette 1992, Loewe 2007), i.e. texts and utterances parallel to the basic text: titles, introductions, prefaces, dedications, epilogues, mottoes, footnotes, editorial notes, commentaries, etc. These issues already constitute a subject of studies and description in the field of text linguistics. Text autonomy is, however, primarily evidenced by the textual world created in it, to use Ryszard Nycz's term (2000). Admittedly, as poststructuralists claim, text meaning depends on the changeable and open context, however, the multiplicity of interpretations does not deny the existence of a text world, which is defined in greater detail and completed by the recipient in the process of reading. Deconstructionism questions the conviction about the existence of a uniformed meaning, as there is more than one way of interpreting a text. This particularly concerns the poetic text and its complex multi-faceted structure of meaning, which compels plurality of interpretations irrespective of the reader's philosophical and interpretative basis. The traditional model of text is characterised by three main properties: 1. autonomy understood as independence of the pragmatic context (the author's intention, communicative situation) and of the historical and ideological one, 2. objectivity, i.e. the recognition of the semantic structure as its stable component, irrespective of the interpretation; 3. unity understood as an internally coherent whole (Nycz 2000: 118). The Polish model, represented by Mayenowa's school (1971, 1974, 1976), verifies these three properties by means of stressing the role of the recipient both in the completion of the semantic structure of the text and in the reconstruction of its coherence. From the point of view of the text recipient text is a coherent informative whole if s/he knows what it speaks about. It concerns not only the reconstruction of meanings together with the presuppositions and implications which are inherent in the text, but also the pragmatic sense lying at its foundation. In reference to Mayenowa's views it is possible to say that text autonomy does not result from its decontextualisation, but from the existence of a context whose influence and causative power allow for the creation of a semantic structure independent of communicative factors, but in such a way that it should contain spaces for a pragmalinguistic content to be filled each time the text is read, interpreted, modified, reconstructed, etc. A model opposite to the traditional one is the deconstructive model (Nycz 2000: 119–120), which treats text as non-autonomous, deprived of an objective semantic structure and unity. Text in itself does not exist, and therefore no interpretation can be adequate and correct as it is not possible to talk about interpreting something which has no objective existence (prior to and independent of interpretation). According to the main representative of deconstruction, the French philosopher Jacques Derrida, it is in no way possible to restrict the number of contexts of a given text, i.e. to deplete the number of its meanings. Interpretation always remains incomplete because there does not exist the ultimate, final context of a text (Burzyńska, Markowski 2006: 378–379).

According to Nycz (2000: 191–196), when applied to the literature of the recent decades the term *postmodernism* forms a meaningful correlation with poststructuralism within the bounds of the reflection of literary studies through the critical attitude towards both the formalist-structuralist tradition and the positivist-sociological heritage. The centre of attention are currently the problems of pragmatic determinants and external references of the literary text. The ultimate meaning of a text is decided by its pragmatic frames which combine the utterance with other forms of discursive practices and with the historical, social and ideological contexts in which it is inscribed. The role of immanent, structural regularities is diminished or they are ignored.

The postmodernist perception of the literary text is a reason why contemporary textology witnesses the formation of tendencies to treat each text, not only a poetic (literary) one, as a process, and thus as something indefinable in its dynamics, developing within social interaction and in strict dependency on the communicative situation, as well as the intertextual context tinted ideologically, historically, socially, politically, etc. This has its advantages, as it broadens the research horizon, and allows one to take up studies on the problems of social, medial, political, etc. communication, within the framework of the so called discourse analysis (Duszak 2010) or a broadly understood discourse stylistics (Witosz 2009), which are characterised by a holistic approach to text. On the other hand, it creates a danger of making the subject of text linguistics completely fuzzy. And the subject is, after all, text and not social communication in all its contemporary dimensions: political, social, economic, biological, etc. It is not ideology or a broadly understood mediality, but textual testimonies of these phenomena. It is text as a document, as a part of text archives of the discourses existing in our times, the discourses expressed by means of language. It is finally text as a representative of a concrete genre, style, and language variety.

The comprehensive approach towards text, its holistic treatment are an important postulate of contemporary textology. However, this theoretical assumption cannot be implemented in research practice in any other way but in stages (Bartmiński, Niebrzegowska-Bartmińska 2009: 348–357). We thus return to the problem of the levels of text description, as it was indicated in the works of a Czech linguist, František Daneš (1970, 1974, 1976, 1985). At this point it is worth referring to the comments of Sambor Grucza (2009: 95–99), who views the widening of the scope of text linguistics as a positive phenomenon, he, however, has a negative attitude towards the shifting of the centre of gravity of its interests onto new elements of its subject matter just recently included in it, which is at the same time accompanied by recognising the former scopes of the field as less important or completely unimportant. And thus, for instance, the shift of the centre of gravity onto the pragmatic and cognitive aspects has resulted, among others, in negligence of the problem of the description of the general essence of textuality and a detailed one for each text genre, which is an important research task of text linguistics. I would add one more aspect here, namely the opposition between writing and speech in the textological interpretation. These two varieties of language generate specific systems and forms of textual behaviour, especially in contemporary public, medial, and electronic communication. To conclude, it is worth quoting the words of Paul Ricoeur (1976: 25), which may constitute the starting point for further consideration:

What happens in writing is the full manifestation of something that is in a virtual state, something nascent and inchoate, in living speech, namely the detachment of meaning from the event.

I also treat these words as a summary of the reflections concerning text autonomy presented in this article.

References

Bartmiński J. 1998. Tekst jako przedmiot tekstologii lingwistycznej. – Bartmiński J., Boniecka B. (eds.) *Tekst. Problemy teoretyczne*. Lublin: 9–25.

Bartmiński J. 2005. Pytania o przedmiot językoznawstwa: pojęcia językowego obrazu świata i tekstu w perspektywie polonistyki integralnej. – Czermińska M., Gajda S., Kłosiński K., Legeżyńska A., Makowiecki A.Z., Nycz R. (eds.) *Polonistyka w przebudowie. Literaturoznawstwo – wiedza o języku – wiedza o kulturze – edukacja*. [Zjazd Polonistów Kraków, 22–25 września 2004]. Kraków: 39–49.

Bartmiński J., Niebrzegowska-Bartmińska S. 2009. *Tekstologia*. Warszawa.

Burzyńska A., Markowski M.P. 2006. *Teorie literatury XX wieku. Podręcznik*. Kraków.

Daneš F. 1970. Zur linguistischen Analyse der Textstruktur. – *Folia Linguistica* IV: 72–78.

Daneš F. 1974. Semantyczna i tematyczna struktura zdania i tekstu. – Mayenowa M.R. (ed.) *Tekst i język. Problemy semantyczne*. Wrocław, Warszawa, Kraków, Gdańsk: 23–40.

Daneš F. 1976. Zur semantischen und thematischen Struktur des Kommunikats. – Daneš F., Viehweger D. (eds.) *Probleme der Textgrammatik. Studia Grammatica*. [vol. XI]. Berlin: 29–40.

Daneš F. 1985. *Věta a text*. Praha.

Dobrzyńska T. 2005. Badanie struktury tekstu i form gatunkowych wypowiedzi jako klucz do opisu kultury i rozumienia literatury. – Czermińska M., Gajda S., Kłosiński K., Legeżynska A., Makowiecki A.Z., Nycz R. (eds.) *Polonistyka w przebudowie. Literaturoznawstwo – wiedza o języku – wiedza o kulturze – edukacja*. [Zjazd Polonistów Kraków, 22–25 września 2004]. Kraków: 87–96.

Duszak A. 1998. *Tekst, dyskurs, komunikacja międzykulturowa*. Warszawa.

Duszak A. 2002. Dokąd zmierza tzw. lingwistyka tekstu? – Krążyńska Z., Zagórski Z. (eds.) *Poznańskie Spotkania Językoznawcze*. [vol. IX]. Poznań: 29–37.

Duszak A. 2010. Styl jako kategoria krytycznej analizy dyskursu. – Bogołębska B., Worsowicz M. (eds.) *Styl – dyskurs – media*. Łódź: 33–43.

Genette G. 1992. Palimpsesty. Literatura drugiego stopnia. – Markiewicz H. (ed.) *Współczesna teoria badań literackich za granicą*. [vol. 4]. Kraków.

Grucza S. 2009. Lingwistyka tekstu – jej przedmiot i cele cząstkowe badań. – Bilut-Homplewicz Z., Czachur W., Smykała M. (eds.) *Lingwistyka tekstu w Polsce i w Niemczech. Pojęcia, problemy, perspektywy*. Wrocław: 95–107.

Labocha J. 1996. Odbiorca w tekście i wypowiedzi. – Gajda S., Balowski M. (eds.) *Styl a tekst*. Opole: 55–60.

Labocha J. 2002. Spójność wypowiedzi retorycznej. – Krążyńska Z., Zagórski Z. (eds.) *Poznańskie Spotkania Językoznawcze*. [vol. IX]. Poznań: 93–99.

Labocha J. 2004. Tekst pisany – tekst zapisany. *Biuletyn Polskiego Towarzystwa Językoznawczego* LX: 5–10.

Labocha J. 2006. Tekst zapisany jako podstawa przemówienia. – Witosz B. (ed.) *Style konwersacyjne*. Katowice: 201–205.

Labocha J. 2008. *Tekst, wypowiedź, dyskurs w procesie komunikacji językowej.* Kraków.

Lalewicz J. 1975. *Komunikacja językowa i literatura.* Wrocław, Warszawa, Kraków, Gdańsk.

Loewe I. 2007. *Gatunki paratekstowe w komunikacji medialnej.* Katowice.

Mayenowa M.R. 1971. Spójność tekstu a postawa odbiorcy. – Mayenowa M.R. (ed.) *O spójności tekstu.* Wrocław, Warszawa, Kraków, Gdańsk: 189–205.

Mayenowa M.R. 1974. *Poetyka teoretyczna. Zagadnienia języka.* Wrocław, Warszawa, Kraków, Gdańsk.

Mayenowa M.R. 1976. Posłowie: Inwentarz pytań teorii tekstu. – Mayenowa M.R. (ed.) *Semantyka tekstu i języka.* Wrocław, Warszawa, Kraków, Gdańsk: 293–294.

Nycz R. 2000. *Tekstowy świat. Poststrukturalizm a wiedza o literaturze.* Kraków.

Pisarek W. 1994. Polszczyzna oficjalna na tle innych jej odmian. – Kurzowa Z., Śliwiński W. (eds.) *Współczesna polszczyzna mówiona w odmianie opracowanej (oficjalnej).* Kraków: 13–21.

Pisarkowa K. 1978. Zdanie mówione a rola kontekstu. – Skubalanka T., Grabias S., Mazur J., Pisarkowa K. (eds.) *Studia nad składnią polszczyzny mówionej.* Wrocław, Warszawa, Kraków, Gdańsk: 7–20.

Ricoeur P. 1976. *Interpretation theory: discourse and the surplus of meaning.* Fort Worth.

Witosz B. 2007. Lingwistyka tekstu – stan aktualny i perspektywy. – *Poradnik Językowy* 7: 4–18.

Witosz B. 2009. *Dyskurs i stylistyka.* Katowice.

Studia Linguistica Universitatis Iagellonicae Cracoviensis
128 (2011)

MICHAŁ NÉMETH
Jagiellonian University, Cracow

A DIFFERENT LOOK AT THE
LUTSK KARAIM SOUND SYSTEM
(FROM THE SECOND HALF OF THE 19TH CENTURY ON)

Keywords: Lutsk Karaim, Karaim phonetics and phonology, Ukrainian dialects

Abstract

After endeavouring to examine the grammatical descriptions published in the literature to date and to reconstruct the sound system of the south-western dialect of Karaim as it was presented in the literature, it can certainly be concluded that the matter is far from clear. This is for the simple reason that these works contradict each other at various points. The reason for such discrepancies should be sought in the historical and linguistic backgrounds of the two main centres of the south-western Karaim population, i.e. Lutsk and Halich. Even though these two centres were always in close communication with one another, and the language that was spoken in them originates beyond any doubt from one common root, they remained for centuries under slightly different linguistic influences as a result of the Slavonic languages surrounding them. The present paper aims to present and, where possible, clarify the differences which follow from the studies on the Karaim sound system we have at our disposal. An attempt is also made to identify some differences between the Lutsk and Halich subdialects of south-western Karaim, and explain their origin. Since the grammatical descriptions we are dealing with here and the written sources we are able to work with concern the end of the first half of the 19th century at the earliest, the time scale of our interest is limited to the second half of the 19th and the first four decades of the 20th century.

1. Preliminary remarks;   2. Unresolved issues regarding the Lutsk Karaim sound system: **2.1.** The question of *e*-type vowels; **2.2** Palatality: **2.2.1** The distribution of [ć], [ś], [ź], [ń], and the special status of [ʒ́]; **2.2.2** The phonetic value of /t/ and /d/ in front of [i];

1. Preliminary remarks

Even though the south-western Karaim phonetic system has been presented several times in a number of articles and grammatical descriptions, a few questions remain unanswered. To be more precise: the questions do have their answers, but at many points the answers contradict each other. Hence, the knowledge we have on this matter remains, in certain areas, confused and hazy. Seen in this light, the present article narrows itself to comparisons of the descriptions of the phonetic features of the Lutsk subdialect of south-western Karaim, with regard to which there is a lack of consensus.

There are at least six authors that should be referred to here. First of all we ought to mention two early works of Grzegorzewski (1903 and 1916–1918), which, although written by a non-Turkologist and therefore not free from certain inaccuracies, provide invaluable material regarding the real pronunciation of Karaim in Halich at the end of the 19th and the beginning of the 20th centuries. Grzegorzewski's work is important in light of the fact that he had the opportunity for personal contact with Karaims. His main informants were Rebeka Leonowicz (born around 1891) the daughter of Jaakow Josef Leonowicz the *chazzan* of Lutsk in the years 1914–1917, and Mordechaj Leonowicz (we can find this information e.g. in Grzegorzewski 1903: 74; 1916–1918: 282, 288). Another important work in this field is Kowalski's "Karaimische Texte", published in 1929, which contains not only an exhaustive description of Trakai Karaim, which was the main subject of the study, but also happens to be enriched with important south-western Karaim linguistic data (see, above all, pp. XLI–XLV, XLVII–XLVIII). Noteworthy is the fact that Kowalski was also able to meet Lutsk Karaims in person in 1926 (see e.g. Dziurzyńska 1999: 51), which allowed him to record south-western Karaim linguistic data in a careful phonetic transcription. The next text is a brief grammar published by A. Zajączkowski (1931) – a native speaker of Trakai Karaim – which contains a very brief phonetic description (pp. 7–9) intended, among others, for "elderly people and school children", as stated in the introductory remarks on pages 3–4. For the latter reason the work is less scientific and less detail-oriented, too. The next author to deal with southern Karaim phonetics was O. Pritsak, a Ukrainian-born researcher, whose contribution to the field was published in *Philologiae Turcicae Fundamenta* (1959). His phonetic description is concise but at the same time fairly detailed, thus it should not be neglected in our research. Chronologically the next study is Musaev's (1964) grammar with a very long chapter devoted to phonetics (pp. 43–93), which is, however, not free from errors and misinterpretations, thus it must be used somewhat cautiously – as will be argued below. Finally, 1978 saw the publication of a 12-page description of southern Karaim phonetics prepared by A. Dubiński – again a Karaim-speaker from Trakai. His article is based on linguistic data collected as a result of consultations with native-speakers from both Lutsk and Halich, too (see Dubiński 1978: 35). Later works, like. e.g. Mosković and Tukan (1993), Berta (1998) or Mireev and Abragamovič (2008), do not cast any additional light to the issue.

2. Unresolved issues regarding the Lutsk Karaim sound system

There is a more or less general consensus on the set of sounds used in Karaim; we have presented this below in Tables 1 and 2.[1] The different opinions we mentioned concern above of all, although not exclusively, the phonetic values of the combinatory variants of some of the sounds. Interestingly enough, the discrepancies we are going to discuss in our paper were not presented within the framework of a discussion, for the simple reason that the authors simply did not quote each other or refer to other, similar works when presenting the Karaim phonetic system. Hence, the differences in the phonetic interpretations of the written and oral materials of southern Karaim must be ascertained by the reader on his or her own.

For the sake of transparency, the most debatable opinions will be presented in the subsequent subchapters chronologically.[2]

		Front		Central		Back	
High		i				y	u
	Close-mid	(ė)					o
Low	**Open-mid**	e					
	Open			a			
		Unrounded	Rounded	Unrounded			Rounded

Table 1. Vowel sounds in Lutsk Karaim

---

[1] Consonants are palatalized in front of [i]. Because of this, and since the palatal element in these sounds is a result of a slight coarticulation, we decided not to indicate this kind of "soft" articulation in the transcription – for the sake of transparency. Graphemes ‹ŧ› and ‹đ› are presented in the table below because they denote consonants which have the status of phonemes. At the same time phonemes /t/ and /d/ have palatal allophones, the articulation of which is shifted to dorsal stops (noted with ‹ŧ› and ‹đ›). To date the acute accent has been used by various authors to note palatality, with the sole exception of the palatal [t́], [d́] – these were always marked with an apostrophe (i.e. with t́ and d́). Moreover, in some works both the dorsal and the palatal combinatory variants of /t/ and /d/ were used with these symbols (cf. e.g. Berta 1998). Therefore we use the acute accent to note palatality, consistently, i.e. also for t́ and d́, while for the dorsal variants we introduce symbols ŧ and đ. We do not use ɣ and ƀ as applied in Kowalski (1929) and Pritsak (1959), since in these works ɣ rendered both /t/ and /k/, while ƀ was used for /d/ and /g/ – all of them in front of [i]. We think, however, that the articulation of these consonant pairs was different (in this position) in Lutsk Karaim.

[2] When quoting linguistic data presented by other authors, we decided to apply it in their transcription, since the transcription used by them also reflects their opinion on the matter.

	Bilabial	Labio-dental	Dental	Palato-dental	Alveolar	Dorsal	Palatal	Palato-velar	Velar	Uvular
Plosives	p b		t d	t́ d́		t d		ḱ ǵ	k g	
Affricates			c ʒ	č ǯ			ć ʒ́			
Fricatives		f v	s z	š ž			ś ź		χ h	ɣ
Nasals	m		n				ń			
Liquids			ł		l					
Trill					r					
Glides	u̯						i̯			

Table 2. Consonant sounds in Lutsk Karaim

2.1 The question of *e*-type vowels

Grzegorzewski was, as far as we are aware, the first to note an open-mid [e] and a close-mid [ė] for Karaim. These sounds are not distinguished either in Latin or in Cyrillic, let alone in Hebrew script.[3] The existence of the former is not in question and it did not arouse doubts in any of the works dealing hitherto with phonetics, either. But the existence and the distribution of the latter is not entirely clear since its appearance was tied to different phonetic environments.

In Grzegorzewski's view, [ė] appeared in Halich Karaim only after /k/ as a result of the *ky* > *kė* change, see Grzegorzewski (1916–1918: 254, 256f.; 1917: 3). This tiny fragment of information is repeated, without presenting any additional data, by Kowalski (1929: XLII), Pritsak (1959: 327) and Musaev (1964: 48).

Somewhat different, however, is the description we find in Dubiński (1978: 36). In this case, the author postulates [ė] in other positions than the above mentioned one:

> [...] Die nächste phonetische Eigentümlichkeit des H. Dialektes beruht auf einem Engvokal *ė*. Diese Erscheinung war bis jetzt sehr wenig untersucht worden und stellt vor allem eine Besonderheit der Umgangssprache dar. [...] Der Engvokal *ė* tritt häufig vor einer den Engvokal *i* enthaltenden Silbe auf. Beispiele: *ałyïyd anï ėzine* 'er hätte ihn zu sich genommen', *k'ełdi mana ėsime* 'es kam mir in den Gedanken' *mėnim icin* 'für mich', *yėdi* 'sieben', *yėngiłrek* 'leichter'. Manchmal haben wir mit dem Engvokal *ė* dann zu tun, wenn in den übrigen Dialekten in derselben Stellung ein *i* nach *k* (*ki*) folgt. Gleichzeitig kommt im H. Dialekt eine Palatalisierung des *k* (*k'*) unter Einwirkung von *ė* vor. Beispiele: T. *akïŋłï* — H. *ak'ėłłi* 'klug', T. *kïbin* — H. *k'ėbin* 'Kuchen', T. *kïłmax* H. *k'ėłmak* 'Tat'. [...]

---

[3]   This is what we read in Dubiński (1978: 36):

> In der Orthographie war der Engvokal niemals angemerkt worden. So war es in den älteren Texten der hebräischen Schrift, wie auch in der Zeitschrift „Karaj Awazy" und literarischen Werken vor dem zweiten Weltkrieg, die auf der Grundlage von Regeln der polnischen Rechtschreibung herausgegeben wurden.

Thus, in Dubiński's opinion the close-mid [ė] emerged in south-western Karaim as a result of two different processes, i.e. due to the same development described by Grzegorzewski and others, and as an outcome of the *e* > *ė* change under the influence of [i] in the subsequent syllable. Both of these processes are, however, in his view irregular and merely reflect a tendency.

With regard to the *ky* > *k̇ė* process, Dubiński repeats Pritsak's opinion that the change took place in Karaim as a result of the influence of Ukrainian dialectal articulatory habits. And, indeed, turning to Zilyńśkyj (1979: 48–49) we discover that in western Ukrainian dialects the segment **ky* was also pronounced as "*k̇ê*" [the symbol *ê* is used by the author to note a "raised mid" *e*-type vowel, see p. 35 of the discussed book[4]]. The only slight disadvantage of identifying this process with the one recorded for Halich Karaim is the fact that in Ukrainian it operates mostly in accented syllables, while for Halich Karaim A. Zajączkowski (1931: 7) notes it in an unaccented position, too, cf. *akył* ~ *akėl* 'intellect' and *kyjyn* ~ *k̇ėjyn* 'torment'. We, however, do not consider this to be a decisive counterargument since Zilyńśkyj (1979: 48, 49) also reports that in western pronunciation the unaccented [y] may undergo a "somewhat lesser narrowing and a lack of tenseness", as a result of which the difference between the y- and *e*-type vowels is often effaced.

Based solely on Karaim philological evidence it is difficult to say anything conclusive with regard to the other positions, in which, according to Dubiński, [ė] appeared (i.e. in front of [i]). The argument supporting Dubiński's observation comes, once again, from Ukrainian dialectal linguistic data, even though we find similar processes on Turkic ground, such as e.g. the umlaut-like changes attested to Uyghur, a good example being Uyg. *kes-* 'to cut' → *kėsip* 'conv. having cut' (see e.g. Räsänen 1949: 79, Tenišev 1984: 82). We would, however, opt for a different argumentation:

Namely, in western Ukrainian dialects [e] is often narrowed to [ė] in front of palatal consonants (see Zilyńśkyj 1979: 55). Bearing in mind the fact that, as is argued below, KarL. [i] in the vast majority of cases palatalizes the preceding consonant or group of consonants, this "definition" in fact covers all the remaining examples enumerated by Dubiński, i.e. [in Dubiński's description] *ėźine, ėśime, mėńim, jėďi* and *jėṅ́iłrek.*

Finally, we should mention A. Zajączkowski's remark, which, although rather brief, casts some additional valuable light on the question. According to his observation, the *y* > *ė* sound change after /k/ was characteristic above all of the pronunciation of Karaim spoken in Halich.[5] This raises the question of whether the close mid [ė] was characteristic of both subdialects or not.

---

[4] Zilyńśkyj's monograph is a translation of his book published in Polish in 1932 (Ziłyński 1932). In the latter we learn that the Ukrainian linguistic data was collected by the author from 1904 till around 1927 (see Ziłyński 1932: vii–x). As a consequence, the information we find in the English translation from 1979 reflects, in practice, the language as it was spoken at the beginning of the 20th century.

[5] See A. Zajączkowski (1931: 7):

> Jedynie *y* po *k* wymawia się jak wąskie *e* (nie tak szerokie jak zwykłe *e* i nie tak wąskie jak zwykłe *y*), przyczem *k* przechodzi w *k'* (miękkie) [...]. Zjawisko to jednak występuje przeważnie w Haliczu.

Turning to Zilyńskyj (1979: 55) we discover that, generally speaking, the $e > \acute{e}$ process in front of palatal consonants appeared in the Transcarpathian, Boikian, Hutsul, Lemkian and Podillian dialects. In other words, it was not recorded for Volhynia, where Lutsk is located, but only for the Halich area. Dejna (1957) did not note it in the Ternopil region either, which is – similarly to Volhynia – situated north of the zone where the change exists. This would suggest the conclusion that the $e > \acute{e}$ sound change was not characteristic of the Lutsk subdialect of Karaim, or, at least, was simply limited to some idiolects.

The case is somewhat similar with the appearance of the $ky > \acute{k}\acute{e}$ process. A well-defined geographical division cannot be made based on both Zilyńskyj (1979: 48–49) and Dejna (1957: 132) since they tie this phenomenon to western Ukrainian dialects in general (without any detailed location provided). At the same time, however, Žylko (1958: 113–117) does not note it for the Volhynian dialect, but ascribes it to the upper Dniestrian dialect (i.e. the territories around Halich), only, see Žylko (1958: 73). This, in the final analysis, seems to support Zajączkowski's observation and allows us to say that the $ky > \acute{k}\acute{e}$ process was at least less characteristic of the Ukrainian dialects spoken in the surroundings of Lutsk, and, therefore, may have been much rarer in Lutsk Karaim pronunciation, too.

2.2 Palatality

The question of the distribution and the phonetic value of the palatal consonants has been presented by several authors in various ways. Since the issue in question concerns one of the most characteristic features of Lutsk Karaim, we decided to take a closer look at the works hitherto published and compare the conclusions – in some cases by quoting more important fragments *in extenso*. As the distribution of the dental [ł] and the alveolar [l] is closely related to that of the palatal consonants, we decided to include the discussion about them in this subchapter.

2.2.1 The distribution of [ć], [ś], [ź], [ń], and the special status of [ʒ́]

2.2.1.1 Grzegorzewski (1903; 1916–1918)

The first commentary on the distribution and the phonetic value of the sounds [ć], [ś], [ź], [ʒ́] and [ń] was provided by Grzegorzewski (1903: 6–7) in a chapter dealing with the dealveolarization process (he calls it *dzetacism*) of [č], [š], [ž] and [ǯ]. The description is as follows:

> Ihr Dzetazismus [= of Halich Karaims – M.N.] [...] erhält sich unbedingt stets (mit Ausnahme einiger aus dem Hebräischen und Slawischen entnommenen

---

This seems to be supported by the testimony of the written sources originating from Lutsk, since they do not show any traces of an *e*-type vowel in the position after [k]. In texts written in Latin script we have, consistently, ‹y›. In those rare ones recorded in Cyrillic script we see ‹ы› and, finally, in the vocalised fragments of manuscripts and printed sources attested in Hebrew script the vowel point *ḥiriq* (◌ִ) is used in this position, which, in the corresponding cases, always reflects the high back [y]. This, however, should be treated rather as supportive evidence and not as decisive proof.

Morpheme) rein und ausdrücklich in den gutturalen Morphemen; in den palatalen dagegen scheint es zu schwanken, so daß z. B. dzetazisierende Spiranten vorwiegend in den akzentuierten Silben [sic! – M.N.] sehr rein auftreten, in anderen hingegen, samt dem palatalen *c* bei vielen Individuen, zu palatalisierten *ś'*, *ž'*, *č'* werden, die den akustischen Eindruck machen, als kämen sie von *š*, *ž*, *č* her [...]. Alle diese Erscheinungen betrachte ich als eine gewissermaßen dem *ś*, *ź*, *ć*, *dź* sich nähernde Abart des Dzetazismus selbst).

Later on Grzegorzewski (1916–1918: 255) changed his reasoning regarding the motive of the palatalization process: he did not repeat his idea of linking it to accentuation (a viewpoint we regard as rather obscure), but remarked that the palatals [ś], [ć], [ź], [ʒ́] appear in front of "palatal sounds"[6]. The latter statement cannot be regarded as an unambiguous definition at all – we cannot but wonder what kind of "palatal sounds" he meant. From the examples he provided using a pure phonetic transcription it transpires that he considered the front [i], and several other segments containing a consonant + [i] to have a palatalizing influence, cf. e.g. [in Grzegorzewski's transcription] *ićki* 'drink', *miśkin* 'poor, needy' or *keźin* 'you eye'[7] (Grzegorzewski 1916–1918: 255). But this is all we can say.

As we can see, Grzegorzewski does not mention here the case of the palatal [ń], which, as will follow from our argumentation below, appears as a combinatory variant of [n] in the same phonetic environment as [ć], [ś] and [ź]. On the one hand, it is reasonable to speculate that perhaps he did not note in his transcription the palatality of [ń] in front of [i] as a mannerism with its roots in Polish orthography, as e.g. in *seznin* 'word (gen)'. On the other hand, however, the fact that he did not list [ń] among the nasals in the table introducing his article Grzegorzewski (1903: 5) testifies decidedly against such an interpretation.

2.2.1.2 Kowalski (1929)

The description we find in Kowalski (1929: XLI) gives us a much more precise picture of the usage and phonetic value of the palatal consonants in question:

> Nur das *i* bewirkt in dem SW-Dialekt eine regelmäßige Palatalisierung der vorangehenden Konsonanten. Geht einem *i* eine aus zwei Bestandteilen zusammengesetzte Konsonantengruppe voran, werden sie meistens beide palatalisiert. [...] Das Konsonanten *s*, *c*, *ʒ* ergeben vor *i* palatale Abarten, die in dem SW-Dialekt dem Klang nach betreffenden polnischen Lauten *ć*, *ś*, *ʒ́* vollständig ähneln, während sie in dem NW-Dialekt den betreffenden russischen Lauten ähnlich klingen.

It is surprising that Kowalski remains silent about [ź] in light of the fact that its pronunciation is also the same as that of the Polish *ź* (cf. A. Zajączkowski 1931: 8), as opposed to KarT. [z′], which tends more to resemble the corresponding Russian sound. Moreover, as the linguistic data shows, it undergoes the same assimilation processes in the palatal environment as the discussed [s], [c] and [ʒ].

---

[6] "Przed palatalnemi głoskami występują palatalne też *ś*, *ć* (*ź*, *ʒ́*)" (Grzegorzewski 1916–1918: 255).

[7] Yet, he notes *ezine* 'self (poss.2.sg.dat)' in place of *eźine* (in the same paragraph), thus his transcription is not consistent.

It is important to bear in mind that in his work Kowalski dealt primarily with the Trakai dialect and his description of the southern Karaim phonetic system served merely as reference material for the reader. However, even though he wrote about tendencies, his short phonetic specification seems to be a bit too general. A number of consonants – more precisely [p], [b], [m], [f], [v] and [r] – do not become palatal when followed by a consonant + [i]. Consequently, the phonetic rule does not apply to such words as e.g. *tenri* 'God', in which the segment *-ri-* does not affect the preceding [n], otherwise it would be indicated at least in those texts written in Latin script (cf., however, 2.2.1.8).

2.2.1.3 Zajączkowski, A. (1931)

In his grammar, Zajączkowski formulates transparent and simple rules that are easy to memorise. According to him:

> Miękkie *ć, ś, ź, ń* brzmią identycznie jak w polskim. Występują w karaimskim w zgłosce zamkniętej [...] przed grupami głosowemi: *ci, di, gi, g'e, ki, k'e, li, ni, si, ti, zi*. [...] Jak polskie *ć, ś, ź*, brzmią również spółgłoski *c, s, z* przed *i* (chociaż w tym przypadku nie zaznacza się tego kreseczką u góry).", see A. Zajączkowski (1931: 8).[8]

This phonetic rule is not only simple, but is also corroborated by the linguistic data. Above all we should mention here texts published in Latin script – even though there are some features which are not reflected either in the Latin or Hebrew script. Luckily for us, however, the linguistic materials recorded and transcribed phonetically by scholars who had the opportunity to hear spoken Lutsk and Halich Karaim also support this notion. The only peculiarity of Zajączkowski's description is that he does not mention [ń] in the last quoted sentence. This would mean that [n] could be not palatalised before [i], which would be rather an inexplicable opinion to have. It is hard to imagine that the vowel which had the strongest palatalising influence did not trigger an [n] > [ń] change. We strongly believe, therefore, that the author's failure to mention [ń] separately was nothing but an oversight, even though Zajączkowski himself did not note the palatality of consonants in front of *i* in his works – following Polish orthography.

2.2.1.4 Pritsak (1959)

What we have missed in Zajączkowski's description is already present in Pritsak's paper – his view on the discussed palatal consonants is almost the same as Zajączkowski's (see Pritsak 1959: 328):

> Im Dialekt von Halič bewirkt nur *i* [...] eine Palatalisierung des vorangehenden Konsonanten [...]. Die Laute *ć, ś, ź, ń* treten außerdem in den geschlossenen Silben vor den Gruppen: *ći, d'i, ǵi, ǵe, k'i, k'ä, li, ńi, śi, t'i, źi* auf [...].

---

[8]   Translation: The palatals *ć, ś, ź, ń* sound identical to those in Polish. In Karaim they occur in closed syllables [...] in front of the segments *ci, di, gi, g'e, ki, k'e, li, ni, si, ti, zi*. [...] The consonants *c, s, z* standing in front of *i* also sound like the Polish *ć, ś, ź* (however in this case we do not note this with a stroke above the letters).

We fully agree with this description, even though we have made a number of supplementary remarks in the conclusion to this subchapter.

2.2.1.5 Musaev (1964; 1977)

The two grammars compiled by Musaev provide hardly any valuable information about the palatal consonant system of Karaim. In fact, almost all we can find as a contribution to the current question in the 50-page chapter devoted to phonetics in Musaev (1964: 65) is the following sentence:

> Большинство согласных в отношении твердости и мягкости нейтральны и в зависимости от окружающих гласных могут артикулироваться с палатали-зацией или без нее: *д — д', л — л', м — м', н — н', с — с', т — т', ш — ш'* и т. д.

This is repeated also in Musaev (1977: 13), with somewhat different examples:

> Некоторые согласные позиционно могут выступать то как передние (мягкие), то как задние (твердые). Таковы, например, звуки *д — д', к — к', м — м', н — н', с — с', з — з', т — т', ш — ш'*.

As we can see, Musaev misinterprets one of the most characteristic features of Karaim. While discussing separately the characteristic features of vowels, he devotes time and space to a discussion of, e.g., all the articulatory variants of [e],[9] but, at the same time he forgets to mention that KarL. *i* has a strong palatalizing influence (cf. e.g. Musaev 1964: 49). The fact that he fails to understand this process is conspicuous especially when turning to the chapter entitled "Переход сочетаний согласных" on page 87 of his work:

> В ряде сочетаний согласных [...] в современном языке звуки полностью или частично заменяются другими:
> *ск > шк: мискин* > Г. *мишкин* 'бедный', 'несчастный', *иске > ишке* 'к делу', *тиске > тишке* 'к зубу'."[10]

From this it clearly transpires that in Musaev's opinion the *s > š* [or *ś*?] process is caused by the neighbouring [k], which is nonsense. He simply forgets to mention that the [k] is palatal in this case and stands in front of [i]. Even though he admits that *ш* can also be pronounced "softly" depending on the phonetic environment (Musaev 1964: 70), his transcription completely eliminates the difference between the south-western Karaim alveolar and palatal consonants in general. Also worth mentioning is the fact that he describes the palatal [ć] as "something between [c] and [č]" (see Musaev 1964: 72), which, again, presents his grammar in an unfavourable light.[11]

---

[9]   He mentions 8 of them: "*ᵊ, э, ᵊ, а, аᵊ; ᵘᵊ, ᵘᵊ, ᵘаᵊ*", see Musaev (1964: 46). We would expect such a statement to be underpinned by an experimental analysis, but it is not. From the structure of the paragraph it does not transpire clearly which dialect this abundance of vowels concerns.

[10] At this point, actually, Musaev contradicts himself, since previously he claimed that "звук *ш* в Г. диалекте встречается лишь в заимствованиях" (Musaev 1964: 70). For the sake of clarity: words *is* 'work' and *tis* 'tooth' are not loanwords.

[11] Our negative critique concerns, however, not only the careless presentation of the south-western material in the grammar, but also a number of misstatements regarding north-western

Moreover, he treats the palatality of Trakai and Lutsk Karaim consonants as the first element of non-existent diphthongs (see Musaev 1964: 43ff., 60–63), which distorts the picture of the palatal consonants in Karaim in principle.[12]

2.2.1.6 Dubiński (1978)

In his article devoted exclusively to the southern Karaim phonetic system Dubiński presents a slightly different picture of the distribution of [ć], [ś], [ź] and [ń] than the one shown above.

To begin with, it clearly transpires from his paper that [i] exerts a strong palatalising influence on these consonants (see Dubiński 1978: 36). Further on, when discussing (among other things) the case of [ć], [ń], [ś] and [ź], the author supports his statement with the following details:

> Diese Konsonanten unterliegen einer Palatalisierung hauptsächlich in der Umgebung von Vordervokalen.
>
> So kommt palatale ć vor e und nach i vor. Beispiele: ćećek 'Blume', ćećeklenme 'blühen', ićki 'Getränk', ićkiri 'Zimmer', kićli 'stark'. [...]
>
> Der Konsonant ń kommt vor e [sic![13] – M.N.] und nach i in geschlossener Silbe im Anlaut und in den weiteren Stellungen innerhalb des Wortes vor. Beispiele: neńdi 'welcher', mersełeńdi 'erhielt als Erbschaft', ekińci 'zweiter', segizińci 'achter', k'etirińdi 'hat sich erhoben'.
>
> Der palatale ś kommt vor und nach dem e sowie nach dem i vor. Beispiele: k'eśk'en 'abgeschnitten', śeśk'endim 'ich erschrak', tańetmeśk'e 'um nicht zu verlieren', iśni 'die Arbeit (Acc.)', miśkin 'armer', k'emińti 'hat verlassen' [...].
>
> Mit dem ź haben wir nach den Vokalen e und i zu tun. [...] Beispiele: eźǵe 'anderer', seźni 'das Wort (Acc.)', teźdi 'wartete', ezimiźni 'uns selbst', k'ergiźdi 'zeigte', ebǵełerimiźǵe 'unseren Vorfahren'.

Karaim, too. So as not to exceed the predetermined limits of our study, let us redirect the reader to Stachowski (2009: 169–173), where a thorough review of Musaev's view on the consonant harmony in north-western Karaim can be found.

[12] On page 47, for instance, we can read the following:

> Дифтонгоидный вариант э выступает в Т. диалекте корнях, а в Г. — и в корнях и в аффиксах после палатализованных согласных (в данной работе для обозначения этого рода э принят знак е): кермен [кйэр'мйэен] 'замок', Г. келем [кйэлэм], Т. келям [кйэлйäм] 'я иду', Г. кисиде [кисидэ] 'у человека'.

This view is unfathomable for several reasons. Firstly, what Musaev notes with an e is not a diphthong, but is simply a [k] palatalised in front of [e], as is usually the case in Turkic languages. Besides, it is not the "diphthongoid e" which appears after a palatal consonant, but the relation of cause and effect is exactly the opposite: the consonant [k] becomes palatal in front of [e], as is usually the case in the Turkic languages. Secondly, the word for 'castle' does not have the sound "[кйэр'мйэен]" either in Lutsk or in Trakai Karaim (cf. KarL. ḱermen and KarT. ḱermań). The nasal [m] never becomes palatal in front of [e] in Lutsk Karaim. Thirdly, the description becomes even more odd if we take into account the fact that Musaev interprets ['a] – in his notation [sic!] ä – in the KarT. word ḱełam as a front [!] vowel (cf. his argumentation about the phonetic value of ä and the vowel harmony in Trakai Karaim e.g. on pages 46 and 50ff.). Finally, frankly speaking we do not really understand where the "diphthongoid e" in "Т. кисиде [кисидэ]" is.

[13] Most probably a misprint. The examples referred to by the author point to a different explanation, namely: "nach e und nach i".

The rules presented here are quite complicated since, in our opinion, they were also supposed to explain such lexemes which should be treated rather as exceptions. Besides, we cannot agree with some of its parts:

Firstly, all the examples enumerated by Dubiński can be explained by Zająckowski's rule supplemented with Pritsak's addition. The only exceptions are *ćećek*, *śeśkendim* and *taśetmeśke* [all examples presented in Dubiński's transcription]. It is not, however, merely the simplicity of the rule that makes us favour it. It also seems more likely that in the words *neńdi*, *merełeńdi*, *keśken*, *eźge*, *seźni* and *teźdi* the palatality of the discussed consonants appears because of the influence of the palatal consonants standing after them (as a result of a regressive assimilation), than supposing that it is due to the vowel [e] standing in front of them. We must remember that [e] does not take part in progressive assimilation processes, but in regressive ones, and influences only [k] and [g] – even [ł] remains dental in front of [e]. The same is the case with [i] standing in front of [ź], [ś] and [ć] – it does not take part in progressive palatalization, either. This can easily be exemplified by the following lexemes: *eźine* 'for itself' (not **ezińe*), *ezende* 'in the river' (not **eźeńde*), *cembir* 'kerchief' (not **ćembir*), *bicen* 'hay' (not **bićen*), *ełcedim* 'I measured' (not **ełćedim*), *icedłer* 'they drink' (not **ićedłer*), *kisenc* 'sadness' (not **kiśeńc*).[14]

On the other hand, one should not neglect Dubiński's idea of explaining the palatal [ć] and [ś] in *ćećek*, *ćećekłenme*, *śeśkendim* and *taśetmeśke* as a result of the influence of [e].[15] However, these words should be treated as exceptions. *Nota bene* they are already listed in KSB and they are also partially mentioned in Grzegorzewski (1916–1918: 254, 267).

2.2.1.7 The special status of [ǯ]

Let us pursue our discussion with an important digression concerning the palatal [ǯ]. It is valid to mention it here as it most probably underwent the same phonetic processes (see below) as [ć], [ś], [ź] and [ń].

The fact is that this sound is almost completely missing from the Lutsk Karaim sound system. The only example we had hitherto encountered is the word *ǯiǵir* 'intestines'[16] attested as ‹dzigirim› (with 1st singular possessive ending) in one of the poems of Sergiusz Rudkowski that we edited (see Németh 2006: 23). As far as we know, there are no examples provided for [ǯ] either in Grzegorzewski (1903: 6–7; 1916–1918: 255) or Kowalski (1929: XLI) let alone Pritsak (1959: 328) – i.e. in those works which list the sound for south-western Karaim. It is interesting to note that the sound in question is not even mentioned by Dubiński (1978: 39).[17] We do not claim that [ǯ] was completely missing from the Lutsk Karaim dialect, but we can say with certainty, that its use was fairly limited.

---

[14]　The examples were taken from Németh (2006), see the morphological index attached to the work.

[15]　Although regressive assimilation (*s – ś > ś – ś*) also appears probable here. Of course in the latter two examples this only concerns the first [ś].

[16]　An interdialectal borrowing from KarK. *ǯijer* '1. liver; 2. intestines' (KRPS 172; Levi 1996: 77: s.v. *потроха*), KarK. *ǯyger* '1. liver; 2. kidney' (KRPS 174; Levi 1996: 68: s.v. *печень*).

[17]　It is also missing from Musaev (1964) and (1977), but these grammars, as shown above, fail to be authoritative in this matter.

2.2.1.8 Final remarks

It is our belief that, based on what we have said above, we should postulate palatal [ć], [ś], [ź], [ń] and [ʒ́] in front of [i] and the palatalized [ć], [d'], [d], [ǵ], [k̈], [l], [ń], [ś], [t'], [t], [ź], with the reservation that the idiolectal realization of this rule might have differed. As an example of the latter phenomenon we should mention the word *tenri* 'God' (cf. 2.2.1.2), which we have also encountered as טֶינִירִי with an additional *yodh* used after *nun* noting, perhaps, palatality (see Németh 2011: 142). This means that the word might be read as *teńŕi*, thus palatal [ń] might also appear after the segment [ŕi]. Such examples should, however, be treated merely as exceptions.

It should be added that [ć], [ń], [ś] also appeared in other positions in Slavonic-origin words, especially in the diminutive forms of personal names, which is supported by the texts written in Latin script, e.g. (*Sabina* →) *Bińća*, (*Šemoel* →) *Semelćo* and the like (for further examples see e.g. Sulimowicz (2004: 147). The only (known to us) native exceptions are *ćećek* 'flower', *śeśken-* 'to get scared' and *taśetme-* 'to lose; to destroy'.

As far as their phonetic value goes, since the appearance of Kowalski's work there has been a consensus in the literature that all four consonants are identical to their Polish (palatal) equivalents, even though Grzegorzewski (1903: 6) writes about soft alveolar [š′], [č′] and [ž′].[18]

2.2.2 The phonetic value of /t/ and /d/ in front of [i]

A number of grammatical descriptions suggest that the pronunciation of the dental [t] and [d] in front of [i] was very similar to that of [k] and [g] in the same position, respectively. The question, however, remains of whether these complementary variants were pronounced identically or merely similarly and what was the reason for such a process. Besides, another issue that needs to be settled is the operational scope of this process.

2.2.2.1 Radloff (1893)

It was Radloff (1893: xv) who first attempted to familiarise readers with the pronunciation of [t] and [k] in front of [i]:

> ħ ist der tonlose Explosivlaut der mittleren Zunge, also ein Palatallaut, der zwischen т und к liegt. Er tritt nur bei den Karaimen von Luzk auf und zwar in Anlaute, statt т vor i, wie ħil statt тil, ħiш statt тiш. Dieses ħ ist immer moullirt [...].

What makes this relation interesting is the fact that Radloff does not mention the voiced counterpart of the sound and according to his observations the phenomenon is limited only to the initial position. However, subsequent works show that such a description does not hold up under scrutiny.

---

[18] The palatal (not palatalized dental) pronunciation of [ś], [ć] and [ź] is also characteristic of the western Ukrainian dialects (see e.g. Dejna 1948: 72). Hence, this feature should be regarded as a rather expansive one.

2.2.2.2 Grzegorzewski (1903; 1916–1918)

Both the voiced and the unvoiced complementary variants of [t] and [d] have already been mentioned by Grzegorzewski (1903: 78). He refers to Radloff's observation, and makes the following remarks:

> Wenn das nicht eine akustische Täuschung ist [...] so könnte man weiter gehen und in Hinblick darauf, daß in Halicz ein ebensolcher Wechsel zwischen den tönenden Lauten derselben Zungenteile zu beobachten ist, annehmen, daß dem ƕ ein tönender Koordinant entspreche [...], ein Mittellaut zwischen *d* und *ǵ* [...], sowie daß in Halicz eine Differenzierung dieser selbständigen Laute, des tönenden und des tonlosen, eingetreten sei in die zwei gewöhnlichen Lautgruppen: *k'*, *t'* und *ǵ*, *d'* [...].

We can see that Grzegorzewski formulates his opinion rather cautiously, and does not want to decide on the phonetic value of /t/ and /d/ when they appeared before [i]. Moreover, he does not raise this issue in his later works. The only information we can extract from Grzegorzewski (1916–1918) is, firstly, that [t] becomes palatalized before [i] and tends to affricatize into [ć],[19] and, secondly, that the word *halidi* 'present, today's' [we note it in Grzegorzewski's transcription] was in his lifetime already being pronounced more like *haliǵi* (Grzegorzewski 1916–1918: 278).[20] The first statement shows that Grzegorzewski had problems identifying the sound, given that previously he had described it as a sound between [t'] and [k'] and not as [ć]. The latter remark, in turn, suggests that he probably heard the auditory difference between *d* + *i* and *g* + *i*.

2.2.2.3 Kowalski (1929)

Kowalski (1929: XLII–XLIII) characterizes the articulation of /t/ and /d/ in front of [i] as being very similar to the pronunciation of [k], [g] in this position, or even identical to it. This assimilation is, in Kowalski's opinion, advanced to such a degree that he transcribes them with separate symbols, namely with ɣ and ƀ.

> Die Artikulationsstelle von *t'* und *d'* erscheint vor einem *i* in dem SW-Dialekt nach hinten verschoben, so daß die Lautgruppen *t'i*, *d'i* den Lautgruppen *k'i*, *ǵi* sehr nahe kommen, ja sogar mit diesem identisch werden können [...]. [...] Die nach hinten verschobene Artikulation der Laute *t'*, *d'* bezeichne ich mit den Zeichen ɣ, ƀ [...].

Kowalski (1929: XLIII, 287) provides us with a number of examples in which we see the alternate use of graphemes rendering [t] ~ [k] and [d] ~ [g] – not only in the

---

[19] See Grzegorzewski (1916–1918: 255): "*t* przed *i* palatalizuje się i ma skłonność afrykatyzowania się, przejścia w *ć*". This sentence introduces a short passage on pages 255–256, in which the author explains the *ti* > *ći* change in a few words. The wording and the style is, however, knotty and figurative to such a degree that we fail to fully understand it.

[20] The chronology of this "change" is surprising as etymologically the "younger" variant (as claimed here) is the original one. The word *haliǵi* is a *-ǵi* derivative (forming adjectives; for a wider semantic field of the suffix cf. A. Zajączkowski 1932: 34) of *hali* 'now' being ultimately of Arabic origin. The word is written as הֲלִידִי in the text the author edited, *vide* p. 269 of the discussed paper.

initial, but also in the medial position.[21] Interestingly, such examples are to be found even in written manuscripts, and this, according to Kowalski (1929: XLIII), points explicitly to the fact that in those texts, in which the authors use an, *sit venia verbo*, etymological notation:

> dieser Unterschied künstlich ist und in dem Sprachbewußtsein der Schreibenden nicht mehr besteht.

Additional information can be derived from a closer look at Kowalski's description. Firstly, the preponderance of examples indicates an unsettled notation of /t/ in front of [i]. There is only one such example mentioned for /d/ in this position, namely [in Kowalski's transcription] *eñбirýin* (Kowalski 1929: XLIII). This fits in well with Dubiński's description that the latter phenomenon was rarer (see below), and to some degree also explains Radloff's observation. Secondly, all the sources used by Kowalski to present the phenomenon in question originate from Halich, and none of them are from Lutsk. This, however, cannot be treated under any circumstances as clear-cut proof, but merely as a supplementary observation.

2.2.2.4 Zajączkowski, A. (1931)

The only information Zajączkowski (1931) provides on this subject is that it is difficult to describe how /t/ and /d/ in front of [i] were pronounced, since they were almost identical to /k/ and /g/ in this position.[22]

2.2.2.5 Pritsak (1959)

Pritsak consistently uses the symbols introduced by Kowalski, namely ɣ and б, to note every /t/ and /d/ in front of [i]. He treats these sounds as "besondere, zwischen *t'* und *k'*, bzw. *d'* und *g'* liegende Laute" (Pritsak 1959: 329) and ascribes this alternation to Ukrainian influences. How accurate this observation was will be discussed below.

2.2.2.6 Dubiński (1978)

Somewhat distinct is the view presented in Dubiński (1978: 40–41). First of all, according to Dubiński this phenomenon is far from being regular:

> Eines der charakteristischen Merkmale des Konsonantensystems im H. Dialekt ist die Alternanz und der Wechsel der Lautgruppen *ti ~ ki* und *di ~ gi*. Regelmässigkeiten konnten in dieser Hinsicht nicht ermittelt werden, obwohl diese Erscheinung von allen Forschern des H. Dialektes bemerkt wurde.

In addition, Dubiński remarks that the *d̓i ~ ǵi* alternation is much rarer:

> Der Lautgruppenwechsel *di ~ gi* ist bedeutend seltener. [...] Ähnliches tritt auch im T. Dialekt auf, wo *k'uṅduź ~ k'uṅǵuź* 'am Tag' als Alternanz vorkommen. Die hier

---

[21] Even though Kowalski (1929: XLIII) states that this phenomenon occurs "in allen Stellungen", this must be treated as a figurative description, as, naturally, a prevocalic consonant cannot stand in the final position.

[22] See A. Zajączkowski (1931: 9): "Trudne do oddania jest brzmienie [...] spółgłosek *t, d* przed *i*, w tym wypadku bowiem spółgłoski te są wymawiane prawie identycznie jak *k, g* [...]".

erörterten Lautwechsel sollen als eine allgemeine Tendenz im Karaimischen betrachtet werden, die sich am deutlichsten im H. Dialekt entwickelt hatte.

The latter statement seems to be especially interesting when compared with what we read in Kowalski (1929: 287–288). From a Trakai Karaim translation of the *Song of Songs* made in 1889 Kowalski extracted examples for the KarT. [ď] ~ [ǵ] and [t'] ~ [k̈] alternation in positions other than in front of [i].[23] He ascribed this phenomenon to southern Karaim influences, saying that this kind of alternation is its characteristic feature. However, if we take into account Dubiński's commentary, the attested alternation in Trakai Karaim is not necessarily a result of the south-western Karaim influence. This question must remain open, especially as we know that in southwestern Karaim such an alternation occurs only in front of [i].

2.2.2.7 Sounds [t] and [d] vs. [t'] and [ď]

We should remember that /t/ and /d/ in front of [i] sounded different from [t'] and [ď]. The latter two sounds only appeared in the final position as the abbreviated 3rd person ending due to a *-tir > -ti > -t'* and *-dir > -di > -ď* change. This difference can be illustrated by the following sketch:

$$(\text{-})t\text{-} + i > t \ \neq \ \text{-}t' < \text{-}ti < \text{-}tir$$
$$(\text{-})d\text{-} + i > d \ \neq \ \text{-}d' < \text{-}di < \text{-}dir$$

As we know from A. Zajączkowski (1931: 9), phonetically [ǵ] and [ď] were equivalent to Russ. *-ть* and *-дь*. If [t] and [d] were pronounced in the same way, they would definitely be described thus. Hence, the exact phonetic value of [t] and [d] remains speculative. In our view, the pronunciation of these two consonants resembled the phonetic value of the dorsal [t] and [d] occurring in Ukrainian dialects (see Zilynśkyj 1979: 36 and 92). The latter ones are also often confused with [k̈] and [ǵ] (see below).

2.2.2.8 Final remarks

The [t] ~ [k̈] and [d] ~ [ǵ] alternation appears above all in those words in which etymologically we have /t/ and /d/, i.e. we have alternating pairs like *tiš ~ kiš* 'tooth' or *tis- ~ kis-* 'to fall' (KRPS 323, 531), but, for instance, there is only *kiśi* 'man' (KRPS 323) without an alternating form **tiśi*.[24]

---

[23] These examples are as follows [in Kowalski's transcription]: *t'eńriďa ~ t'eńriǵa* 'God (dat)', *t'ut'agilďań ~ t'ut'agilǵań* 'to smell (part.perf)', *koladalar ~ kolaǵalar* 'shadow (pl)', *t'oźleidir ~ koźleidir* 'to watch (praes.3.sg)', *t'ult'ular ~ t'ulk̈ular* 'fox (pl)'. There is only one example in the discussed position, and that is to *ielpit't'iń ~ ielpit'k̈iń* 'to blow (imperat.2.sg)'.

[24] This is supported by the orthography of some private Lutsk Karaim manuscripts written in Hebrew script, the critical edition of which was prepared by us (Németh 2011). There, the sounds in question are in the vast majority of cases marked with the letters *teth* and *daleth*, respectively. Thus, the consonants, which were marked with the symbols ɣ and β in Kowalski (1929) or Pritsak (1959) were perceived as the combinatory variants of [t] and [d] rather than those of [k] and [g]. The number of lexemes in which this alternation is evident is very small.

Then, the fragments written by Radloff and Grzegorzewski themselves indicate that the phenomenon occurred in Halich (Grzegorzewski did not work with Lutsk Karaim linguistic materials) and only partially in Lutsk, where according to Radloff it concerns only the unvoiced consonant pair. This, combined with the fact that the materials which constituted the basis for Kowalski's (1929) phonetic analysis also originated from Halich (rather sketchily perhaps but nonetheless true) leads to the conclusion that this alternation should be ascribed above all to Halich Karaim.

When we turn to descriptions of the Ukrainian dialects spoken in the analysed territories – at the same time bearing in mind among others Pritsak's laconic remark about the Ukrainian origin of this phenomenon – all the above mentioned features gain additional value. This is because there is a Ukr. dial. *t́, d́ > ḱ, ǵ* change that is typical of some south-western Ukrainian dialects (see Žylko 1958: 93–94). Thus, a Ukrainian influence is more than plausible here, and the "direction" of this change explains why the alternation in Karaim appears only in words that etymologically have /t/ and /d/ in the discussed position (no *ḱ, ǵ > t́, d́* change is encountered in these dialects). Additionally, we know that this particular process in Ukrainian was applied most consistently in front of [i], as e.g. in *t́isno ~ ḱisno* 'tightly', and in this position the pronunciation of *t́, d́* is rather dorsal (Zilyńskyj 1979: 36 and 92). However there are also less common examples of such a change in front of the continuants of *'a < *ę*, such as e.g. in *t́eśki ~ ḱeśki* 'heavy', see Dejna (1957: 64–65). Moreover, the similarity between the alternation in Karaim and in Ukrainian dialects also becomes visible in Dejna's description, according to which occasionally there is almost no auditory difference in Ukrainian between these sounds (Dejna 1957: 66).

As far as the geographical range of this process is concerned, it primarily covers the Ternopil, Hutsul, Transcarpathian, Boiko and Dniestrian regions (see Dejna 1957: 67), i.e. the central and the southern territories of western Ukraine. In the Volhynia region, i.e. in the area around Lutsk, such a change only appears occasionally (see Zilyńskyj 1979: 92). This again strengthens and makes highly likely our supposition that the alternation was characteristic above all of the Halich subdialect of Karaim. Seen in this light, the rare examples of this change in Lutsk Karaim should be explained either by the articulatory influence of Halich Karaim (since contacts between these two communities were constant), or by contacts with the Ukrainian inhabitants of the territories south of Lutsk. Additionally, the phenomenon should be treated rather as an idiolectal one[25] – similarly to its idiolectal status in Ukrainian dialects, see Dejna (1957: 64). If this is true, this would be the second subdialectal difference between Halich and Lutsk Karaim caused by Ukrainian influence besides the *y > e* sound change in front of /k/ discussed above.

The case is similar with the pronunciation of the segment /sti/. In Kowalski (1929: XLI–XLII) and later also in Pritsak (1959: 329) we read that in this segment [t] is not pronounced as [t], but as [ć]. The only similar statement in the literature is made by Grzegorzewski (1916–1918: 255), cited above, according to which [t] tends to be

---

[25] The idiolectal character of this phenomenon should also be deduced from Kowalski (1929: XLIII), where the author writes that "[…] der Unterschied zwischen *t́i, d́i*, und *ḱi, ǵi* im Sprachbewußtsein mancher Individuen nicht mehr besteht […]".

pronounced as [ć]. Thus, the descriptions hitherto made report this change based primarily on Halich Karaim linguistic data. As far as the Lutsk Karaim written sources go, we have not found any orthographical evidence supporting this change, even in carelessly (i.e. phonetically) written manuscripts. This can be supported by the fact that the *s + ti > śći* change is also characteristic only of those Ukrainian dialects which were in use in, among other places, the Halich area (see Dejna 1957: 61–63). The isogloss of this feature separates the dialects used around Lutsk from those spoken in the south.

In the final analysis, it seems that the pronunciation of the above mentioned consonants was often idiolectal, a fact which appears to be supported by Kowalski's and Grzegorzewski's observations mentioned above, and could have differed in the subdialects of Lutsk and Halich.

2.2.3 The distribution of [ł] and [l]

2.2.3.1 Grzegorzewski (1903; 1916–1918)

The first observer to describe the system of liquids in Karaim was Grzegorzewski (1903: 5). He noted three liquids for Karaim used in Halich: "[l], [ł] and [ł']". To better understand the results of Grzegorzewski's research let us, again, cite his viewpoint *in extenso*:

> [...] Sonorlauten: *n, m, r, ł, l* (dabei die 4 ersten auch mouilliert) (*l* in Verbindung *le, el* klingt fast wie kroatisch *l*: ich transkribiere es durch mouilliertes *ł* [*ł'*]). [In a footnote attached to the latter sentence:] Die jüngste Generation macht zwischen diesen Lauten fast durchaus keinen Unterschied mehr: das *ł'* klingt bei ihr beinahe oder auch ganz so wie *ł*.

The description is far from being entirely clear. As far as we understand it, Grzegorzewski postulates a dental [ł], which remains dental when surrounded by [e], unlike what is usually the case in the Turkic languages. At the same time, in Grzegorzewski's opinion, in such a position it also sounds somewhat palatalized, which he marks with an *ł'*. Finally, there is also the alveolar [l]. Thus, based on the description quoted above, as well as on the transcription employed in Grzegorzewski's (1903) article, we can say that according to the author [l] appeared before [i], [ł] was used in front of the back vowels, and, finally, "ł'" in front of or after [e]. Nonetheless, the exact phonetic difference between [l] and [ł'] as well as between [l] and [ł'] cannot be determined solely on the basis of Grzegorzewski's explanation.[26] This is not disambiguated in Grzegorzewski (1917: 3) either.

This viewpoint on the distribution of the above mentioned three liquids was slightly modified in Grzegorzewski (1916–1918: 257). In the later case, namely, the

---

[26]　This system partially reflects the *l*-type sound system in Ukrainian dialects: (1) Grzegorzewski's "l" resembles the "weakly softened" Ukr. *l*, which appears in the Dniestrian and occasionally in the Hutsul dialects also in front of [i] (see Zilynśkyj 1979: 101), (2) Grzegorzewski's "ł'" stands probably for an alveolar [l], and, finally, (3) Grzegorzewski's "ł" should be described as a dental liquid.

author claimed that [l] also sometimes occurs after [e] and [i], especially when followed by dental plosives. This observation is perceptive, although not entirely acceptable. Firstly, from subsequent works based on the knowledge of native speakers it clearly transpires that [l] does not occur "simply" after [e] and [i] – as is argued below. Secondly, it is not clear to us why dental plosives would palatalize a neighbouring consonant.

2.2.3.2 Kowalski (1929)

Kowalski's position on the issue is much simpler. When discussing the palatalizing feature of [i] Kowalski (1929: XLI) mentions the following:

> Nur das *i* bewirkt in dem SW-Dialekt eine regelmäßige Palatalisierung der vorangehenden Konsonanten. Geht einem *i* eine aus zwei Bestandteilen zusammengesetzte Konsonantengruppe voran, werden sie meistens beide palatalisiert. Nur wenn der erste Bestandteil ein *ł* ist, bleibt er unverändert.

From this we know that Kowalski postulates only two liquids, [ł] and [l] – the latter only in front of [i]. This can be supported by analysing his transcription, where we find e.g. *ekśiklikten* 'lack (abl)', *kiłбiłer* 'to laugh (praet.3.pl)' or *śiriłeбiłer* 'to be chased away (praes.3.pl)', see Kowalski (1929: 286–287).

2.2.3.3 Zajączkowski, A. (1931)

A. Zajączkowski (1931: 9) once again provides us with a different definition. According to this text [l] occurs in front of [i] as well as (unlike what we learn in earlier works) in a closed syllable, if there is a segment /ti/ or /di/ positioned after it. Besides, he remarks that [l] may also appear in front of other palatal consonants, but only as a result of careful pronunciation, exemplifying it with the word *elǵen* 'the deceased' (~ *ełǵen*)".[27]

2.2.3.4 Pritsak (1959)

In *Philologie Turcicae Fundamenta* we find almost the same information as in the previous work, namely a short statement that "*l* erscheint nur vor *i*, *ɣi* und *бi*" (see Pritsak 1959: 329; cf. however, also *äłбi* on page 328, which is probably a printing error).

2.2.3.5 Dubiński (1978)

In Dubiński (1978: 39–40) the distribution of [l] is explained somewhat differently, again:

> Einer getrennten Betrachtung bedarf das palatale *l*. Im H. Dialekt trifft man insbesondere das velare *ł*, dagegen das palatale *l* kommt einzig in der Umgebung des Vokals *i* vor. Beispiele: *biliwli* 'bekannt', *esitildi* 'man hat gehört', *k'eliredi* 'er kam',

---

[27] In Zajączkowski's words:

> Miękkie *l* występuje przed *i* lub w zgłosce zamkniętej o ile po niej następuje *ti*, *di*. […] Czasem także przed innemi, miękkiemi spółgłoskami może wystąpić *l*, ale tylko w starannej wymowie: *elg'en* „zmarły, nieboszczyk" (obok *ełg'en*).

tiğellik 'Vollkommenheit', *tili* 'seine Zunge (Sprache)' aber *til* 'Zunge (Sprache)'. Das palatale *l* kann auch sporadisch nach dem Vokal *e* vorkommen. Beispiele: *belgi* 'Merkmal', *belgiłedi* 'hat bemerkt'.

As we can see, Dubiński interprets the linguistic data in the following way: he postulates the alveolar [l] "in the surrounding" of [i], probably meaning that such a shift in pronunciation could also be a result of a progressive assimilation, as exemplified by the word *esitildi*. A similar progressive assimilation, but after [e], would explain the alveolar character of [l] in the last two examples. We do not think, however, that this would be a suitable explanation, and this is for the same reason that we rejected the possibility of a progressive palatalization process in chapter 2.2.1.6 in the case of [ć], [ś], [ź] and [ń] (for the argumentation see there). This can be seen e.g. in the word *til* mentioned by Dubiński, in which *l* remains dental after [i]. Additionally, if we take a closer look at the examples Dubiński enumerates, we can see that they are all to be explained by Zajączkowski's "definition", which appears to us to be a credible one.

2.2.3.6 Musaev (1964)
Musaev (1964: 73) does not devote much time and space to this issue. The only thing he writes, in fact, and quite laconically, too, is:

> В Г. диалекте *л* часто в соседстве с палатализованными согласными и передними гласными произносится твердо.

2.2.3.7 Conclusion
In our view, and as the orthography based on Polish writing used in the inter-war period shows, the alveolar [l] appeared in Karaim in front of the segments /ti/, /di/ and in front of [d'] and [i]. This is even more likely as we know that [i] and the two above mentioned segments exerted the strongest palatalizing influence in Lutsk Karaim. Nevertheless, it is important to recall the appearance of the alveolar [l] in eloquent pronunciation in front of other palatal consonants, too, as stated by A. Zajączkowski (1931: 9). This explains such rare attestations as e.g. the 2nd plural imperative form *kełńiz* noted as "*kelniz*" in Mardkowicz (1933: 6) in place of the expected "*kełniz*".

2.3 The alveolar [č], [š], [ž] and [ǯ]

The dealveolarization of the alveolar affricates and fricatives is a widely known feature of Lutsk Karaim (see e.g. Räsänen 1949: 173). However, this primarily concerns the inherited vocabulary and loanwords from the older layers of the lexicon. In the case of the younger Hebrew and Slavonic loanwords, however, the alveolar consonants could have been pronounced in the same way as they were articulated in the donor language, as was already mentioned by Grzegorzewski (1916–1918: 254–255). In the latter work we read that such articulation was for some individuals quite difficult to render. Turning to A. Zajączkowski (1931: 7) and Pritsak (1959: 328) we even found that [š] was uttered among south-western Karaim phonemes. Nevertheless, we cannot explain why the other sounds, namely [č], [ž] and [ǯ], were neglected by them. In Mardkowicz's dictionary for instance, we find words like [in the original writing] *czufut* 'Jew' [č-] or *szewet* 'tribe, clan' [š-] (KSB 21, 59), which would already justify treating all of these sounds equally. Probably such words gave grounds for Pritsak (1959: 328) to list additionally [č] for south-western Karaim. But in the journal *Karaj Awazy* we find the sound [ǯ] in the word *džuwaher* 'diamond' in a Lutsk Karaim text (Rudkowski 1931: 19), thus, theoretically, even Pritsak's description is not complete. It is true that the number of such attestations is low, but nevertheless we do not see any arguments in favour of the the idea of listing only [š] or [š] and [č] in the column containing the alveolar consonants. For this reason we also enumerated them in Table 2.

2.4. The question of the fricative [χ], [h], and [ɣ] and its continuants

The system of the velar and uvular fricatives was presented for the first time in Grzegorzewski's article published in Vienna in 1903. Since then, works dealing with this topic have offered various viewpoints on this system. Below we have outlined the most important trouble spots in the discussion, again, chronologically.

2.4.1 Grzegorzewski (1903; 1916–1918)

Grzegorzewski (1903: 5) notes the following sounds in this category: the voiceless "*x, χ*" and the voiced "*ɣ (h)*", with the annotation that all of them might have their palatal equivalents ("*dabei auch mouilliert*"). Furthermore, he writes that:

> dem *x* (*χ*) entsprechende tönende Spiranten (‖ arab. ġ̣) fehlen ganz und gar, sie sind durch ihre Divergenten [...] *g, h* [...] vertreten.

Such a not entirely clear notion is augmented by a footnote (Grzegorzewski 1903: 5–6) in which, additionally, the symbol "*gh*" is introduced and described as follows:

> Nur bei manchen Personen der älteren Generation, die der Schriftsprache vollkommen mächtig sind, hört man zuweilen *gh*, und zwar nur bei solchen die aus Troki (oder aus dem Oriente) stammen oder längere Zeit dort zugebracht haben; sonst hat es sich zu zwei besonderen Lauten differenziert — zu *g* und *h*, so daß in dem betreffenden Ausdrücken statt des *gh* willkürlich *g* oder *h* gebraucht wird.

Finally, Grzegorzewski (1903: 5) remarks the following – complicating even more his already barely comprehensible reasoning:

> [Aspirierter Vokalleinsatz — *h*.][28]

It is difficult to assign the correct phonetic value to some of the symbols that Grzegorzewski used here. Even his later work does not disambiguate things for us, since the description we find here contains different symbols, and reports only two sounds from this category (the voiced velar fricative rendered with *h* and the voiced uvular

---

[28] We ignore this statement in our comments below as we fail to fully understand it.

fricative noted with γ, see Grzegorzewski 1916–1918: 257). Besides, his archaic and somewhat bizarre style is another difficulty that has to be overcome when reading the article. Still, to clarify our opinion about Grzegorzewski's notation and his viewpoint on the system of fricative consonants discussed in this part, we have ventured to draw the following table:

Grzegorzew-ski (1903)	Its equivalent	Description	In our transcription
x	Pol. ‹ch› in *chata* 'cottage'	voiceless velar fricative	χ
χ	Class. Ar. ھ h	voiceless glottal fricative	–
h	Pol. ‹ch› in *niechże* 'may; let'	voiced velar fricative	h
γ ~ gh	Class. Ar. غ ġ	voiced uvular fricative	γ

Table 3. Lutsk Karaim fricatives as noted by Grzegorzewski (1903)

Interesting to note is the case of the sound noted by Grzegorzewski with γ. For as we see, it does not occur in his article in Karaim examples, although it is mentioned as part of the Karaim sound system (Grzegorzewski 1903: 5). We see it mentioned, in fact, only in that part devoted to the KTkc. -Vγ > -Vu̯ change (Grzegorzewski 1903: 29ff.), which took place in Karaim and serves as one of the criteria used to classify the Turkic languages (see e.g. Tekin 1991: 13). The fact that this sound should be equated with what Grzegorzewski notes as *gh* remains hidden from the reader except on page 78 of the 80-page long article, where in footnote 32 (attached to the word *kiri* 'alive' on page 69) we read in a completely different context the following:

> [...] ebenso wie sich der ursprünglich selbständige Laut *gh* (γ ‖ arab. غ) zu *g* und *h* differenziert hat.

The voiceless glottal fricative χ, which appears in Grzegorzewski's work only in Persian and Arabic loanwords, is not mentioned in the subsequent works, except in Musaev's (1964) grammar (see below).

It is worth noting that according to Grzegorzewski the voiced uvular fricative [ɣ] was already on the verge of disappearing from Halich Karaim at the very beginning of the 20th century and was scarcely used even by the older generation. Furthermore, it was only present in the pronunciation of those elderly people who had their roots in the community of Troki or the Crimea. And, indeed, we can hear this even today in Troki Karaim in the recordings made by É.Á. Csató-Johanson[29]. Finally, as we quoted above, in Grzegorzewski's view it developed into [g] ~ [h].[30]

---

[29] *Spoken Karaim. Multimedia CD-ROM* prepared by Éva Ágnes Csató-Johanson in cooperation with David Nathan in 2002.

[30] This was confirmed in Grzegorzewski (1917: 3).

2.4.2 Kowalski (1929)

This problem is not discussed by Kowalski (1929). He merely mentions [h] in a slightly different context, namely when discussing the changes the final [k] and [ḱ] underwent in the intervocalic position (on morphologic boundaries). This observation can be presented as follows (Kowalski 1929: xlii):

$$-Vḱ + V > -Vh̭V-$$
$$-Vk + V > -VgV- \sim -VhV-$$

2.4.3 Zajączkowski, A. (1931)

In his grammar Zajączkowski does not devote too much time and space to the fricatives in Karaim either. He simply mentions "*ch*" and "*h*" in a table as velar voiceless and voiced consonants (see page 9 of his work). In addition, he remarks that [k] changes into [h] when surrounded by back vowels and into [ǵ] in a front vowel environment, see A. Zajączkowski (1931: 10). Thus, we can reconstruct the following view:

$$-Vḱ + V > -VǵV-$$
$$-Vk + V > -VhV-$$

2.4.4 Pritsak (1959)

Pritsak (1959: 328) enumerates in this group "χ, γ, γ̂" as velar consonants. He also presents the changes in which the final [k] and [ḱ] take part in the intervocalic position, although, again, somewhat differently than had been done before him:

$$-Vḱ + V > -VǵV- \sim -Vh̭V-$$
$$-Vk + V > -VgV- \sim -VhV-$$

2.4.5 Musaev (1964; 1977)

The system Musaev (1964: 71–72) presents is "somewhere between Grzegorzewski and Zajączkowski". He introduces three fricatives in this group: "*x*", "*ɜ*" and "*h*". The first one, "*x*", is a velar voiceless fricative, i.e. [χ] in our transcription. The "*ɜ*" is considered to be its voiced counterpart, i.e. [h] in our transcription. The latter sound, according to Musaev (1964: 71), also appears as a result of a [k] > [h] change in the intervocalic position, which, consequently, seems to be a simplified description of the process discussed by Kowalski, Zajączkowski an Pritsak. The last one, the sound noted as "*h*" is, according to Musaev (1964: 72), a glottal voiceless fricative – i.e. the same that was noted by (Grzegorzewski 1903: 5) with the Greek letter χ. In Musaev's view "*h*" appears only in loanwords.

This description is repeated – although in a much more concise, slightly different and somewhat less comprehensible way – in Musaev (1977: 12). It remains, however, unclear to us why Musaev (1977: 13) claims that the (extinct) uvular plosive "*къ* (*q*)" was the velar counterpart of the fricative (*спирант*) "*гъ*". He also mentions that:

попадая в интервокальное положение, звук *гъ* спирантизуется и приближается к проточному звуку *h* […], which gives rise to the question of how can a fricative become (more?) fricative. Moreover, he lists native examples with "*h*" (Musaev 1977: 13), although in his previous grammar he claims that it appears only in loanwords (Musaev 1964: 72). The author must have confused the sound "*г*" from his first work with the uvular plosive "*гъ*" introduced in his short grammar from 1977.[31] The plosive feature of the sound "*гъ*" seems to be corroborated by Musaev's (1977: 13) other statement that:

Глубокозаднеязычный звук *гъ* в обоих диалектах произносится гораздо тверже, чем русское *г* в слове гора.

2.4.6 Dubiński (1978)

Dubiński writes about two consonants belonging to the discussed group: a velar fricative "*x*" and, surprisingly, a "guttural *γ*". The term "guttural", however, is most probably used here in the broad sense encompassing postpalatal, velar and uvular sounds in the older German linguistic terminology (see e.g. von Essen 1979: 75) and refers, in fact, to a voiced velar fricative. The sound in question was described by the author while discussing the change of the final -*k* in the intervocalic position (Dubiński 1978: 42):

In der Umgebung den Hintervokalen geht *k* in das stimmhafte gutturale *γ* über. Dagegen ist der Zustand im Falle von Vordervokalen unbeständig. Hier wechselt *k* in *g* oder vereinzelt auch in *γ* über. Regelmässigkeiten konnten in dieser Hinsicht nicht ermittelt werden.

Thus, the following sketch can be set out here:

$$-V\acute{k} + V \; > \; -V\acute{g}V\text{-} \sim \text{-}V\acute{h}V\text{-}$$
$$-Vk + V \; > \; -VhV\text{-}$$

2.4.7 The palatal variants

As we already know, Grzegorzewski (1903: 5) was the first person who also postulated the palatal [ҳ] and [ḣ] for south-western Karaim. This has only been partially reinforced in later works, given that Pritsak (1959: 328) mentions only [ḣ] and remains silent about the other sound. Turning to Kowalski (1929) we cannot find words with the sound [χ] in front of [i] – merely [h] in front of [i], which is noted – similarly to what we can see in Pritsak (1959) – with *ý*. The lack of [χ] in this position as an example in these works is obviously due to the fact that such a segment is unusual both for Turkic and Slavonic phonotactics.[32]

Even though later works do not support it, Grzegorzewski's idea must not be entirely neglected in light of the strong palatalizing influence of [i]. We must also remember that the vast majority of Karaim written sources and a number of scholarly works do not note any palatality in front of [i].

---

[31] Let us only mention that none of the other authors mention the uvular plosives for Lutsk Karaim.

[32] In KRPS (p. 602) for instance, in the initial position we only find this group of sounds in the KarL. word *χiʒet* 'riddle'. As far as we know this is the only example for the segment [χi] in KRPS.

2.4.8 Conclusion

At the outset let us summarize in a table the system of fricatives as outlined in the above presented works:

GRZEGORZEW-SKI (1903)	KOWALSKI (1929)	A. ZAJĄCZ-KOWSKI (1931)	PRITSAK (1959)	MUSAEV (1964)	MUSAEV (1977)	DUBIŃSKI (1978)	Description & transcription
x	*χ*	*ch*	*χ*	*x*	*x*	*x*	voiceless velar fricative (χ)
χ	–	–	–	*h*	*h*	–	voiceless glottal fricative
h	*h*	*h*	*γ*	*ɛ*	*ɛʋ* [(?)]	*γ*	voiced velar fricative (h)
γ ~ gh	–	–	–	–	–	–	voiced uvular fricative (ɣ)

Table 4. System of fricatives in Lutsk Karaim as presented by different authors

The descriptions are far from being consistent on this matter. The most conspicuous peculiarity is the postulating of a voiceless glottal fricative by Grzegorzewski and Musaev. Since the writing systems used for Karaim do not distinguish between the two voiceless fricatives (*ch* performs this role in Latin script, *x* in Cyrillic and *cheth* (ח) in Hebrew script), we cannot say anything about their distribution with certainty. This is also because of the fact that in the Persian and Arabic loanwords, in which the voiceless glottal fricative occurs (according to the two authors), the corresponding Arabic and Persian sounds are adopted on Karaim ground in different ways – both by voiced and voiceless fricatives. This can be illustrated by tracing back the reflexes of, for instance, the following consonants: Ar. ح ḥ (fricative, pharyngeal, voiceless), Ar. ع ʿ (fricative, pharyngeal, voiced), Pers. خ x (fricative, uvular, voiceless), Pers. ه h (fricative, glottal, voiceless) and the Pers. غ ġ (plosive, uvular, voiceless). The examples have been collected on the basis of W. Zajączkowski (1961):

Ar. ح ḥ > KarL. χ ~ h: Ar. حجرة ḥuǧra 'room, chamber' ≫ KarL. χuʒura 'room, chamber; bureau' vs. Ar. حيوان ḥayawān 'animal' ≫ KarL. hajvan 'animal' (see Wehr 1952: 142; 198, s.v. حى)
Ar. رحمة raḥma 'mercy' ≫ KarL. raχmet 'mercy, charity' vs. Ar. لوحة lawḥa 'signboard' ≫ KarL. łevha 'signboard, table' (see Wehr 1952: 299, s.v. رحم; 786)

Ar. ع ʿ > KarL. χ ~ h: Ar. قعره qaʿra 'pit' ≫ KarL. kaχra 'hall' vs. Ar. ساعة sāʿa 'hour' ≫ KarL. sahat 'hour' (see Wehr 1952: 696, s.v. قعر; 402)

Pers. خ *x* > KarL. *χ ~ h*: Pers. خاج *xāğ* 'cross' ≫ KarL. *χač* 'cross' vs. Pers. خرمن *xar-*
man 'harvest' ≫ KarL. *harman* 'threshing machine'
(see Steingass 1892: 437, 456–457)

Pers. ه *h* > KarL. *χ ~ h*: Pers. گناه *gunāh* 'sin, crime' ≫ KarL. *gineχ* 'sin' vs. Pers. پادشاه
pādšāh 'king' ≫ KarL. *patsah* 'nobleman, dignitary'
(see Steingass 1892: 1097, 229)

Pers. غ *ġ* > KarL. *χ ~ h*: Pers. باغچه *bāġča* 'garden' ≫ KarL. *baχca* 'garden' vs. Pers. کاغذ
kāġad 'paper, letter' ≫ *kahyt* 'paper' (see Steingass 1892:
148, 1006)

Let us also sum up the case of the final -*k*. In the table below we compared the views
on the changes it underwent in south-western Karaim when followed by a suffix
with an initial vowel (we cannot be sure about Musaev's and Grzegorzewski's positions on this matter).[33]

KOWALSKI (1929)	A. ZAJĄCZKOWSKI (1931)	PRITSAK (1959)	DUBIŃSKI (1978)
-Vǩ + V > -Vǩ̇V-	*-Vǩ + V > -Vġ́V-*	*-Vǩ + V > -V$\frac{h}{g}$V-*	*-Vǩ + V > -V$\frac{h}{g}$V-*
-Vk + V > -V$\frac{h}{g}$V-	*-Vk + V > -VhV-*	*-Vk + V > -V$\frac{h}{g}$V-*	*-Vk + V > -VhV-*

Table 5. The development of /-k/

We believe that the description of this process differed depending on the articulatory
habits of the corresponding linguistic informants. Thus it is very likely that the use
of [g] and [h] in this position was highly idiolectal.

In addition, the pronunciation of these alternating variants was, in our view,
connected with the case of the continuants of the uvular [ɣ]. It is our belief that the
final -*k* first changed into -*γ*- in the intervocalic position and, subsequently, as already
reported by Grzegorzewski, this sound underwent, more or less at the beginning of
the 19th century, a [ɣ] > [g] ~ [h] sound change. Establishing the exact chronology
and distribution of these consonants is, however, an impossible task, in the first
place because all of these sounds, namely [ɣ], [g] and [h], could have been denoted
in older texts with the same letter *ghimel* (ג). On the other hand, if the letter *he* (ה)
or *ghimel* with a macron (ḡ) was written in older manuscripts to render the sound
in this position, the proper reading might be both [ɣ] and [h]. Hence, also in this
case we cannot establish its exact phonetic value.

Based on the philological evidence, however, we can say that Lutsk Karaim in
the 19th century exhibited a [g] ~ [h] alternation in place of the original uvular [ɣ]
solely in a back-vowel environment. In a front-vowel environment, above all in front
of [e], we only have *ghimel* noted in this place – the letters *he* and *ghimel* with a macron, which would unambiguously point to [h] or [ɣ], never occur in this position.

---

[33] Worth mentioning is the fact that these descriptions, where applicable, also differ regarding
which of the alternating variants was the more frequent.

This fact is supported by the texts recorded in Latin script, good examples being the dative case suffix and the perfect participle markers. This is because in the older text the dative case suffix variants are *-ga* ~ *-ha* ~ *-ǵe* used after vowels and voiced consonants and *-ka* ~ *-ǩe* attached to voiceless coda. The same is the case with the perfect participle suffix, namely we have *-gan* ~ *-han* ~ *-ǵen* attested after a voiced stem ending and *-kan* ~ *-ǩen* after a voiceless stem ending. This state is confirmed by the vast majority of texts published in Latin script in the interwar period, although a small number of them exhibit an *-he* and *-hen* ending, as is noticeable, for example, in the words *połełerhe* 'to the fields' (Rudkowski 1939: 9) or *isihen* 'chilled, freezing cold' (Rudkowski 1932: 14, in original writing). The considerably small number of the latter kind of attestations combined with the evidence provided from the older texts written in Hebrew script suggest that the latter two variants occurred in Karaim later, probably by way of analogy with a set of suffix variants occurring in a back-vowel environment.

The following sketch aims to recapitulate what we said above (A = back vowel; E = front vowel):

$$-Ak- + A- \; > \; -A\gamma A- \; > \; -AgA- \; \sim \; -AhA-$$
$$-E\ǩ- + E- \; > \; -E\ǵE- \; > \; -E\ǵE- \; > \; -E\ǵE- \; \sim \; -Ehe- \; \sim \; -E\hbar i-$$

2.5. The question of the glide [u̯] and the labiodental [v]

There is likewise a lack of a general consensus as far as the distribution of the labiodental [v] and the glide [u̯] is concerned. The phonetic value of [u̯] has been debated and described in different ways. Below we take a brief look at what grammarians have hitherto written about this matter.

2.5.1 Grzegorzewski (1903; 1916–1918)

At the very beginning of his early work Grzegorzewski (1903: 5) presents the Halich Karaim phonetic system, in which he distinguishes between a "Geräuschlaut *v*" and a "Halbvokal *w*". It is, however, difficult to determine the distribution of these two sounds based on his description, because on the one hand he delivers only a fragmentary explanation, mentioning merely the development of the word-final *-Vγ* into *-Vu̯* in Halich Karaim.[34] On the other hand, however, from the enumerated examples of Persian or Slavonic borrowings it follows that these sounds were adopted on Karaim ground in a highly irregular fashion. This can be illustrated by the following [in Grzegorzewski's transcription]:

Pers. و *v* > KarL. *v* ~ *u̯*: Pers. گاوُر *gāvur* 'infidel' ≫ KarH. *g'avur* id. vs. Pers. ویران *verān* 'ruined, depopulated' ≫ KarH. *veren* ~ *weren* id. (see Steingass 1892: 1073, 1483; Grzegorzewski 1903: 14, 18, 54)

---

[34] See Grzegorzewski (1903: 29; 1916–1918: 262–263). Berta (1994: 168–170) presents the entire Kiptchak system as inherited in Karaim, where the author postulates a labiodental [v] in word-final position.

Pol. *v* > KarL. *v* ~ *u̯*: Pol. *więc* 'thus' ≫ KarH. *v'enc* id. vs. Pol. *bawić* 'to play' ≫
KarL. *bau̯cet-* id. (see Grzegorzewski 1903: 23, 30)

Additionally, we cannot be entirely certain if the symbols "u̯" and "w" refer to the same labial glide. Such an interpretation seems to be the most probable interpretation.

2.5.2. Kowalski (1929)

Kowalski (1929) devotes little attention to the question of these sounds in Lutsk Karaim. The only relevant information we can find in this case is that:

> Der labiodentalen Spirante *v* der NW-Mundart entspricht in der SW-Mundart der Halbvokal *u̯*. (Kowalski 1929: xliv)

The south-western Karaim fragments cited by Kowalski of course support this statement: the symbol [u̯] is noted consistently, also e.g. in the word *u̯eren* 'ruined, depopulated' (see Kowalski 1929: 286) mentioned by Grzegorzewski as *"veren"* ~ *"weren"*. The only hint that would suggest that Kowalski postulated a labiodental [v] for south-western Karaim in loanwords is the word *vinadan* 'fault (abl.)' < Pol. *wina* 'blame, fault', see Kowalski (1929: 288).

Kowalski's description of these sounds in Trakai Karaim might, in fact, shed valuable light on the possible situation in Lutsk. This is because in two places Kowalski emphasizes that the pronunciation of the labiodental [v] is above all characteristic of the younger generation. In his view:

> Doch findet man *u̯* als individuelle Aussprache, namentlich bei Leuten aus der älteren Generation auch in der NW-Mundart. (Kowalski 1929: xliv);

> *v* ‖ *u̯*. Die ältere Generation spricht halbkonsonantisches *u̯* aus, wo man bei der jüngeren Generation ein labiodentales *v* hört. Ich schreibe überall *v*. (Kowalski 1929: lxxiv–lxxv).

We can argue that in the late twenties the pronunciation of [u̯] as a glide gradually disappeared in north-western Karaim and gave place to the labiodental articulation. This also concerned the final position – where the glide [u̯] developed during the already mentioned vocalization process of the KTkc. *-y* (Kowalski 1929: xxxi) – as transpires from Kowalski's field work. We will return to this description when summing up the conclusions in 2.5.7, and compare it with the situation in Lutsk Karaim.

2.5.3 Zajączkowski, A. (1931)

In a table listing the south-western Karaim consonants A. Zajączkowski (1931: 9) describes a sound noted with a "w" as a voiced "labial" one. This information, however, is not of any use to us, as in his work this term is applied both to labiodental and labial consonants – the phonemes [f], [p] and [b] are in the same group. The fact that double-u is used in this work is obviously due to the influence of Polish orthography – it does not have any additional, linguistic sense. The only remark which would enable us to reconstruct, although very cautiously, Zajączkowski's view is that he compared the Karaim consonants with their Polish counterparts and stated that they are, in general, pronounced in the same way as in Polish, the only consonants which would need further explanation being the palatal consonants.[35]

2.5.4 Pritsak (1959)

Pritsak (1959: 328) does not note the labiodental [v] at all when discussing the set of consonants existing in south-western Karaim – he classifies "w" as a "Halbvokal". Nevertheless, at the same time he notes "v" in the Slavonic examples he enumerates throughout his article. Thus, he probably distinguished between labiodental [v] and the glide [u̯] postulating a [v] in Slavonic, above all Polish and Russian, loanwords.[36]

2.5.5 Musaev (1964; 1977)

In his grammars Musaev (1964: 69; 1977: 14) mentions the bilabial "β" and labiodental [v]. In his view the latter appears in loanwords only (he mentions a Hebrew, a Russian and a Persian example). Therefore, he does not postulate a glide, but rather a bilabial consonant instead. At the same time, similarly to Kowalski (1929), he remarks that the bilabial "β" is often pronounced labiodentally among younger speakers.[37] Noteworthy is the fact that his description does not clarify whether what we read in this fragment is valid for both north-western and south-western dialects or only for one of them. Probably, since he does not specify this, it concerns both dialects. One must, however, bear in mind the fact that the vast majority of materials constituting the base of Musaev's grammars originated from present-day Lithuania.

2.5.6 Dubiński (1978)

Finally, Dubiński (1978: 36) provides us with an additional piece of information, saying that the glide [u̯]:

> erscheint vor allem in der Umgangssprache, dagegen in der Schriftsprache wird er selten vermerkt. Im T. Dialekt tritt in gleicher Stellung das labiodentale *v* auf.

This information seems to be especially important. Therefore, we should add some comments to it in the conclusions below – combining it with Kowalski's observation.

2.5.7 Conclusion

To sum up, we see that various authors present slightly different views on this subject, while the amount of reliable information is scant. Since none of the writing

---

[35]   See Zajączkowski (1931: 9):

> Spółgłoski w karaimskim wymawia się naogół podobnie jak ich odpowiedniki w języku polskim. Szerszego omówienia wymagają spółgłoski miękkie (palatalne): ć, d', g', k', l, ń, ś, t', ź.

[36]   Still, we can find examples that make this notion a little less clear: even though he notes rather consistently [v] in Slavonic loanwords (as e.g. in the Ukr. *-ovyj* suffix, see Pritsak 1959: 330), we can find examples, such as "mäläχuwna" 'queen' (with the Pol. *-ówna* [Pol. *-v-*] suffix), in which Pritsak notes "w" and mentions a Kar. "-uwna" suffix. The question remains open as to whether the glide appears in the latter case under the influence of the labial [u].

[37]   This observation is surprising as it suggests that the generation that was considered to be younger in Kowalski's time is still the younger generation in Musaev's time – i.e. four decades later.

systems used by Karaims distinguished between these sounds, we cannot go any further based only on philological evidence. The opinions we have presented here can be summarised in the following table:

	Grzegorzew-ski (1903; 1916–1918)	Kowalski (1929)	A. Zając-kowski (1931)	Pritsak (1959)	Musaev (1964; 1977)	Dubiński (1978)
labiodental [v]	+	+ (?)	+ (?)	+ (?)	+	+
bilabial [β]	–	–	–	–	+	–
glide [u̯]	+	+	?	+	–	+

Table 6. The question of the glide [u̯], the labiodental [v] and bilabial [β]

As we can see, Musaev (1964; 1977) is the only scholar who clearly refutes the opinion that the [u̯] in south-western Karaim was a glide and claims it to be a bilabial consonant instead. We cannot be sure about Zajączkowski's view as the terminology he uses is ambiguous. The existence of the labiodental [v] is confirmed by three authors.

It seems that there were two different tendencies in western Karaim. On the one hand, in north-western Karaim the labiodental [v] at the beginning of the 20th century was characteristic of the pronunciation of the younger generation as opposed to the glide [u̯], which was pronounced only by what was then the older generation, see Kowalski (1929: LXXIV–LXXV). Thus the glide was about to disappear. On the other hand, in the south-western dialect, as Dubiński (1978: 36) reports, the glide was still in use in the colloquial language and gave way to [v] only in the literary language.

Such a picture prompts the conclusion that we should treat such a divergence as a result of different external influences. Namely, in the northern dialect the disappearance of the glide should be put down above all to Russian and Polish influences, while in Lutsk and Halich the preservation of the glide must have happened as a consequence of the wide use of this sound, in certain positions, in the Ukrainian dialects (cf. e.g. Dejna 1957: 74ff.). Finally, the fact that the labiodental [v] became dominant in literary south-western Karaim can be explained by the higher status of Polish and Russian in the territories in question (see e.g. Kurzowa 1985: 29–30).

Thus we can say that at least for the period encompassing the end of the first half and all of the second half of the 19th century, as well as in the initial decades of the 20th century, i.e. for the period covered by the grammatical descriptions, both sounds were present in the south-western Karaim used in Lutsk. The use of the semivocal [u̯] was still widespread at the beginning of the 20th century, as is also testified by Dubiński (1978), i.e. the latest work based on research conducted with the assistance of south-western Karaim native speakers (both from Lutsk and Halich). We are afraid, however, that the question as to the exact distribution of them will remain unanswered since the glide [u̯], the labiodental [v] and even the bilabial [β] – which would explain Musaev's opinion – were used interchangeably in the western Ukrainian dialects even in the same idiolect, as was reported in Zilynśkyj (1979: 81–82). Even though the glide and the bilabial sound were replaced with [v] in all positions, except in front of vowels, this was merely a tendency.

The glide could have appeared in Karaim in the word-final position due to two different processes: (1) as a continuant of the above mentioned KTkc. -γ, thus as the outcome of an indigenous process, and (2) as an influence of the irregular articulation of the sound noted with ‹в› in Ukrainian. This would, in fact, explain Pritsak's and Grzegorzewski's inconsistent notation, i.e. the transcription of the suffixes -uu̯na vs. -ovyj and v́enc vs. bau̯cet- (see above).

3. Final remarks

The foregoing discussion attempted to explain to the reader that some phonetic features of Lutsk Karaim remain debatable. The differences between the juxtaposed grammatical descriptions arise not only from different observations, but are probably also due to the different pronunciation of the informants with whom the authors of the presented works cooperated. Finally, as we argued above, the pronunciation of Karaim as used in Lutsk and Halich was, in all probability, not the same. The diverse Slavonic (Polish, Russian and Ukrainian) influences which gained strength in the 19th century lead to articulatory and subdialectal differences. Moreover, the territories in which the Halich subdialect of Karaim was spoken remained under the influence of the Ukrainian Dniestrian dialect, while Lutsk was in contact with some transitional dialects exhibiting features lying between the south-western and northwestern (Polissian) dialects. Despite the latter, these two Karaim subdialects were, and still are, usually treated in the grammatical descriptions as one homogeneous dialect. Of course, to a certain degree this is more than reasonable, but one must bear in mind that the differing historical and linguistic backgrounds could have resulted, and apparently did result, in different linguistic features.

4. Abbreviations

abl. = ablative; **acc.** = accusative; **Ar.** = Arabic; **conv.** = converb; **dat.** = dative; **dial.** = dialectal; **gen.** = genitive; **imperat.** = imperative; **Kar.** = Karaim; **KarK.** = Crimean Karaim; **KarL.** = Lutsk Karaim; **KarT.** = Trakai Karaim; **KTkc.** = Kipchak Turkic; **part.** = participle; **perf.** = perfect; **Pers.** = Persian; **Pol.** = Polish; **poss.** = possessive; **praes.** = *praesens*, present tense; **praet.** = *praeteritum*, simple past tense; **Russ.** = Russian; **Ukr.** = Ukrainian; **Uyg.** = Uyghur.

5. References

Berta Á., 1994, Zum Wandel des auslautenden -G im Kiptschakischen. – *Journal of Turkology* 2/2: 163–195.

Berta Á. 1998. West Kipchak languages. – Johanson L., Csató É.Á. (eds.) *The Turkic languages*. London, New York: 301–317.

Dejna K. 1948. Elementy polskie w gwarach zachodnio-małoruskich. – *Język Polski* 28.3: 72–79.

Dejna K. 1957. *Gwary ukraińskie tarnopolszczyzny*. [*Prace Językoznawcze Komitetu Językoznawczego Polskiej Akademii Nauk* 13]. Wrocław.

Dubiński A. 1978. Phonetische Merkmale des Łuck-Halicz Dialektes der karaimischen Sprache. – *Rocznik Orientalistyczny* 39.2: 33–44.

Dziurzyńska E. 1999. Podróże naukowe Tadeusza Kowalskiego w świetle materiałów archiwalnych. – Bieńkowski W. (ed.) *Tadeusz Kowalski 1889–1948*. [*Materiały z Posiedzenia Naukowego PAN w dniu 19 czerwca 1998 r., Polska Akademia Umiejętności. W służbie nauki* 4]. Kraków.

Eilers W. 1967. *Deutsch-persisches Wörterbuch*. vol. 1. Wiesbaden.

von Essen O. 1979⁵. *Allgemeine und angewandte Phonetik*. Berlin.

Grzegorzewski J. 1903. Ein türk-tatarischer Dialekt in Galizien. Vokalharmonie in den entlehnten Wörtern der karaitischen Sprache in Halicz. [Mit Einleitung, Texten und Erklärungen zu den Texten]. – *Sitzungsberichte der kais[erlichen] Akademie der Wissenschaften in Wien. Philosophisch-historische Klasse* 146: 1–80.

Grzegorzewski J. 1916–1918. Caraimica. Język Łach-Karaitów. – *Rocznik Oryentalistyczny* 1.2: 252–296.

Grzegorzewski J. 1917. Narzecze południowe Karaitów polskich czyli t. zw. Łach-Karaimów. – *Sprawozdania z czynności posiedzeń Akademii Umiejętności w Krakowie* 22.3: 2–6.

Kowalski T. 1929. *Karaimische Texte im Dialekt von Troki*. [*Prace Komisji Orjentalistycznej Polskiej Akademji Umiejętności* 11]. Kraków.

KRPS = Baskakov N.A., Šapšal S.M., Zajončkovskij A. (eds.) 1974. *Karaimsko-russko-pol'skij slovar'*. Moskva.

KSB = Mardkowicz A. 1935. *Karaj sez-bitigi. Słownik karaimski. Karaimisches Wörterbuch*. Łuck.

Kurzowa Z. 1985. *Polszczyzna Lwowa i Kresów południowo-wschodnich do 1939 roku*. Kraków [reprinted in 2006].

Levi B.Z. 1996. *Russko-karaimskij slovar'. Krymskij dialekt*. Odessa.

Mardkowicz A. 1933. Jedi bitik. – *Karaj Awazy* 6: 6–10.

Mireev V.A., Abragamovič N.D. 2008. *Jazyk karaimov zapadnoj Ukrainy (Čast' pervaja. Kratkij očerk)*. Simferopol', Polevskoj, Slippery Rock.

Moskovič W., Tukan B. 1993. The Slavic component in the dialects of the Karaim language. – Moskovič W., Shvarzband Sh., Alekseev A. (eds.) *Jews & Slavs*. vol. 1. Jerusalem, St. Petersburg: 296–303.

Musaev K.M. 1964. *Grammatika karaimskogo jazyka. Fonetika i morfologija*. Moskva.

Musaev K.M. 1977. *Kratkij grammatičeskij očerk karaimskogo jazyka*. Moskva.

Németh M. 2006. *Nieznane wiersze karaimskie Sergiusza Rudkowskiego (dialekt łucko-halicki). Edycja krytyczna* [unpublished M.A.]. Kraków.

Németh M. 2011. *Unknown Lutsk Karaim letters in Hebrew script (19ᵗʰ–20ᵗʰ centuries). A critical Edition* [Studia Turcologica Cracoviensia 12]. Kraków.

Pritsak O. 1959. Das Karaimische. – Deny J. et al. (eds.) *Philologiae Turcicae Fundamenta.* Wiesbaden: 318–340.

Radloff W. 1893. *Versuch eines Wörterbuches der Türk-Dialecte.* vol. 1. Sanktpeterburg.

Räsänen M. 1949. *Zur Lautgeschichte der türkischen Sprachen* [*Studia Orientalia* 15]. Helsinki.

Rudkowski S. 1931. *Korutkan dżuwaherłer.* – *Karaj Awazy* 2: 19–20.

Rudkowski S. 1932. Kisencłer. – *Karaj Awazy* 4 (1932.2): 14.

Rudkowski S. 1939. *Dostłar (II ilisi). Caja kotarmak caja ucurłaricin.* Łuck.

Stachowski K. 2009. The discussion on consonant harmony in northwestern Karaim. – *Türkbilig* 18: 158–193.

Steingass F. 1892. *Persian-English dictionary.* London.

Sulimowicz A. 2004. Imiona Karaimów z Halicza. – Siemeniec-Gołaś E., Georgiewa-Okoń J. (eds.) *Wśród jarłyków i fermanów.* [*Materiały z sesji naukowej poświęconej pamięci dra Zygmunta Abrahamowicza*]. Kraków: 143–149.

Tekin T. 1991. A New classification of the Turkic languages. – *Türk Dilleri Araştırmaları*: 5–18.

Tenišev È.R. 1984. *Sravnitel'no-istoričeskaja grammatika tjurkskich jazykov. Fonetika.* Moskva.

Wehr H. 1952. *Arabisches Wörterbuch für die Schriftsprache der Gegenwart* [two-volume edition]. Leipzig.

Zajączkowski A. 1931. *Krótki wykład gramatyki języka zachodnio-karaimskiego (narzecze łucko-halickie).* Łuck.

Zajączkowski A. 1932. *Sufiksy imienne i czasownikowe w języku zachodniokaraimskim (przyczynek do morfologji języków tureckich). Les suffixes nominaux et verbaux dans la langue des Karaïms occidentaux (contribution à la morphologie des langues turques).* [*Prace Komisji Orjentalistycznej Polskiej Akademji Umiejętności* 15]. Kraków.

Zajączkowski W. 1961. Die arabischen und neupersischen Lehnwörter im Karaimischen. – *Folia Orientalia* 3.1–2: 177–212.

Zilynśkyj I. 1932. *Opis fonetyczny języka ukraińskiego* [*Prace Komisji Językowej Polskiej Akademji Umiejętności* 19]. Kraków.

Zilynśkyj I. 1979. *A Phonetic description of the Ukrainian language.* Cambridge [USA].

Ziłyński see Zilynśkyj.

Žylko F.T. 1958. *Govory ukrajinśkoji movy.* Kyjiv.

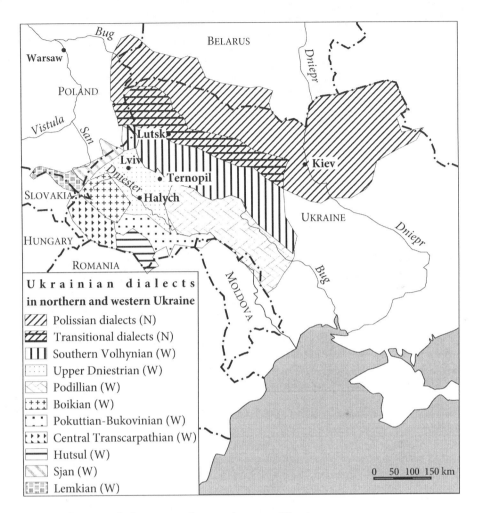

Map 1. Ukrainian dialects in northern and western Ukraine.
Based on Zilynśkyj (1979: 202; facing page)

Studia Linguistica Universitatis Iagellonicae Cracoviensis
128 (2011)

DARIUSZ R. PIWOWARCZYK
Jagiellonian University, Cracow

FORMATIONS OF THE PERFECT IN THE SABELLIC LANGUAGES WITH THE ITALIC AND INDO-EUROPEAN BACKGROUND*

Keywords: Sabellic languages, Oscan-Umbrian verb, perfect

Abstract

The problem of the origin of the Sabellic perfects (in the older literature called Oscan-Umbrian) has been discussed at length very often in Indo-European linguistics ever since the 19th century and the monumental work of Robert von Planta (1892–1897). Still, to this very day it remains a mystery. Various hypotheses have been proposed but none of them explained everything clearly and without problems. Especially intriguing is the fact that the multiple formations of the perfect found in Sabellic languages (reduplicated, simple, -f-, -tt- and -nky-perfects) perform essentially the same function of the preterite tense, being the syncretism of both the Proto-Indo-European aorist and perfect, similarly as in Latin.

In the present article the author seeks to present the compelling hypotheses of the origin of the formations of the perfect in the Sabellic languages, evaluate them according to their supposed probability and present the most probable solution to the problem. The Sabellic perfects are classified into groups and each group is discussed as to its origin and development with the Indo-European background in mind. This is followed by some reconstructions underlying the attested forms. The Sabellic formations treated in this article are the reduplicated perfect, long-vowel perfect, s-perfect, simple perfect, -f-perfect, -tt-perfect, -k-perfect, -nky-perfect and the Sabellic future perfect with the characteristic -us- suffix. The discussion is closed by conclusions and the appendix with the complete list of the attested forms of the perfect.

* This article is a revised version of the author's M.A. thesis in Classics (Cracow 2009), written under the supervision of Dr. hab. Hubert Wolanin (Cracow). It began as a seminar paper written at Leiden University under the supervision of Dr. Michiel de Vaan (Leiden). I am grateful to both my supervisors for comments and remarks and to Kristen de Joseph (Leiden) for correcting my English. Needless to add, the remaining errors are solely my responsibility.

The main conclusion of the article is the following: we have generally three tendencies of explaining the origin of the Sabellic perfects: periphrastic, analogical and phonological. The phonological explanation is forceful and therefore not very probable. On the other hand, periphrastic and analogical solutions are extreme and the author thinks that the most probable explanation is the middle solution combining all three approaches.

1. Introduction

Ever since the beginning of Indo-European linguistics, the Sabellic languages (or rather Oscan-Umbrian, as it was called then) have been investigated with their better-attested sister language, Latin, in mind. The disproportion in the state of attestation of the Sabellic languages and Latin is enormous, due to the historical developments in ancient Italy in general and the Roman conquest in particular. Analogically, within the Indo-European family, Hittite was considered the main Anatolian language and for some time thought of as the only representative of this group of languages worth researching, while the other languages were almost completely neglected in historical-linguistic research [e.g. in Kronasser's (1956) historical grammar]. Only in recent times has it been shown that the other languages have some important things to say about the overall picture of the Anatolian branch. The same goes for the Sabellic languages, often neglected in research due to the superiority of the Latin material. Yet they can tell us much about the overall linguistic history of the Italic branch (especially the more conservative Oscan language) and provide insights into some of the controversial issues.

One of those controversial issues is the origin of the whole variety of the formations of the perfect in the Italic languages. The Proto-Indo-European perfect essentially had only two distinct formations, an old simple perfect of the type of Greek *oîda* and Latin *uīdī* and a reduplicated perfect of the type of Greek *mémona*, Skt. *cakára* and Latin *meminī*. Yet, over time several different formations were created in the history of the Italic branch, and the precise origin of these formations has never been fully and exhaustively explained. This article does not pretend to find the ultimate solution for the aforementioned problem; its major aim is instead to outline the proposed hypotheses and evaluate them according to their probability in the general framework while trying to present new paths toward the solution.

2. The Italic languages

The Italic languages, constituting one of the language groups of the Indo-European family of languages, are generally divided into Latino-Faliscan and Sabellic (or Sabellian; in the older literature also Osco-Umbrian[1]) group. The Latino-Faliscan subgroup consists of Latin (from 600 BC) and Faliscan (600–150 BC), while the Sabellic

---

[1] The term "Sabellian" was previously used to denote the minor Italic languages, i.e. all of those apart from Latin, Faliscan, Oscan and Umbrian. Since the decipherment of South Picene in the 1980s and its establishment as a sister branch of both Oscan and Umbrian, the term "Sabellian"

consists of Oscan (500–100 BC), Umbrian (400–150 BC) and some minor languages (scantily attested): Paelignian, Marrucinian, Vestinian, Marsian, Aequian, Hernican, Volscian, South Picene (550–350 BC) and Pre-Samnite (500 BC). Within the Sabellic languages the division is made between the Oscan group, the Umbrian group and the Picene group. The Oscan languages are Oscan proper, Paelignian, Marrucinian, Vestinian and Hernican. The Umbrian group consists of: Umbrian proper, Aequian, Marsian and Volscian. Finally, the Picene group comprises South Picene and Pre-Samnite (cf. Wallace 2007: 1–10). Following the scheme of Ringe (2006: 16), the chronological development of the Italic languages would thus be as follows: Proto-Indo-European > North IE (after the separation of Anatolian) > West IE (after the separation of Tocharian) > Italo-Celtic > Proto-Italic > Proto-Latino-Faliscan (Latin, Faliscan), Proto-Sabellic (Oscan, Umbrian, South Picene, Pre-Samnite, etc.). The Sabellic languages use three different scripts: the Latin alphabet, the national Oscan and Umbrian alphabet (derived from Etruscan) and the Greek alphabet.

The position of other languages from within the geographical bounds of Italy (Venetic, Sicel, Etruscan, North Picene, Raetic) is unclear. Etruscan, attested by nearly 6,000 inscriptions, and North Picene are clearly non-Indo-European, along with Raetic, which is probably related to Etruscan. Venetic is an Indo-European language but its genetic affiliation has not been confirmed. Some scholars would count it also as Italic since it shares several important features with this branch (cf. van der Staaij 1995: 193–210).

3. The Indo-European verb

The reconstruction of the PIE verb is one of the most controversial topics of contemporary Indo-European linguistics, mostly because of the Anatolian material, especially Hittite. The main problem lies in incorporating the verbal system found in Hittite (with only two tenses – present and preterite – and no optative or subjunctive) with the "Graeco-Aryan" reconstructed model of PIE (based essentially on Vedic Sanskrit and Homeric Greek, with elaborate categories of present, aorist and perfect-stems, three moods, etc.). The tendency seems to favour the hypothesis that Anatolian split off first from the PIE language and attests the older stage of development rather than loss of categories present in Vedic and Greek (cf. Jasanoff 2003, Clackson 2007: 129–151). However, other scholars, most notably the "Erlangen school", seem to favour the traditional explanation (Tichy 2004). For our purposes it is irrelevant whether we consider our point of departure to be West Indo European or the PIE of the German school. It still is essentially the same reconstructed system (the so-called "Cowgill-Rix verb") with three aspect-stems present (denoting imperfective aspect), aorist (denoting perfective aspect) and perfect stem (denoting a sort of stative-resultative aspect).

---

or "Sabellic" has been used to denote the former and now imprecise (due to the omission of South Picene) term "Oscan-Umbrian".

3.1. Proto-Indo-European perfect

The formation of the perfect stem in PIE follows the pattern of o-graded root in the singular and zero-grade in the plural and e-reduplication. The endings used in the perfect are completely separate from the primary and secondary endings. The basis for such reconstruction of the perfect are the perfect stems of Homeric Greek and Vedic Sanskrit. The endings of the perfect are the basis of the Hittite *hi*-conjugation – a conjugation of the present found in Hittite with the endings essentially continuing the PIE perfect – in contrast to the *mi*-conjugation, which continues the PIE athematic present. The explanation of the development of the Hittite *hi*-conjugation still remains controversial (cf. Jasanoff 2003 for a new hypothesis on the topic).

3.2. Indo-Iranian perfect

In Vedic Sanskrit, the oldest language of the Indic branch, the perfect is made with reduplication and still very frequently has the stative meaning as inherited from PIE (Fortson 2004: 192). Examples of Vedic forms are *cakára* 'make,' *tutóda* 'strike,' *dadháu* 'place' or *véda* 'know' (Burrow 2001: 341–346). In Avestan, the other oldest member of the Iranian branch, the perfect is also still clearly visible: *vaēdā* 'know'.

3.3. Greek perfect

In Greek, the PIE perfect is still visible in Homeric Greek, frequently with stative meaning. There is only one attested personal form of the perfect tense from the Mycenaean period: **e-pi-de-da-to** PY Vn 20.1 /epidedastoy/ '(he, she, it) distributed' (Sowa 1998: 292). Even in the language of the Greek inscriptions,

> the perfect expresses a past event and its continuing consequences, while the aorist expresses the event and leaves the consequences to be inferred (Ringe 1984: 533).

3.4. Latin perfect

In Latin the PIE perfect and aorist merged into one category of the past perfective tense. Remnants of the old stative meaning are visible in forms like *odī* 'I hate', *meminī* 'I remember' and *nouī* 'I know'. The remnants of the PIE aorists are visible in the following Latin forms (after Safarewicz 1953: 216–217 and Kümmel 2007: 28–29): *fuī*, continuing *b^hū(w)-ed, i.e. the reanalyzed PIE root aorist *e-b^huh$_2$-t (cf. Greek *éphun*, Skt. *ábhūt*), *cecidī*, continuing the reduplicated aorist (cf. Greek *kekádonto*), *fēcī*, continuing the root aorist with *k*-suffix[2] *d^heh$_1$-k- (cf. Greek *éthēka*); and *dīxī*, continuing *deik-s-ai, i.e. the reanalyzed form of the PIE sigmatic aorist *e-dēik̂-s-m (cf. Greek *édeiksa*, Avestan *dāiš*). On the other hand, the PIE perfect is

---

[2]   That is, an independent formation or just root aorist with -*k*- suffix giving the synchronic long-vowel -*k*-perfect. The origin of the formations with -*k*- suffix present in Latin, Greek and Phrygian is dubious (Meiser 2003: 199–200).

continued in Latin in forms such as *uīdī*, from *woidh$_2$ei (cf. Greek *oîda*, Skt. *véda*), or *meminī*, from PIE *me-mon-h$_2$ei (cf. Greek *mémona*). The synchronic long-vowel perfect in Latin goes back partly to the PIE reduplicated perfect with roots in the first laryngeal (so perfect *ēd-* < *h$_1$e-h$_1$d- to the present *ĕdō* and then *uēn-* to *uĕniō* analogically), and partly to the ablauting PIE root aorist ending in laryngeals (*fēc-* < *d^{h}eh$_1$k- to the present *făciō* < *d^{h}h$_1$k-yō and then *cēp-* to *căpiō* analogically). There is also a typically inner-Latin formation of the perfect, the so-called *u*-perfect like in *portāuī* 'I carried', *nēuī* 'I sewed' or *audīuī* 'I heard'. There are generally three hypotheses concerning the origin of this formation:

> some have tried to connect it with the -*u* in Sanskrit perfects like Ved. *dadáu* 'I/he gave' (root *dā-*), *tastháu* 'I stood' (root *sthā-*); others have preferred to say that the pattern began with a verb whose perfect stem could have originally ended in *-Vw-, such as perhaps *gnōuī* 'I knew' (*ĝneh$_3$w-) (Fortson 2004: 256–257).

Recently, Seldeslachts (2001) published an extensive monograph on the origin of the Latin perfect. The newest treatment of the Latin perfect formation is the work of Meiser (2003). Meiser essentially follows a third hypothesis, established by Helmut Rix (1992), that posits a periphrastic origin for Latin *u*-perfect. Rix argues that the Latin *u*-perfect has its origin in the periphrasis of the perfect participle active and the form of 'to be' *est*. He traces it to *portāwos est which is in turn simplified into *portāwist and gives the attested Latin *portāvit* (Rix 1992: 229–233). As we shall see later, same kind of analysis is employed by Rix when dealing with the Sabellic formations of the perfect.

4. Sabellic perfect

The main problem which the current article investigates is concerned with the formation of the perfect stem in the Sabellic languages and its origin. It is generally assumed that the PIE aorist and perfect merged in Proto-Italic. However, the complete merger must have occurred after the separation of Latino-Faliscan and Sabellic languages, as we find different types of perfect stem formation which are exclusive to Latin, Oscan or Umbrian, respectively, and also different endings in Latino-Faliscan and in Sabellic (cf. Rix 2003a: "aorist and perfect were still distinct in P[roto]It[alic], even if their signification became more similar to each other"). In Latin, the endings of the perfect continue the PIE perfect endings (with different contaminations), whereas in Sabellic they continue the secondary aorist PIE endings (thematic aorist endings, according to Rix 2003a: 15). Moreover, we find differences in the creation of perfect subjunctive, which in Latin is created by means of the suffix -*ī*- and in Sabellic by -*ē*-, and in the future perfect, which in Latin is signalled by -*er*- < -*is*- and in Sabellic by -*us*- (Meiser 2003: 32). There are more or less (depending on differences in classification among scholars) nine different types of perfect stem formation in the Italic languages: reduplicated, with long stem vowel, simple, *s*-perfect, *k*-perfect, *u*-perfect, *f*-perfect, *tt*-perfect and *nky*-perfect. The latter three (*f*-perfect, *tt*-perfect and *nky*-perfect) are exclusive to Sabellic languages, the *tt*-perfect exclusive to Oscan (and minor languages related to Oscan) and the *nky*-perfect exclusive to Umbrian. On the contrary, the *u*-perfect is present only in Latin and the same might account for the *s*-perfect, as the forms pointing to its existence in Sabellic are scanty and dubious. Although the matter of the origin of such a varied scope of different perfect formations in Sabellic was touched upon quite often (Osthoff 1884: 191–263, von Planta 1892–1897: 326–401, Brugmann 1893: 1234–1245, Sommer 1926, Olzscha 1958, Diels 1959, Olzscha 1963, and Markey 1985, among others), no complete answer has ever been given. It is especially worth noting that "there is essentially no adequate explanation of the multiplicity of forms alongside their presumed uniformity of function" (Silvestri 1998).

The present article does not claim to find an ultimate solution to the problem mentioned above. As has been already observed,

> Due first of all to the limited number of inscriptions we have in Sabellic and second to their inconsistent spelling, any sketch of Sabellic phonology, both historical and synchronic, must be tentative (Fortson 2004: 264).

Obviously, the same also goes for morphology. It is then the general aim to investigate in detail the attested perfect formations and the proposed hypotheses concerning their origin, with an evaluation of their plausibility. As regards evaluation of the plausibility of the hypotheses, I follow Ringe (1990: 221) in stating that irregular sound change is less plausible than a regular one; between two regular but incompatible sound changes phonetic plausibility should give us the answer, and in terms of reckoning with analogical change,

> it must be judged in the specific context of the paradigm in which it is supposed to have taken place; and in order to render such judgements possible, that paradigm, as well as other relevant paradigms in the language, must be reconstructed in the greatest possible detail (Ringe 1990: 221).

It should be noted, however, that as in many other cases in Indo-European linguistics, the complete answer to the question of the origin of the Sabellic perfects may be hidden in the depths of the irretrievable and forgotten past, and we must also be prepared to accept this fact rather than multiply the hypotheses based on dubious evidence. In the author's opinion, *facta non sunt multiplicanda*, and therefore we should not present other theories of probable origin of these formations unless we gather a clear evidence in support of such claims.

What follows is the classification of the attested perfects with the proposed reconstruction. Every class is closed with some general remarks as to the proposed hypotheses concerning its origin and its evaluation. The division of the formations of the perfect in classes is made on diachronic-synchronic terms, that is, the analysis is neither completely diachronic nor completely synchronic. It follows the custom present in Indo-European linguistics to analyze the form basically according to its origin, while keeping in mind its synchronic stance. If we were to analyze the forms synchronically, only some of the original reduplicated perfects should be classified as simple perfects and several other specific classes should be postulated. Besides, we are unable to tell how the speakers of the language perceived the forms. Pure diachronic analysis again would imply the non-existence of the -*tt*-perfect, -*f*-perfect and -*nky*-perfect, as those forms are clearly inner-Sabellic developments.

4.1. Reduplicated perfect

This formation originally goes back to PIE, where it was a typical pattern of perfect formation, that is, *e*-reduplication, *o*-grade of the root and stative aspect (at least for West Indo European, i.e. after the separation of the Anatolian branch and possibly also Tocharian), e.g. *ste-stoh$_2$-h$_2$e 'I am standing'; cf. Gk. *gégona*, *mémona*, Skt. *cakára*, etc.

The reduplication syllable was uniformly */e/, and it was preserved as such in Sabellic (e.g. O. **deded** 'dedit', U. *dirsust* [< *dedust], O. *fefacid* 'fecerit', U. *peperscust* 'posuerit'), but assimilated in Latin to the vowel of the root if it was /i/, /o/ or /u/ (e.g. *momordī*, *cucurrī* for earlier *memordī*, *cecurrī* but *pepulī* [Buck 1904: 170]). The Oscan form *fifikus* 'feceris / fixeris' with /i/ in the reduplication syllable may appear to be a trace of a similar phenomenon in Sabellic to some (Buck 1904: 170), and even enough evidence for others to claim that the "colouring of the reduplicated syllable probably took place independently in the Italic languages" (van der Staaij 1995: 164). As we have only one form attested, I find such hypotheses highly speculative. After all, "it would be imprudent to try to develop any theories about the vocalism of a hapax legomenon for which there is no obvious explanation" (Cowgill 1957: 108). As to the root syllable there is, as van der Staaij (1995: 164) correctly observes, no trace of original PIE ablaut, i.e. *o*-grade in singular and zero-grade in plural, e.g. O. **deded** 3 sg., O. **dedens** 3 pl., U. *dersicust* 3 sg., U. *dersicurent* 3 pl.

There is no unanimity whether the forms like O. **aamanaffed** 'mandavit', O. **prúffed** 'probavit' or O. **fufens** 'fuerunt' should be classified as reduplicated perfects according to their probable origin [so Buck (1904: 170) and others claim for the first two forms; von Planta (1892–1897: 330–331) on O. **fufens**: "schwerlich starkes reduplicirtes Perfect") or as *f*-perfects (van der Staaij 1995: 169)]. The forms synchronically have /f/ phonemes and therefore might be seen as *f*-perfects, though their origin is different. They will be discussed in the section devoted to *f*-perfects (see 4.5. below).

The following reconstructions illustrate the origin of some of the Sabellic reduplicated perfects presenting the general pattern (cf. van der Staaij 1995: 164, Meiser 2003: 158–166):

O. **deded** < *de-dh$_3$-ed (root *deh$_3$- 'to give')
> This form has the generalized zero-grade instead of the expected full grade in the root. The respective 3 pl. form is found in the O. **dedens**.

O. **dadid** /dādīd/ < *dād + dedid < *de-dh$_3$-ih$_1$-t
> This form consists of the preverb *dād* and the reduplicated perfect subjunctive reconstructed as the zero-grade *-ih$_1$- suffix. The reduplication syllable is in turn syncopated.

O. **fifikus** < *fi-fig-us < *dʰe-dʰiĝʰ-(bʰ)us(t) (root *dʰeiĝʰ- 'to form')

This form shows an irregularity in the reduplication vowel. It may have been assimilated to the root vowel which was itself generalized from the full grade to the zero-grade. The future perfect suffix -*us*- (see 4.9. below) probably goes back to the univerbation of the participle and the future of the verb "to be" *fust*.

U. *dersicust* < *dedikust < *de-dik-(bʰ)us(t)-t (root *deik- 'to show')

This form shows a typical perfect reduplication and the generalized zero-grade in the root. The intervocalic */d/ is changed to the typical Umbrian sound /ř/, written as <rs> in the Latin alphabet. The future perfect suffix -*us*- is followed by the ending of 3 sg. The respective 3 pl. form is attested as Umbrian *dersicurent*.

Generally, this type of perfect is the least controversial. It stems from both the PIE perfect and the PIE reduplicated aorist.

4.2. Long-vowel perfect

This formation goes back partly to the PIE aorist (Lat. *fēcī* < *dʰeh₁-ĝ-h₂ei, O. *hipust* < *gʰeh₁bʰ-) partly to the long-vowel preterites, whose status in PIE is unclear (Cowgill 1957, Pike 2003), and partly to the PIE reduplicated perfect (Lat. *fūgī* < *bhe-bhough-h₂ei). The Oscan forms **upsed**, **uupsens**, **upsens**, ουπσενς 'operaverunt' are classified by some as *s*-perfects (Wallace 2007: 29), which seems improbable to me as the non-perfective gerundival form **úpsannam** 'operandum' also contains /s/. Others (van der Staaij 1995: 165) consider them to be reduplicated perfects (*He-Hop-) in origin. The fact is that we have /ō/ in the perfect and /ŏ/ in the present. Whether this is the result of morphological vowel lengthening or reduplication is impossible to tell. The forms of *hipid* /hēpēd/ 'habuerit' as compared to the present *hafiest* with short vowel basically follow the same pattern.

The following reconstructions illustrate the origin of some of the Sabellic long-vowel perfects presenting the general pattern: (cf. van der Staaij 1995: 165, Meiser 2003: 153–157)

O. **uupsens** < *ōps- lengthened morphologically < *h₃ep-s- (root *h₃ep-) 'to work' or from < *ōps- < *He-Hop-s- < *He-h₃ep-s-.

As mentioned above, we are not able to tell whether the form is reduplicated or morphologically lengthened in origin. It seems, however, that this verb is denominal. Firstly, the Proto-Italic noun *opes 'work' was created (cf. Latin *opus*) from the PIE root *h₃ep- 'to produce, to work.' This noun formed the denominal present *opesāye- [cf. Latin *operāri* (De Vaan 2008: 432)], from which the present stem *ops-, with syncope of the internal /e/, was abstracted, and used either with reduplication or lengthening to form the Oscan perfect **uupsens**.

O. *hipid* < (cont.) *h₁ēp-ih₁-t < *h₁e-h₁op/h₁p-ih₁-t (root *h₁ep- 'to catch, to have')

This form has been partly contaminated by the form *hafiest* 'habebit' (the Oscan stem *haf*- from PIE *gʰHbʰ-; cf. Latin *habeō* < *gʰHbʰ-h₁ye?, De Vaan 2008: 277–278), from which the /h/ in anlaut has been taken over. The root vowel is lengthened either through morphological lengthening or reduplication. The case is the same with the Oscan future perfect form *hipust*.

4.3. -*s*-perfect

Originally, this formation most probably goes back to the PIE sigmatic aorist. In Latin it may be represented by forms like *dīxī* (cf. Gk. *édeiksa*) and also by futures of the type *faxo*. In Sabellic, the status of this formation is dubious. Two forms point to this type of perfect: Pael. *lexe* and U. *sesust* 'sederit'. According to Wallace (2007: 29), O. **upsed** 'operavit' should also be classified as an *s*-perfect, though I prefer different a classification [see 4.2. above; compare also von Planta (1892–1897: 338)]. As for Paelignian *lexe*, it may well be a simple present formation as compared to Latin *legistis* (Silvestri 1998: 338). The interpretation is controversial. The U. *sesust* form has been analyzed as going back to the participial stem in *sesso-* (Buck 1904: 170). A different analysis is postulated by Rix (2003a: 16):

> the sigmatic aorist disappeared in Sabellian, two isolated, especially motivated stems excepted: *sess-* < **sed-s-* 'sit' (Umb. *sesust*) can be understood as a reduplicated perfect, and **ōp-s-* 'produce' (Osc. *uupsens*) was supported by the suppletive present *ope-sā-*.

Additionally, it must be observed that the absence of this very productive type of aorist in Sabellic, which underlies the very frequent *s*-perfects in Latin, is rather odd.

The attestation of the Paelignian form is as follows:

P. *lexe* Ve. 213,7 / Pg 9 (Corfinium) 2 pl. pr.?

The probable reconstructions of the two forms are:

P. *lexe* < **leg-e-se (Meiser 2003) or *leg-s-te or *leg-is-te
U. *sesust* < **se-sd-us-e-t or <**sed-us-e-t

Both examples of the probable Sabellic *s*-perfect are dubious, and therefore the existence of this formation in Sabellic should rather be rejected (cf. van der Staaij 1995: 166).

4.4. Simple perfect

The simple perfect (i.e. without reduplication) may go back to the PIE aorist (root, thematic), or may have lost its perfect marker due to the analogy to with the present stem (van der Staaij 1995: 167). The examples of the loss of the reduplication are: O. *dicust* to the reduplicated U. *dersicust*; U. **fakust** 'fecerit' to the reduplicated O. *fefacid* (though the examples are drawn from different languages). Other examples of this class are O. **kúmbened** 'convenit', O. *cebnust*, U. *benust* 'venerit' and O. αναϝακετ 'dedicavit'.

The following reconstructions illustrate the origin of some of the Sabellic simple perfects presenting the general pattern: (cf. van der Staaij 1995: 167, Meiser 2003: 209)

O. **kúmbened** < *kom-g^{w}em-ed (root *g^{w}em 'to go')

This form presents the outcome of the root of the verb 'to go', widely attested within the Indo-European languages (cf. Greek *baínō* and Latin *věniō* from the zero-grade *g^{w}m̥-yo). The nasal vowel is changed to /n/ as in the other languages. Particularly interesting is the behaviour of the PIE labiovelars, which turn into labials in Sabellic.

U. *benust* < *g^{w}em-(b^h)us-t

This form again represents the same root as above with the same sound development. The only difference is that it is attested in Umbrian and that it is the future perfect with the characteristic *-us-* suffix. The case is the same with the Oscan *cebnust*, where we have the preverb *ce-* and the form with syncope of internal /e/.

A similar example would be O. αναφακετ from *ana-d^{h}h$_1$-k-ed (root *d^{h}eh$_1$-).

We should also mention that in the older literature, the Sabellic *l*-perfect was postulated. The issue has been solved by Meiser in 1986.

> The Umbrian forms *entelust*, **apelust** which were formerly taken as *l*-perfect forms of **entento**, **ampentu**, have turned out to be future perfect forms built from root aorists from roots in *-l*. The underlying roots of these verbs are probably *telh$_2$- 'carry', cf. Latin *tollere*, and *pelh$_2$- 'beat', cf. Latin *pellere*, respectively. **entento**, **ampentu**, then, reflect *-tel-n-h$_2$-tōd, *pel-n-h$_2$-tōd, respectively, with a development *-ln- > *-nn- > -n-. (van der Staaij 1995: 171 summarising Meiser 1986: 164).

Mention must also be made of the so-called 'thematic perfect.' Forms such as Oscan **manafum** or South Picene **ad-staíúh** and **opsút** are sometimes classified as thematic because of their supposed thematization (thus van der Staaij 1995: 165). The ending of the former would come to the thematic aorist *-o-m, while that of the latter is sometimes interpreted as the alleged ō-perfect of South Picene (for details, see Adiego Lajara 1992: 121).

4.5. -*f*-perfect

This formation is absent from Latino-Faliscan but present exclusively in Sabellic languages. Its origins are disputed. According to Rix (1992: 239), the source of this *-f-* is the reduplicated perfect stem, whether *fef- < *d^{h}ed^{h}h$_1$- (as in **prúffed**) or fuf- < *fefw- < *b^{h}eb^{h}w- (as in **fufens**). The same analysis is posited by Buck (1904: 172), though he classifies **aamanaffed** and **prúffed** as reduplicated perfects (see 4.1. above). The competing hypothesis of Hamp (1990), who traces the origin of this formation to the rounded laryngeal *x^w, does not seem very plausible. Rix traces the origin of the reduplication itself to the univerbation of the periphrasis, explaining e.g. Oscan **staieffud** as going back to the construction of the present participle *staients and the perfect *fefud < *steh$_2$-yeh$_2$-nt-s + *b^{h}e-b^{h}uH-t.

Recently, three new forms of the reduplicated perfect were found in the so-called Tortora inscription. The forms belong to the archaic Pre-Samnite dialect of the South Picene group of the Sabellic languages. Of those the most important is the Pre-Samnite form *fufυϝοδ*, analyzed as /fufuwond/ (Beckwith 2008), which shows the Italic perfect paradigm of the verb 'to be' with the thematization of the older *fufuwēr (Beckwith *ibid.*).

The following reconstructions illustrate the origin of some of the Sabellic *f*-perfects presenting the general pattern (cf. van der Staaij 1995: 169–170):

O. **manafum** < *man-fe-fom < *man-d^{h}e-d^{h}h$_1$-o-m

This form is probably a thematization of the original form (see 4.4. above for the thematic perfect classification). Observe also the Latin counterpart *mandāre* which is, as in Oscan, the compound of *manus* + *dāre* 'to put at hands.' O. **aamanaffed** is the same root only with a preverb **aa-** and with double -**ff**- reflecting earlier *a-man-fefed and *a-man-d^{h}e-d^{h}h$_1$-ed.

O. **fufens** < *b^{h}e-b^{h}woh$_2$/b^{h}uh$_2$-

This word attests the Sabellic form of the perfect of the verb 'to be.' It is possible that this form has been reanalyzed and its /f/ element used as a marker of the perfect. The Pre-Samnite form *fυfυϝοδ* with the -*ond* ending is a thematization of the earlier 3. pl. perfect ending *-ēr.

O. **aíkdafed** < *h$_2$eyk̂-dā-d^{h}h$_1$-ed or from Proto-Italic *aikidans fufed (WOU 2000: 68)

O. **prúffed** < *pro-fefed < *pro-d^{h}e-d^{h}eh$_1$-d

U. *andirsafust* < *andi-daf fust < *am-di-da-nt-s fust

4.5. -*tt*-perfect

This formation is only present in Oscan and some minor Sabellic languages related to Oscan (Paelignian, Volscian, Marrucinian). The inscriptions with *tt*-perfect attestations come mainly from the 2nd century BC and from the places of Pietrabbondante (×6), Pompeii (×7) and Rossano (×4). According to some (Buck 1904: 172, Rix 1992: 238), it is based on the periphrastic construction with a *to*-participle and a past form of the verb 'to do,' e.g. *termnātom fefakom [theoretical *CeC-ā-to-d^{h}h$_1$- as in van der Staaij (1995: 170)]. In Oscan it is only present in *ā*-stems. Several other hypotheses have been developed to explain the origin of this formation (see von Planta 1892–1897: 342–348 for a good survey), including the change of *ky > *tt* as in Greek and the connection of the Oscan *tt*-perfects to the Umbrian *nky*-perfects and Latin *u*-perfects (Saint John 1973a), which is a very forceful hypothesis. It seems that even more modern theories (e.g. the one mentioned above by Saint John 1973a) go back to the ones already posited long ago (von Planta 1892–1897: 347–348). The Volscian *sistiatiens* form has been investigated several times (cf. Wallace 1985) and still remains a problem.

Recently, however, Beckwith (2005), criticizing Rix's (1992, 2003a, 2003b) periphrastic explanations for lack of economy, has come out with an analogical explanation (or rather a series of analogical extensions and reanalyzes). He creates a proportion *sista- (pres.): *sistatt- (perf.) = *dōnā- (pres.): X (perf.), X = *dōnā-tt, where the -*tt*- element has been reanalyzed as a perfect marker by the speakers. And although the more or less contemporary date of the attested *tt*-perfects could in principle point to an analogical explanation, the sound change of *twV > *ttV that he assumes is not without difficulties (cf. Buck 1904: 172).

The following reconstructions illustrate the origin of some of the Sabellic tt-perfects presenting the general pattern: (cf. van der Staaij 1995: 170)

O. **dadikatted** < *dat-dikā-tt-ed

This form is a complete rendering of the Latin *dedicauit* perfect. It is attested from an inscription dating back to the end of the 2nd century BC.

duunated < *dōnā-t-ed < *deh₃-no- (or periphrasis with *duunatom fefakom)

famatted < *fāmā-tt-ed < *bʰeh₂-meh₂-

prufatted < *profā-tt-ed < *probʰ-

seganatted < *sek-na-

teremnattens < *teremna-/termen-ā-tt-ēr(i)

tribarakattins < *trēb-ark-ā-t-ē-nd (Rix 2003a: 18) (denominative verb)

tribarakattuset < *trēb-ark-a-tt-us-ed < *trēb-h₂erk-

M. *amatens* < *h₂emh₃- (LIV² 2001: 266)

4.7. -k-perfect

This formation is scarcely attested in the Sabellic languages. It is possible that it can be compared to the -k- suffixes present in Latin, cf. *fēcī* < *dʰeh₁-k̂-h₂ei, and to the k-perfects present in Greek, e.g. *héstaka*. The etymology of this -k- both in Sabellic and in Latin and Greek still remains a mystery (Meiser 2003: 199–200, van der Staaij 1995: 171).

O. λιοκακειτ Ve. 184,5 / Lu 39 (Anzi)

O. *kellaked* Pocc. 14,15 / Sa 10,12 (Pietrabbondante) 3 sg. pf.

4.8. -nky-perfect

The *nky*-perfect formation is exclusive to Umbrian and appears in the future perfect forms. Rix (1992) [building on the idea of Sommer (1926)] traces its origin to a univerbation of the instrumental of an *ā*-stem with a preterite of the *i*-present of the root *h₁nek̂- 'to bring', which gives Umbrian *ankie/o-. Poultney (1959: 135) traces the origin of these perfects to "a combination of an accusative noun in -*am*, -*im* + *ke + *iust* and other forms of the perfect system of the verb 'go'." The hypothesis of Saint John (1973a), connecting the Oscan *f*-, Umbrian *nky*- and Latin *u*-perfects, has already been mentioned and refuted above. The periphrastic theory of Jerrett (1974) is less convincing than the one by Rix (1992), as he comes up with an IE root *kei unattested in Sabellic.

The following reconstructions illustrate the origin of some of the Sabellic *nky*-perfects presenting the general pattern:

U. *purdinşiust* < *por-d(o)uh₃-nky-us-t (van der Staaij 1995: 171)

U. *combifianşiust* < *kom-βιβιιā-nkyom < -bʰidʰiiām h₁nkyom (Rix 2003b: 158)

4.9. Future perfect

It is characteristic for the Sabellic languages to form the future perfect stem with the -*us*- suffix. Examples of this formation are numerous.

Rix (1992) traces the origin of this suffix to another periphrastic construction – the active perfect participle and the future of the auxiliary verb 'to be,' e.g. *gʷegʷen-wos bʰusti > *bebenwos fust > *-wos fust > *-usfust > -ust. The traditional explanation is given by Buck (1904: 173) and Poultney (1959: 136), who assume that the -us- suffix has been taken analogically from the Sabellic future form of the verb 'to be,' i.e. *fust*. This solution is in turn criticized by Saint John (1973b), who postulates a u-perfect in Sabellic [an idea also mentioned by von Planta (1892–1897)]. This idea in turn is criticized by Xodorkovskaya (1993), who suggests that the suffix is a combination of two formants: the *-u- and *-s-. Recently, Jasanoff also proposed the same explanation, adding some arguments for the similar analogical spread of the Latin -is- preterital suffix (Jasanoff 1987; similarly, Jasanoff 1991: 86). The exact origin of this suffix remains unknown. It has also been postulated earlier that the -us- suffix might be related to the Latin u-perfect (von Planta 1892–1897: 373) or the PIE perfect participle in *-wos-/-wes-/-us- (Schultze 1887: 272–274). The theory of the participial origin has been also taken over by Pulgram (1978: 117). He traces -us- back to the nominative singular of an

> ancient active perfect participle in -us- which has been provided with the regular inflexional endings: 2 sg. -us-ses, 3 sg. -us-set, from which later, by syncope, -us(s), -ust, and 3 pl. -us-sent, whence Oscan -uset, -**uzet**, Umbrian -urent (Pulgram 1978: *ibid.*).

The following reconstructions illustrate the origin of some of the Sabellic future perfects with the characteristic -us- suffix presenting the general pattern:
U. *dersicurent* < *dedikus fusent < *dedik-wos fus-ent (Rix 2003a: 20)
U. *portust* < *portus fust < *port-wos fust (Rix 2003a: 20)
O. **tribarakattuset** < *trēb-ark-ā-t-us-ed < *trēb-ark-ā-t-wos fust

All of the analyzed forms are in origin univerbations of an active perfect participle in *-wos- and the future of the verb 'to be' -*fust*. The double /tt/ in the Oscan form is explained by Rix as an optional *littera*-rule by means of which the "long /ā/ plus single /t/ became short /a/ plus geminated /t/ (...) V:K -> VKK" (Rix 2003a: 20).

5. Conclusions

From what has been shown it follows that there are generally three tendencies of explaining the divergent Sabellic formations of the perfect in today's Indo-European linguistics. The first tendency would be to explain the forms by periphrasis. Postulated initially by Buck and Sommer, this hypothesis is nowadays identified with Rix and Meiser. The second option would be to explain the different perfects as originating from single forms and then expanded to the other forms analogically. This hypothesis is now identified with Beckwith's 2005 article. The third option would be the explanation posited by Jack Saint John whereby all of the divergent perfect formations (including the Latin u-perfect) are explained in a single theory, though very forceful and therefore not convincing.

If the third hypothesis is not very probable, the first one is also not without problems. Exhaustive criticism is voiced by Beckwith (2005: 148):

> this would require that proto-Italic had at least three different isofunctional periphrastic formations to yield the attested forms: one to generate the Latin -v-perfect, one for the Oscan -tt-perfect, and one for the Umbrian *-nky-perfect. Worse, these three formations would have to be radically different from one another: an active perfect participle *portāwos est for the Latin formation, but a past passive participle with *fefakom for the Oscan along with another formation for the Umbrian (…), and yet these divergent formations would have *exactly the same function*.

On the other hand, Beckwith's analogical explanation has problems with the sound development of *tw > tt, and in the fact that analogy requires an explicit motive, which we are not always able to observe, and a model on which to operate.

It is also worthwhile to observe that the respective Sabellic counterparts of the Latin perfects have either tt-perfect forms or f-perfect so **prúffed**: *posuit*, **prúfatted**: *probauit*, **manafum**: *mandaui*, **dadíkatted**: *dedicauit*. The Latin always has its u-perfect here as counterpart.

In my opinion, neither of the extreme theories, as I would call them, that trace the origin of the perfect formations only to periphrasis (Rix) or only to analogy (Beckwith) is correct. We do not normally observe such strict operations of either analogy or periphrasis within the languages and we have to keep in mind that the Sabellic languages are actual attested languages of the specific region and specific time. They are not our models of reconstructed, hypothetical proto-languages.

And even within our reconstructed languages we should remember that we are actually unearthing a system and not hundreds of unattached elements:

> (…) we view Proto-Indo-European as a **language**, from which the attested Indo-European languages have developed, and not as a **storehouse** of roots, stems and affixes from which the speakers of the various languages were free to select what they wanted, like children playing with building blocks (Cowgill 1973: 273).

Keeping that in mind, the middle solution might prove to be correct: namely, that the divergent Sabellic perfects are just the effect of regular sound changes within the attested lexemes (reduplicated perfects of the **aamanaffed** type, giving f-perfects), analogical reshapings (taking over the -f- from the reduplicated perfect **fufens** and introducing it elsewhere, the same with the -tt-perfect) and univerbation (the nky-perfect) of the type postulated by Rix. Yet problems with that solution are also numerous. For one, analogy is very difficult to prove. Univerbations do occur in Latin and Sabellic but we do not have a single uncontracted form to prove our point of the periphrasis, other than the typical Latin elided perfect passives or the Sabellic forms like **teremnatust**.

However, I think that our main problem is that the material at our disposal is relatively small and incomplete. Therefore there is always the chance that the key to our mystery is still buried somewhere in the grounds of the hidden past of ancient Italy, waiting to be unearthed.

APPENDIX

LIST OF THE ATTESTED FORMATIONS OF THE PERFECT IN THE SABELLIC LANGUAGES

Following is the alphabetical list of the attested formations of the perfect in the Sabellic languages (listed as evidenced in WOU). Compounded forms are marked with a hyphen between the preverb and the verbal stem. Question marks indicate dubious forms or interpretations. The glosses normally indicate the number of the inscription in the handbook of Emil Vetter (1953, abbreviated as Ve.); sometimes, if the inscription was found later, in its supplement by Paolo Poccetti (1979, abbreviated as Pocc.); and always in the newest edition of the texts by Helmut Rix (2002, all the other abbreviations). Umbrian forms are glossed with the number of the Iguvine table they are found on (i.e. IIb is the second table, side "b" and VIIa is the seventh table, side "a", etc.).

Form	Language	Person & Tense	Gloss
afđed	Paelignian	3 sg. pf.	Ve. 213,6 / Pg 9
aflakus	Oscan	2 sg. fut. II	Ve. 6,10,11 / Cp 37
αfλκειτ	Oscan	3 sg. perf. ?	Ve. 183 / Lu 13
aikdafed	Oscan	3 sg. ind. pf.	Ve. 150 / Sa 7
amatens	Marrucinian	3 pl. pf.	Ve. 218,11 / MV 1
apelus	Umbrian	3 sg. fut. II	IIb 27
apelust	Umbrian	3 sg. fut. II	Va 17
angetuzet	Oscan	3 pl. fut. II	TB 20
angitu[st or [zet	Oscan	3 sg. or pl. fut II.	TB 2
anter.vakaze	Umbrian	3 sg. subj. perf. pass.?	Ib 8
ander.uacose	Umbrian	3 sg. subj. perf. pass.?	VI b 47
atahus	Volscian	3 sg. fut. II	Ve. 222,1 VM 2
benus	Umbrian	2 or 3 sg. fut. II	IIb 16
benust	Umbrian	3 sg. fut II	VIb 53
benurent	Umbrian	3 pl. fut. II	Va 25, 28, Vb 5
benurent	Umbrian	3 pl. fut. II	VIb 57
benuso	Umbrian	3 pl. fut. II	VIb 64, 65 VIIa 2
kúm-bened	Oscan	3 sg. pf.	CA A 10
ce-bnust	Oscan	3 sg. fut. II	TB 20
dadíkatted	Oscan	3 sg. pf.	Ve. 151 / Pocc. 19 / Sa 21

Form	Language	Person & Tense	Gloss
dersicust	Umbrian	3 sg. fut. II	VIb 63
dersicurent	Umbrian	3 pl. fut. II	VIb 62
deded	Oscan	3 sg. pf.	Ve. 11 (two times) / Po 3 Ve 13, 19 / Po 5, 10 Ve 140 / Sa 22 Ve 153 / Sa 5
de]ded	Oscan	3 sg. pf.	Ve 152 / Sa 3
δεδετ	Oscan	3 sg. pf.	Ve 191 / Lu 19
ded.	Marsian	3 sg. pf.	Ve 223 / VM 3
tetet	Pre-Samnite	3 sg. pf.	Ve. 101 / Ps 3
dede	Umbrian	3 sg. pf.	Ve 230 / Um 11
dedens	Oscan	3 pl. pf.	Ve 108 / Pocc 132 / Cm 9 Pocc 133 / Cm 4 Cm 2
ded[ens	Oscan	3 pl. pf.	Pocc. 16 / Sa 24
δεδενς	Oscan	3 pl. pf.	Pocc. 148 / Lu 2
teřust	Umbrian	3 sg. fut. II	Ib 34
dirsust	Umbrian	3 sg. fut. II	VIIa 43
dadid	Oscan	3 sg. subj. pf.	Ve. 6, 4
a-teřafust	Umbrian	3 sg. fut. II	Ib 40
an-dersafust	Umbrian	3 sg. fut. II	VIIb 3
an-dirsafust	Umbrian	3 sg. fut. II	VIIa 46
disleralinsust	Umbrian	3 sg. fut. II	VIa 7
duunated	Oscan	3 sg. pf.	Ve. 149,8 / Sa 4
ehpeílatasset	Oscan	3 pl. pf. pass.	Ve. 81 / Cp 24
eiscurent	Umbrian	3 pl. fut. II	Vb 10, 15
iust	Umbrian	3 sg. fut. II	VIa 7
am-pre-fu\<u>s	Umbrian	3 sg. fut. II	Ib 20
am-bre-furent	Umbrian	3 pl. fut. II	VIb 56
da-etom est	Umbrian	3 sg. perf. pass.	VIa 28,37,47, VIb 30
per-etom est	Umbrian	3 sg. perf. pass.	VIa 27,37,47, VIb 30
eitipes	Umbrian	3 pl. pf.	Va 2,14

Form	Language	Person & Tense	Gloss
emps (*est*)	Umbrian	3 sg. pf. pass.	Ve. 236 / Um 6
emmens	Oscan	3 pl. pf. act.	Pocc. 134 / Cm 5
per-emust	Oscan	3 sg. fut. II	TB 15
pert-emust	Oscan	3 sg. fut. II	TB 4
fufens	Oscan	3 pl. pf.	Ve. 84, 85 / Cp. 29, 30
fɛfικεδ	Pre-Samnite		Ps 20
fυfϝοδ	Pre-Samnite		Ps 20
fυfυϝοδ	Pre-Samnite		Ps 20
fuid	Oscan	3 sg. subj. pf.	TB 28, 29
fust	Oscan	3 sg. fut. II	TB 19–30 (6 times), TB Pocc. 185,8
fust	Umbrian	3 sg. fut. II	Ib 7,39 III 6 Va 4,11,19,20
fust	Umbrian	3 sg. fut. II	VIa 7, VIb 39,41,42,47 (two times), VIIa 45, VIIb 1
fus	Umbrian	3 sg. fut. II	VIb 40
furent	Umbrian	3 pl. fut. II	Va 22
fefure	Umbrian	3 pl. fut. II	IIa 4
ad-fust	Oscan	3 sg. fut. II	Ve. 86 / Cp 31
(ad)fust	Oscan	3 sg. fut. II	Ve. 87 / Cp 32
famatted	Oscan	3 sg. pf.	Ve. 163 / Hi 1
faamated	Oscan	3 sg. pf.	Ve. 154 / Pocc. 18 / Sa 13
α-fααματεδ	Oscan	3 sg. pf.	Pocc. 167 / Lu 6
α-fααμα[	Oscan	3 sg. pf.	Pocc. 168 / Lu 7
α-fαματεδ/τ	Oscan	3 sg. pf.	Pocc. 175,6 / Lu 5
ατ-fαματτενς	Oscan	3 pl. pf.	Pocc. 150 / Lu 3
fe\<f\>acid	Oscan	3 sg. subj. pf.	TB 10
fefacust	Oscan	3 sg. fut. II	TB 11,17
fecront	Marsian	3 pl. pf.	Pocc. 223
fec(ed ?)	Marrucinian	3 pl. pf.	Pocc. 206 / MV 3
face	Umbrian	3 sg. pf.	Um 3
fakust	Umbrian	3 sg. fut. II	IV 31

Form	Language	Person & Tense	Gloss
fakurent	Umbrian	3 pl. fut. II	Ib 34
facurent	Umbrian	3 pl. fut. II	VII 43
ανα-ϝακετ	Oscan	3 sg. pf.	Ve. 190 / Lu 18
fifikus	Oscan	2 sg. fut. II	Ve. 6,5 / Cp 37
fi]r[i]mens	Oscan	3 pl. pf.	Ve. 9+10 / Po 2
frosetom est	Umbrian	3 sg. pf. pass.	VIa 28, 37, 47 VIb 30 3
habus	Umbrian	3 sg. fut. II	VIb 40
haburent	Umbrian	3 pl. fut. II	VIIa 52
hipid	Oscan	3 sg. subj. pf.	TB 8,14,17
hipust	Oscan	3 sg. fut. II	TB 11, TB Pocc. 185,8
pru-hipid	Oscan	3 sg. subj. pf.	TB 25
pru-hipust	Oscan	3 sg. fut. II	TB 26
iocatin	Paelignian	3 pl. pf.	Ve. 212 / Pg 1
pro-canurent	Umbrian	3 pl. fut. II	VIa 16
kellaked	Oscan	3 sg. pf.	Pocc. 14,15 / Sa 10,12
censas fust	Oscan	3 sg. fut. II pass.	TB Pocc. 185,8
şersnatur furent	Umbrian	3 pl. fut. II pass.	Va 22
clisuist	Paelignian	3 sg. pf. pass. f.	Ve. 213,4 / Pg 9
coisatens	Paelignian	3 pl. pf.	Ve. 216 / Pg 2
kuratu eru	Umbrian	inf. pf. pass.	Va 26,29
combifianşi	Umbrian	3 sg. subj. pf.	VIb 52
combifianşiust	Umbrian	3 sg. fut. II	VIb 49
combifianşust	Umbrian	3 sg. fut. II	VIIa 5
combifiansiust	Umbrian	3 sg. fut. II	VIb 52
λιοκακειτ	Oscan	?	Ve. 184,5 / Lu 39
manafum	Oscan	1 sg. pf.	Ve. 6,3
ma]nafum	Oscan	1 sg. pf.	Ve. 6,1 / Cp 37
aa-manaffed	Oscan	3. sg. pf.	Ve. 12,14,15,17 / Po. 4,6,7,9
aa-man[aff]ed	Oscan	3 sg. pf.	Ve. 18 / Po. 14
aa-manafed	Oscan	3 sg. pf.	Pocc. 34 / Sa 2, Pocc. 20 / Sa 9

Form	Language	Person & Tense	Gloss
a]-manafed	Oscan	3 sg. pf.	Pocc. 15 / Sa 12
a-m[a]nafed	Oscan	3 sg. pf.	Pocc. 13 / Sa 11
aa-[m]ana[ff]e[d	Oscan	3 sg. pf.	Pocc. 17 / Sa 8
e-manafed	Oscan	3 sg. pf.	Pocc. 14 / Sa 10
pepurkurent	Umbrian	3 pl. fut. II	Vb 5
com-parascuster	Oscan	3 sg. fut. II pass.	TB 4
persnis fust	Umbrian	3 sg. fut. II	VIb 39
pesnis fus(t)	Umbrian	3 sg. fut. II	VIb 40,41
peperscust	Umbrian	3 sg. fut. II	VIb 5
pepescus	Umbrian	3 sg. fut. II	VIIa 8
pesetom est	Umbrian	3 sg. pf. pass.	VIa 27,37,47, VIb 30
pperci	Paelignian	3 sg. pf.	Ve. 203 / Pg 4
prúfatted	Oscan	3 sg. pf.	Ve. 11,14 / Po 3,6 Ve 152, 153 / Sa 3,5 Pocc. 13,14,15 / Sa 11,10,12
prúfatte[d	Oscan	3 sg. pf.	Cm 3
prúfated	Oscan	3 sg. pf.	Pocc. 20 / Sa 9
προφατεδ	Oscan	3 sg. pf.	Pocc. 175, 7 / Lu 5
prúfatt(e)d	Oscan	3 sg. pf.	Ve. 13 / Po 5
prúf]atted	Oscan	3 sg. pf.	Ve. 19 / Po 10
pr[ú]fated	Oscan	3 sg. pf.	Pocc. 34 / Sa 2
prúfattens	Oscan	3 pl. pf.	Ve. 8 / Po. 1, Cm 2
p]rúfatt[ens	Oscan	3 pl. pf.	Ve. 143 / Sa 14
prúffed	Oscan	3 sg. pf.	Ve. 107 / Cm 10 Ve. 156 / Sa 25
prúftúset	Oscan	3 pl. pf. pass. n.	CA A 16
prúftas sú[nt	Oscan	3 pl. pf. pass. f.	Ve. 141 / Sa 17
pru-sikurent	Umbrian	3 pl. fut. II	Va 26, 28
purtiius	Umbrian	3 sg. fut. II	Ia 27, 30, IIa 7, 9
purtitius	Umbrian	3 sg. fut. II	Ia 33
purtinşus	Umbrian	3 sg. fut. II	Ib 33

Form	Language	Person & Tense	Gloss
purdinşiust	Umbrian	3 sg. fut. II	VIIa 43
purdinşus	Umbrian	3 sg. fut. II	VIb 23,37,38
purdinsust	Umbrian	3 sg. fut. II	VIb 16, 24
purditom fust	Umbrian	3 sg. fut. II pass.	VIIa 45
purdito fust	Umbrian	3 sg. fut. II pass.	VIb 42
purtitu fust	Umbrian	3 sg. fut. II pass.	Ib 39, Va 18
portust	Umbrian	3 sg. fut. II	VIIb 3
seganatted	Oscan	3 sg. pf.	Pocc. 21 / Sa 35
sistiatiens	Volscian	3 pl. pf.	Ve. 222,4 / VM 2
sesust	Umbrian	3 sg. fut. II	VIa 5
ander-sesus<t>	Umbrian	3 sg. fut. II	VIa 7
spa<t>u fust	Umbrian	3 sg. fut. II pass.	Va 20
staflatasset	Oscan	3 pl. pf. pass.	Ve. 81 / Cp 24
sta̲i̲effud	Oscan	3 sg. pf. ?	Ve. 86 / Cp 31
ad-staíúh	South Picene	3 pl. pf. ?	AP 2
pra]istaiúh	South Picene	3 pl. pf. ?	RI 1
stakaz est	Umbrian	3 sg. pf. pass.	IIa 15
subator sent	Umbrian	3 pl. pf. pass.	VIa 27,36,46, VIb 29
entelust	Umbrian	3 sg. fut. II	VIb 50
entelus	Umbrian	3 sg. fut. II	Ib 12
teremnattens	Oscan	3 pl. pf.	Ve. 8, 5–6
teremna[t]tens	Oscan	3 pl. pf.	Ve. 8,2–3 / Po 1
teremnattens	Oscan	3 pl. pf.	Ve. 9+10 / Po 2
teremnatust	Oscan	3 sg. pf. pass.	Ve. 8,4 / Po 1
termnas (est)	Umbrian	3 sg. pf. pass.	Ve. 236 / Um 6
tríbarakat.tíns	Oscan	3 pl. pf. subj.	CA B 22
tríbarakat.tuset	Oscan	3 pl. fut. II	CA B 13, 16
tuderato est	Umbrian	3 sg. pf. pass. n.	VIa 8
úpsed	Oscan	3 sg. pf.	Pocc. 34 / Sa 2

Form	Language	Person & Tense	Gloss
upsed	Oscan	3 sg. pf.	Ve. 142 / Sa 18, Ve. 177 Pocc. 56 / Sa 33
ups(e)d	Oscan	3 sg. pf.	Sa 34
upse[d	Oscan	3 sg. pf.	Hi 8
ups(ed)	Oscan	3 sg. pf.	Ve. 176 / Sa 32
opsút	South Picene	3 sg. pf.	AQ 2
o]psúq	South Picene	3 sg. pf.	TE 7
uupsens	Oscan	3 pl. pf.	Ve. 8 / Po. 1
upsens	Oscan	3 pl. pf.	Ve. 16 / Po. 8
ουπσενς	Oscan	3 pl. pf.	Ve. 196 / Me 1,3
oşens	Vestinian	3 pl. pf.	Pocc. 207 / MV 2
opset(*a est*)	Umbrian	3 sg. pf. pass.	Ve. 234 / Um 7
oseto (*est*)	Umbrian	3 sg. pf. pass.	Ve. 233 / Um 8
upsatuh sent	Oscan	3 pl. pf. pass.	Ve. 124a-c / Si 4–6
ortom est	Umbrian	3 sg. pf.	VIa 46
orto est	Umbrian	3 sg. pf.	VIa 26,36, VIb 29
urtu fefure	Umbrian	3 sg. fut. II ?	IIa 4
urust	Oscan	3 sg. fut. II	TB 14, 16
usaşe	Umbrian	3 sg. pf. ?	IIa 44
usaie	Umbrian	3 sg. pf. ?	Ib 45
uaśetom est	Umbrian	3 sg. pf. pass.	VIa 37
uasetom est	Umbrian	3 sg. pf. pass.	VIa 47, VIb 30
uaseto est	Umbrian	3 sg. pf. pass.	VIa 27
uesticos (*fust*)	Umbrian	3 sg. fut. II pass.	VIb 25
vurtus	Umbrian	3 sg. fut. II	IIa 2
kuvurtus	Umbrian	3 sg. fut. II	Ib 11
couortus	Umbrian	3 sg. fut. II	VIIa 39
courtust	Umbrian	3 sg. fut. II	VIa 6
couortuso	Umbrian	3 sg. fut. II pass.	VIb 64

List of abbreviations

Attestations:

CA = cippus Abella
Cm = Cetera Campania
Cp = Capua
Fr = Frentani
He = Hernici
Hi = Hirpini
Lu = Lucani
Me = Messina
MV = Marrucini, Vestini
Pg = Paeligni
Po = Pompei
Ps = Pre-Samnites
Sa = Samnites
Si = Sidcini
Sp = South Picene
TB = Tabula Bantina
Um = Umbri
VM = Volsci, Marsi, Aequiculi, Sabini
Ve. = Vetter (1953)
Pocc. = Poccetti (1979)

Grammatical and linguistic:

PIE = Proto-Indo-European
IE = Indo-European
O. = Oscan
U. = Umbrian
M. = Marrucinian
P. = Paelignian
sg. = singular
pl. = plural
pres. = present
fut. = future
perf. = perfect
act. = active
pass. = passive
ind. = indicative
subj. = subjunctive
inf. = infinitive

As is common in scientific literature, Sabellic forms written in native alphabets are printed in bold, those written in the Latin alphabet in cursive and those in the Greek alphabet in Greek.

Bibliography

Adiego Lajara I. 1992. *Protosabelio, osco-umbro, sudpiceno*. Barcelona.

Beckwith M. 2005. Volscian sistiatiens and the Oscan -*tt*- perfect. – *Historische Sprachforschung* 118: 145–159.

Beckwith M. 2006. The old Italic ō-perfect and the Tortora inscription. [Abstract from the 18th annual UCLA Indo-European conference. Los Angeles 03.11–04.11.2006]. Los Angeles.

Beckwith M. 2008. The Latin imperfect and *v*-perfect: A paradigm split. [Abstract from the 20th annual UCLA Indo-European conference. Los Angeles 31.10–01.11.2008]. Los Angeles.

Brugmann K. 1893. *Grundriss der vergleichenden Grammatik der indogermanischen Sprachen*. [Dritter Band]. Strassburg.

Buck C.D. 1904. *A grammar of Oscan and Umbrian*. Boston.

Burrow T. 2001. *The Sanskrit language*. Delhi.

Clackson J. 2007. *Indo-European linguistics. An introduction*. Cambridge.

Cowgill W.C. 1957. *Indo-European long-vowel preterits*. [Unpublished Ph.D. dissertation. Yale University]. New Haven.

Cowgill W.C. 1973. The source of Latin *stāre*, with notes on comparable forms elsewhere in Indo-European. – *The Journal of Indo-European Studies* 1.3: 271–303.

Diels P. 1959. Zur umbrischen Konjugation. – *Münchener Studien zur Sprachwissenschaft* 15: 17–22.

Fortson B.W. 2004. *Indo-European language and culture. An introduction.* Oxford.

Hamp E.P. 1990. On the Oscan-Umbrian *f*-perfect. – *Glotta* 68: 211–215.

Xodorkovskaya V.V. 1993. K predystorii sistemy vremen infekta / perfekta v latinskom i oksko-umbrskom yazykax. – *Voprosy yazykoznaniya* 1993.2: 58–68

Hoffmann K. 1970. Das Kategoriensystem des indogermanischen Verbums. – *Münchener Studien zur Sprachwissenschaft* 28: 19–41.

Jasanoff J. 1987. The tenses of the Latin perfect system. – Cardona G., Zide N.H. (eds.) *Festschrift for Henry Hoenigswald on the occasion of his seventieth birthday.* Tübingen: 177–183.

Jasanoff J. 1991. The origin of the Italic imperfect subjunctive. – *Historische Sprachforschung* 104: 84–105.

Jasanoff J. 2003. *Hittite and the Indo-European verb.* Oxford.

Jerrett D.H. 1974. The Umbrian -*nky*- perfect. – *Transactions of the American Philological Association* 104: 169–178.

Kronasser H. 1956. *Historische Laut- und Formenlehre des Hethitischen.* Heidelberg.

Kümmel M.J. 2007. *Grundzüge der historischen lateinischen Sprachwissenschaft.* [Skriptum. Sprachwissenschaftliches Seminar der Albert-Ludwigs-Universitat]. Freiburg.

LIV² 2001 = Rix H. et al. (eds.) 2001. *Lexikon der indogermanischen Verben.* Wiesbaden.

Markey T.L. 1985. Some Italic perfects revisited. – *Word* 6: 26–41.

Meiser G. 1986. *Lautgeschichte der umbrischen Sprache.* Innsbruck.

Meiser G. 2003. *Veni vidi vici. Die Vorgeschichte der lateinischen Perfektsystems.* München.

Olzscha K. 1958. Das umbrische Perfekt auf -*nki*. – *Glotta* 36: 300–304.

Olzscha K. 1963. Das *f*-Perfektum im Oskisch-Umbrischen. – *Glotta* 41: 290–299.

Osthoff H. 1884. *Zur Geschichte des Perfects im Indogermanischen.* Strassburg.

Pike M. 2003. The Indo-European long-vowel preterite: New Latin evidence. [Paper presented at the International Conference on Historical Linguistics. 14 August 2003, Copenhagen]. Copenhagen.

von Planta R. 1892–1897. *Grammatik der oskisch-umbrischen Dialekte.* [2 vols]. Strassburg.

Poccetti P. 1979. *Nuovi documenti italici.* Pisa.

Poultney J.W. 1959. *The bronze tables of Iguvium.* Baltimore.

Pulgram E. 1978. *Italic, Latin, Italian.* Heidelberg.

Ringe D. 1984. *The perfect tenses in Greek inscriptions.* [Unpublished Ph.D. dissertation. Yale University]. New Haven.

Ringe D. 1990. The Tocharian active s-preterite: A classical sigmatic aorist. – *Münchener Studien zur Sprachwissenschaft* 51: 183–242.

Ringe D. 1996. *On the chronology of sound changes in Tocharian.* [vol. 1]. New Haven.

Ringe D. 2006. *A linguistic history of English.* [vol. 1]. Oxford.

Rix H. 1992. Zur Entstehung des lateinischen Perfektparadigmas. – Panagl O., Krisch T. (eds.) *Latein und Indogermanisch.* [Akten des Kolloquiums der Indogermanischen Gesellschaft, Salzburg, 23.–26.09.1986]. Innsbruck: 221–240.

Rix H. 2002. *Sabellische Texte.* Heidelberg.

Rix H. 2003a. Towards a reconstruction of Proto-Italic: the verbal system. – Huld M. et al. (eds.) *Journal of Indo-European Studies Monograph* 47: 1–24.

Rix H. 2003b. Ausgliederung und Aufgliederung der italischen Sprachen. – Bammesberger A., Vennemann T. (eds.) *Languages in prehistoric Europe.* Heidelberg: 147–172.

Safarewicz J. 1953. *Zarys gramatyki historycznej języka łacińskiego. Fonetyka historyczna i fleksja.* Warszawa.

Safarewicz J. 1967. *Studia językoznawcze*. Warszawa.

Saint John J. 1973a. The perfect in Oscan and Umbrian. – *Canadian Journal of Linguistics* 18: 1–6.

Saint John J. 1973b. The Oscan-Umbrian future perfect in *-us-*. – *Orbis* 22: 155–160.

Schultze W. 1887. Das lateinische *v*-perfectum. – *Zeitschrift für vergleichende Sprachforschung* 28: 266–274.

Seldeslachts H. 2001. *Études de morphologie historique du verbe latin et indo-européen*. Louvain.

Silvestri D. 1998. The Italic languages. – Ramat A., Ramat P. (eds.) *Indo-European languages*. London, New York: 322–344.

Sommer F. 1926. Oskisch-Umbrisches. – *Indogermanische Forschungen* 43: 40–46.

Sowa W. 1998. Notes on the Mycenaean verbal morphology: The finite verb forms. – *Linguistica Baltica* 7: 271–297.

van der Staaij R.J. 1995. *A reconstruction of Proto-Italic*. [Unpublished Ph.D. dissertation. Universiteit Leiden]. Leiden.

Tichy E. 2004. *Indogermanistisches Grundwissen*. Bremen.

Untermann J. 2002. Das Perfekt der Sekundärverben im Oskisch-Umbrischen. – Fritz M., Zeilfelder S. (eds.) *Novalis Indogermanica: Festschrift für Günter Neumann zum 80. Geburtstag*. Graz: 489–495.

De Vaan M. 2008. *Etymological dictionary of Latin and the other Italic languages*. Leiden.

Vetter E. 1953. *Handbuch der italischen Dialekte*. Heidelberg.

Wallace R. 1985. Volscian sistiatiens. – *Glotta* 63: 93–101.

Wallace R. 2007. *The Sabellic languages of ancient Italy*. München.

WOU 2000 = Untermann J. 2000. *Wörterbuch des Oskisch-Umbrischen*. Heidelberg.

Studia Linguistica Universitatis Iagellonicae Cracoviensis
128 (2011)

MARZANNA POMORSKA
Jagiellonian University, Cracow

MONTH NAMES IN THE CHULYM TURKIC DIALECTS – THEIR ORIGIN AND MEANING

Keywords: Chulym Turkic, month names, etymology, comparative linguistics

Abstract

Our article presents not just a review of the traditional month names in the Chulym Turkic dialects, but also its analysis from a lexical, etymological, semantic and ethnographic point of view.

Studying the traditional month names may uncover interesting and important information about aspects of the lives of their users, e.g. their main occupations, means of obtaining food, impact of natural phenomena, plants and animals important to them, the influences of foreign cultures or religions. It is especially important to investigate less well-known peoples like the Turkic peoples in Siberia, among them the Chulym Turkic peoples.

Our aim is not just a review of the existing material,[1] but also its analysis from a lexical, etymological, semantic and ethnographic point of view. Among younger generations of the Chulym Turkic peoples, we may expect the use of Russian names for the months, but they are not recorded in the literature, not even in the most recent monograph by Li Yong-Sŏng (2008).

Traditional Chulym names for the months of the year were first recorded by J.P. Falk[2] in his *Beiträge zur topographischen Kenntnis des Russischen Reichs*, III, St. Petersburg 1786: 467ff. (cf. Dułzon 1952: 117ff.) or 557 (cf. Alekseev 1991: 84). Chulym month names are recorded in several other publications: Küärik names

---

[1] For sources of Chulym Turkic lexical materials and the transcription used see Pomorska 2004.
[2] We quote Falk's material after Alekseev (1995) but, in some cases, we query the phonetics and present alternatives.

are quoted by Radloff (1893) in the first volume of his dictionary s.v. *aj* (Radloff I 7), Lower- and Middle-Chulym names are quoted in Dułzon's articles[3] and Birjukovič's monographs (Dułzon 1952: 117ff., Dułzon 1966: 463, Birjukovič 1984: 11f.). Li Yong-Sŏng (2008: 111) quote two MČ names, one of them (*kozan aj*) does not occur in the works by Dułzon and Birjukovič. Alekseev's ethnographic study on the Chulym Turkic peoples (1991) also contains relevant data: [4] the author lists Lower- and Middle-Chulym names which in most cases are quotations from Dułzon 1952 and from an unavailable to us work by Bojaršinova, Z. Ja.: *Naselenie Zapadnoj Sibiri do načala russkoj kolonizacii*, Tomsk 1960.

Falk and Radloff list twelve month names, Dułzon and Birjukovič – thirteen. Alekseev quotes thirteen names for Lower Chulym and fiveteen names for Middle Chulym. All the authors present the month names in ordered lists. Radloff, Dułzon and Birjukovič number their month names, Alekseev does not. Dułzon and Alekseev translate them, Birjukovič additionally compares them to Russian month names. Radloff indicates the first name as „January" only and does not translate his month names at all.

It is probable that the first month in Falk, Dułzon, Birjukovič and Alekseev's lists (i.e. the month they refer to as „January") is not actually the first month of the Chulym calendar. According to Dułzon, the year for Middle Chulym Turks begins in our May or August or September.[5] Falk indicates our September, the month of the first snowfall, as the beginning of the year (Alekseev 1991: 84).

All translations of Chulym month names are quoted in their original languages, as recorded by the authors of the sources. Our English translations (in bold text) result from the meaning of Chulym compositions.

Most compositions listed below contain the noun for 'month; moon': Küä. *aj* '1. Mond; 2. mondförmig; 3. Monat' (Radloff I 3ff.), MČ *aj* 'месяц (календарный)' (Birjukovič 1979: 134), LČ *aj* 'месяц, луна' (Dułzon 1952: 141) = Tu. *aj* 'month; moon' (cf. Radloff I 3ff., ÈSTJa I 98ff.).

The month names in the Chulym Turkic dialects

1. **'big cold (month)'** ~ **'big month'** (Küä, LČ, MČ[6]):

   1.1 Küä. *uluğ suak* 'Januar' (Radloff I 7 and 1695);

---

[3] Dułzon's article *Sistema sčeta vremeni u čulymskich tatar* (published in *Kratkie soobščenija Instituta Ètnografii AN SSSR*, X, Moskva – Leningrad 1950) has not been available, but it is very likely that the lexical analysis of the month names was quoted without change in his article from 1952 and his further works as well as by other researchers.

[4] Alekseev's material differs in some cases from Dułzon and Birjukovič's recordings so we quote it here despite their sometimes strange and probably misprinted or mistaken notation or semantics. We shall highlight these when encountered.

[5] „В части Чулыма, расположенной выше владения Кии, нам чаще всего указывали на май, как на начало года, реже на август – сентябрь. Для нас это приобретает особый интерес в связи с тем, что у кетов год начинается в мае, а у самоедов, по данным академика Шифнера в августе" (Dułzon 1952: 119f.).

[6] Our notation indicates that the given name is quoted by each author (i.e. Radloff, Dułzon, Birjukovič, Alekseev). If this is not the case, it will be noted.

1.2 LČ *ulug aj suagy* 'месяц большого мороза' (Birjukovič 1984: 12) ~ 'большой месяц мороза' (Dulzon 1966: 463, Alekseev 1991: 85) ~ *ulug aj* 'большой месяц' (Alekseev 1991: 86);

1.3 MČ *ulug sōk* 'сильный мороз' (Dulzon 1952: 119, Dulzon 1966: 463) ~ *ulug sōk aj* 'месяц сильного мороза (соотв. декабрю)' (Birjukovič 1984: 27) ~ *ulug sug aj* ~ *ulug sugbaj* 'большой мороз' (Alekseev 1991: 85, hapax legomenon);

1.4 1.4 Čul. *ulu aj* 'большой месяц – декабрь' (Falk).

Cf. Küä. *ulug* 'hoch' (Radloff 1868: 701) ~ 'gross' (ibid. 697) ~ 'gewaltig' (ibid. 1868: 692), LČ *ulug* 'большой' (Dulzon 1952: 175), MČ *ulug* 'id.' (Birjukovič 1979: 105) ~ *ulu* in *kičizi uluzu* 'самый молодой' (Birjukovič 1981: 11) = Tuv., Šr., Sag., Koib., Kač. *uluɣ* 'gross, erhaben' (Radloff I 1695), Tel., Alt., Šr., etc., Ott. *ulu* 'id.' (ibid. 1692; cf. ÈSTJa I 593ff.).

Cf. Küä. *suak* 'Kälte' (Pritsak 1959: 632),[7] LČ *suvak* ~ *sugak* 'холод, холодный, холодно' (Birjukovič 1984: 58) ~ *suak* 'холодный' (Dulzon 1952: 117), MČ *sugak* 'холодно' (Birjukovič 1979: 5) ~ *sōk* 'id.' (ibid.) ~ *suak* 'холод, холодный, холодно' (Birjukovič 1984: 58) = Alt., Tel., Leb., Šr., etc. *sōk* 'kalt, Kälte' (Radloff IV 518), Ott. *souk* '1. id.; 2. feindlich, nicht gut' (ibid. 516f.) ~ *soyuk* 'id.' (ibid. 530), Tel., Kzk., Kas. *sūk* 'kalt, Kälte' (ibid. 751), Tr. *soğuk* '1. cold; cold weather; 2. frigid, unfriendly; inemotional in disposition; 3. out of place, in bad taste' (Redhouse 1026).

2. **'small cold (month)'** ~ **'small (short) month'** (Küä., LČ, MČ):

2.1 Küä. *kiʒig suak* (Radloff I 7);

2.2 LČ *kiʒig aj suagy* 'маленький месяц (месяц маленького мороза)' (Dulzon 1966: 463, Alekseev 1991: 85) ~ 'месяц маленького мороза' (Birjukovič 1984: 12) ~ *kiʒigaj* 'маленький месяц' (Alekseev 1991: 86);

2.3 MČ *kičig sōk aj* 'месяц маленького мороза (соотв. примерно ноябрю)' (Birjukovič 1984: 27) ~ *kičig sōk* 'маленький мороз' (Dulzon 1952: 119, Dulzon 1966: 463) ~ *kičig sok* 'малый мороз' (Alekseev 1991: 85);

2.4 Čul. *kiča aj* 'короткий месяц – ноябрь' (Falk), LČ *kiʒigaj* 'маленький месяц' (Alekseev 1991: 86).

Cf. Küä. *kiʒig* 'klein' (Radloff 1968: 696) ~ *kiʒïk* 'klein' (Radloff II 1384), LČ *kiʒig* 'young' in *kiʒig palavys* '(наш) младшый сын' (Birjukovič 1979a: 34), MČ *kičig* 'маленький' (Birjukovič 1984: 18) ~ 'младшый' (ibid. 41) ~ *kičik* 'младшый' (Dulzon 1973: 19) ~ *kiči* ~ *kičä* in *kičäzinä* 'small-3-Dat' (Birjukovič 1979a: 34), *kičizi uluzu* 'самый молодой' (Birjukovič 1981: 11, cf. also No. 10 below) = Tel., Tar., Čag. *kičik* 'klein, gering' (Radloff II 1381), Ott. *küčük* 'klein, unbedeutend, jünger, niedriger' (ibid. 1493), Tr. *küçük* '1. small, little; 2. young, younger' (Redhouse 693; cf. Clauson 696a-b, ÈSTJa V 75ff.).

---

[7] The word has been recorded by Radloff in compositions for months only.

3. **'hare month'** (MČ: Li Yong-Sŏng):
   MČ *kozan aj* 'January, lit. hare month' (Li Yong-Sŏng et al. 2008: 111).

   Cf. MČ *kozan* 'hare' (Li Yong-Sŏng et al. 2008: 157), LČ *kojan* 'id.' (Dulzon
   1952: 130) = Sag., Koib. *kozan* 'Hase' (Radloff II 629), Čag. *kojan* 'id.' (ibid. 526),
   Alt., Tel. *kojon* 'id.' (ibid.), Alt., Tel., Leb. *köjön* 'id.' (ibid. 1240; cf. ÈSTJa VI 29f.,
   Ščerbak 1961: 136).

4. **'ridge of a year (month)'** (LČ, MČ; Falk):
   4.1 LČ *jyl syrty aj* 'месяц большого хребта года' (Dulzon 1966: 463, Alekseev
        1991: 85) ~ 'хребет года' (Birjukovič 1984: 11) ~ *jylsyrty* 'январь' (Birjukovič
        1984: 35);
   4.2 MČ *čylzyrty* 'хребет года (соответствует приблизительно январю)'
        (Dulzon 1952: 119, Dulzon 1966: 463, Birjukovič 1984: 11) ~ *čylsyrty* 'январь'
        (Birjukovič 1984: 75) ~ *čälsyrty aj* 'длинная ночь, большой мороз' (Alek-
        seev 1991: 85) ~ *čälyšty* (!, M.P.) *aj* 'id.' (ibid.);
   4.3 Čul. *jäl särtä* 'половина зимы – январь' (Falk).

   Cf. LČ *jyl* 'год' (Dulzon 1952: 156), MČ *čyl* 'id.' (Birjukovič 1979a: 15), Küä. *jyl*
   'Jahr' (Radloff 1868: 702) = Alt., Tel., Leb., Kirg., Ott., etc. *jyl* '1. id.; 2. Lebensjahr'
   (Radloff III 480f.), Tr. *yıl* 'year' (Redhouse 1257), Sag., Koib., Šr. *čyl* 'id.' (ibid.
   2084; cf. ÈSTJa IV 275).
       Cf. Čul. *syrt* 'back; ridge'[8] = Alt., Leb., Sag. Koib., Kač., Ott., etc. *syrt* '1. Hin-
   terseite, Rücken; 2. Äussere, Aussenseite; 3. Erhöhung, Hügel' (Radloff IV 646f.),
   Tr. *sırt* '1. upper part of a person's back, back; 2. ridge of an animal's back; ridge
   (of a mountain)' (Redhouse 1014).

5. **'small ridge of a year (month)'** (Küä., LČ):
   5.1 Küä. *kyrlaŋ* (Radloff I 7);
   5.2 LČ *kyrlaŋ aj* 'месяц малого хребта года' (Dulzon 1966: 463) ~ *kyrdan aj*
        (!, M.P.) ~ *kylau* ~ *kyrlyu aj* 'id.' (Birjukovič 1984: 11) ~ *kurlaŋaj* (!, M.P.)
        'id., месяц бури' (Alekseev 1991: 85) ~ *kylancaj* (!, M.P.) 'id.' (ibid.).

   Cf. Čul. *kyrlaŋ* 'small ridge (of a mountain)'[9] = Alt., Tel., Leb., Šr., Sag., Koib.
   kyrlaŋ 'kleiner Bergrücken, Hügel, bergiges Land' (Radloff II 753f.).
       Following such semantics, Alekseev's translation 'месяц бури = stormy month'
   is incorrect.

6. **'fox month'** (LČ: Birjukovič, MČ; Falk):
   6.1 LČ *tülgaj* 'месяц лисы' (Birjukovič 1984: 11, Dulzon does not record this
        name for Lower Chulym);

---

[8] The word has been recorded for LČ and MČ in the names for the months only.
[9] The word has been recorded in Čul. dialects in the names for the months only.

6.2   MČ *tülgü aj* 'February, lit. fox month' (Li Yong-Sŏng et al. 2008: 111) ~ *tülgaj* 'месяц лисицы' (Dulzon 1952: 119, Dulzon 1966: 463) ~ *tülgajä* 'месяц лисы' (Birjukovič 1984: 11) ~ *tülgu* (!) *aj* 'лисий месяц, гон лис' (Alekseev 1991: 85);

6.3   Čul. *tulg aj* 'месяц лис – февраль' (Falk).

Cf. LČ *tülgü* 'лисица' (Dulzon 1952: 167), MČ *tülgü* 'id.' (Birjukovič 1979: 123, Li Yong-Sŏng 2008: 174), Küä. *tülgü* 'Fuchs' (Radloff 1868: 691) ~ *tülkü* 'id.' (ibid. 696) = Kom., Alt., Tel., Tuba, Kzk. *tülkü* 'id.' (Radloff III 1570), Leb. *tülgö* 'id.' (ibid.), Uig., Čag. *tülki* 'id.' (ibid.), Ott. *tilki* 'id.' (ibid. 1385), Tr. *tilki* '1. fox; 2. cunning person; sly fellow' (Redhouse 1177; cf. Clauson 498b-499a., Ščerbak 1961: 135).

7.   **'eagle month'** (Küä., LČ, MČ; Falk):
   7.1   Küä. *küzägän* (Radloff I 7);
   7.2   LČ *küzügän aj* 'месяц прилета орла' (Dulzon 1966: 463) ~ *kuzugan aj* 'месяц орла' (Birjukovič 1984: 11, Alekseev 1991: 85);
   7.3   MČ *küčügän aj* 'месяц орла' (Dulzon 1952: 119, Dulzon 1966: 463) ~ 'месяц орла (соотв. марту)' (Birjukovič 1984: 27) ~ *kučugan aj* 'месяц орла' (ib. 11) ~ 'месяц орла (коршуна), орел поднимается' (Alekseev 1991: 85);
   7.4   Čul. *kučugän aj* 'месяц орла – март' (Falk).

Cf. LČ *küzügän* 'орел' (Dulzon 1966: 463, Birjukovič 1984: 45)[10] = Bar. *küzügän* 'Adler' (Radloff II 1499), Kür. *küčügän* 'eine kleine Adlerart, der weissgeschwänzte Adler' (Radloff II 1495), Tel. *küčüyän* 'id.' (ibid.), Kzk. *küšügön* 'Geierart' (ibid. 1512), Ott. *güčügän* ~ *güčän* 'id.' (ibid. 1645; cf. ÈSTJa V 130, VEWT 306).

7.a   **'big bird month' = 'eagle month'** (MČ: Dulzon):
MČ *ulug kuš aj* 'месяц большой птицы' (Dulzon 1952: 119).

Although Dulzon translates this as 'месяц большой птицы = big bird month', it is probably 'eagle month', cf. MČ *ulugus* 'орел' (Birjukovič 1984: 6) ~ **'owl'*, cf. MČ *ulug kušlap* 'по совиному' (Birjukovič 1981: 94, cf. also Pomorska 2004: 151) < **ulug kušla-* 'to be / to behave like an owl', cf. also Küä. *kušta-* 'Vögel jagen' (Radloff 1868: 696) ~ 'Vögel schiessen' (ibid. 695) = Tar., Čag. *kušla-* 'mit einem Jagdvogel auf die Jagd gehen' (Radloff II 1030), Alt., Tel., Leb., Šr. *kušta-* 'Vögel schiessen, auf die Vogeljagd gehen' (ibid.) < MČ *kuš* ~ *kus* 'птица' (Birjukovič 1984: 24), cf. LČ *kuš* 'id.' (Dulzon 1952: 153), Küä. *kuš* 'Vogel' (Radloff 1868: 702) ~ *kus* 'id.' (ibid. 696, a hapax legomenon) = Tu. *kuš* 'id.' (cf. Clauson 670b, ÈSTJa VI 185ff.).

8.   **'crow month'** (Küä, LČ, MČ; Falk):
   8.1   Küä. *karɣyj aj* (Radloff I 7);

---

[10]   For MČ and Küä. this word has been recorded in the names for the month only.

8.2 LČ *kargaj* 'месяц вороны' (Dulzon 1966: 463, Birjukovič 1984: 11) ~ 'месяц вороны (галки)' (Alekseev 1991: 85);

8.3 MČ *kargaj* 'месяц вороны' (Dulzon 1952: 119, Dulzon 1966: 463) ~ 'id. (соотв. апрелю)' (Birjukovič 1984: 27) ~ 'вороний месять; ворона кричит' (Alekseev 1991: 85);

8.4 Čul. *karga aj* 'месяц вороны – апрель' (Falk).

Cf. Küä. *karya* 'Krähe' (Radloff II 191), LČ *karga* 'ворона' (Dulzon 1952: 137), MČ *karga* 'id.' (Birjukovič 1979: 21) = Tel., Alt., Šr., Koib., Kač., Čag., Ott., etc. *karya* 'Krähe' (Radloff II 191), Tr. *karga* 'crow' (Redhouse 606), Tuv. *kāryan* 'id.' (Ölmez 2007: 186; cf. Clauson 653a, ÈSTJa V 303f., VEWT 232, Li Yong-Sŏng 1997: 259, esp. 266, fn. 99, Erdal 1991: 83, Tekin 1995: 173).

9. **'cuckoo month'** (Küä., LČ, MČ; Falk):
   9.1 Küä. *kök aj* (Radloff I 7);
   9.2 LČ *kögaj* 'месяц кукушки' (Dulzon 1966: 463) ~ *kogaj* 'id.' (Birjukovič 1984: 11, Alekseev 1991: 85);
   9.3 MČ *kögaj* ~ *kȫgaj* 'месяц кукушки' (Birjukovič 1984: 11) ~ *kögäj* 'месяц кукушки' (Dulzon 1966: 463) ~ 'месяц кукушки (соотв. маю)' (Birjukovič 1984: 27) ~ *kogaj* 'месяц кукушки' (Dulzon 1952: 119) ~ *kokaj* ~ *kogaä* 'кукушкин месяц' (Alekseev 1991: 85);
   9.4 Čul. *koj aj* (!, M.P.) 'месяц кукушки – май' (Falk).

Cf. LČ *küök* 'кукушка' (Dulzon 1966: 142), MČ *kȫk* 'id.' (Birjukovič 1979: 27)[11] = Šr., Sag., Koib. *kȫk* 'Kuckuck, als Teil eines Eigennamens' (Radloff II 1223), Khak. *kȫk* 'кукушка' (KhakRS 90), Khak.dial. *käkük* 'id.' (ibid. 73), Šr. *kȫk* 'id.' (ŠorTS 55), Tr. *guguk kuşu* 'cuckoo' (Redhouse 415).

10. **'small hot month'** (Küä., LČ: Dulzon 1952; Falk):
   10.1 Küä. *kiʒiǧ iziǧ aj* (Radloff I 7);
   10.2 LČ *kičig* (!, probably misprintly for *kicig*, M.P.) *isig aj* 'месяц малой жары' (Dulzon 1952: 119).

Cf. LČ *isig* ~ *izig* 'жаркий' (Dulzon 1952: 161) ~ 'жара' (ibid. 158), MČ *isig* 'жаркий' (Birjukovič 1979a: 53) ~ 'жара' (ibid. 47)[12] ~ *izig* 'id.', cf. No. 15 below = Šr., Leb., Sag. *iziǧ* 'heiss' (Radloff I 1540), Tuv. *izig* 'warm' (Ölmez 2007: 186; cf. Clauson 246a-b, ÈSTJa I 668ff.).

10.3 Čul. *kiči šilgai* 'small hot month', in Falk it is incorrectly: 'малое лето – июнь' (cf. 'big hot month' below).

---

[11] For Küä. the word has been recorded in the names for the months only.

[12] For Küä. the word has been recorded in the names for the months only.

Cf. Čul. *šilVg[13] = MČ *čylyg* 'тепло; теплый' (Pomorska 2004: 96), LČ *jylyg* 'id.' (ibid.), Küä., Leb., Koib., Kač. *jylyḡ* 'warm' (Radloff III 484), Tuv. *čylyg* 'id.' (Ölmez 2007: 118; cf. Clauson 925a, ÈSTJa IV 276).

For Küä. *kiʒiḡ* 'small' ~ LČ *kiʒig* 'id.' ~ MČ *kiči* 'id.' see No. 2 above.

11. 'lean fish month' (MČ):

MČ *aryk palyk aj* 'месяц тощей рыбы' (Dulzon 1952: 119, Dulzon 1966: 463) ~ *aryk pālyk aj* 'месяц тощей рыбы (соотв. июню)' (Birjukovič 1984: 27) ~ *arkpal-gaj* 'месяц сухой (худой) рыбы; начинает рыба жиреть' (Alekseev 1991: 85).

Cf. MČ *aryk* 'тощий' (ibid. 15) ~ *āruk* 'тощий' (Birjukovič 1979: 79) ~ 'худой' (Birjukovič 1984: 30), LČ *aruk* 'худой' (Dulzon 1952: 133) = Küä., Alt., Tel., Leb., Ott., etc. *aryk* 'mager, abgemagert, schwach, matt, siech' (Radloff I 268), Tuv. *aryk* 'mager' (Ölmez 2007: 78), Tr.dial. *arık* 'lean, thin' (Redhouse 71; cf. Clauson 214a, ÈSTJa I 161).

Cf. MČ *pālyk* 'рыба' (Birjukovič 1979: 51f.), LČ *pālyk* 'id.' (Birjukovič 1979a: 15) ~ *palyk* 'id.' (Dulzon 1952: 134) = Küä., Alt., Tel., Leb., Šr., Sag., Koib., Kač., Uig. *palyk* 'Fisch' (Radloff IV 1166), Ott., Kar., etc. *balyk* 'id.' (ibid. 1496), Tuv. *balyk* 'id.' (Ölmez 2007: 86), Tr. *balık* 'id.' (Redhouse 127; cf. Clauson 335b, ÈSTJa II 59f.).

12. 'riverbank fish trap month' (LČ):

LČ *kyr dug aj* 'месяц маленьких береговых запоров для ловли рыбы' (Dulzon 1966: 463) ~ 'месяц береговых запоров (для ловли рыбы)' (Birjukovič 1984: 11) ~ *kur* (!, M.P.) *dug aj* 'месяц маленьких береговых запоров (для ловли рыбы)' (Alekseev 1991: 85).

The semantic analysis of this composition leads us to the conclusion that Dulzon's and Alekseev's translations as 'small riverbank fish trap month' has no lexical support. It is probable that this error was caused by the comparison with another Čul. month name, i.e. *ulug tug aj* 'big fish trap month' (↓). Our sources note LČ *kъr* 'берег' (Birjukovič 1979a: 36), MČ *kyr* 'id.' (ibid. 19) ~ 'степ' (Birjukovič 1984: 18) ~ 'пашня' (ibid. 46), Küä. *kyr* '1. Ecke, Kante; 2. hohes Ufer, Bergrücken' (Radloff II 732) ~ 'Niederung' (Radloff 1868: 694) = Alt., Tel., Šr., etc. *kyr* '1. Ecke, Kante; 2. hohes Ufer, Bergrücken' (ibid.), Tuv. *kyr* 'Grenze, Rand' (Ölmez 2007: 199), Ott. *kyr* 'Steppe, Ebene' (Radloff II 732), Tr. *kır* 'countryside, uncultivated land' (Redhouse 653; cf. also Clauson 641a-b (1), ÈSTJa VI 225), so the translation of this composition should be 'riverbank fish trap' only.

In his etnographic study on Chulym Turkic peoples, Alekseev describes the ways and tools traditionally used for fishing, among them *tyunek*, a kind of standing, woven fish trap constructed of spruce or pine wood, cf. LČ *tünök* 'ловушка на рыбы' (Dulzon 1952: 141, Dulzon 1973: 20, cf. also Rus.dial. *тюнék* 'зимняя ловушка для рыбы' (Anikin 1997: 600) using for catching different kinds of fish in all seasons. The *tyuneks* were stood in the deep part of the river, against the water flow

---

[13] For the *č-* ~ *š-* alternation in MČ see Pomorska (2000: 255).

and they were equipped with landing nets, e.g. LČ *sügän* 'рыболовная морда' (Dul-zon 1952: 158) ~ MČ *sügän* 'id.' (Birjukovič 1979: 123), and this dam was named a *tug* (in *kyr dug aj* with a positional sonorisation between two voiced sounds).

Summing up, LČ *kyr dug aj* < LČ *kyr* 'river bank' + LČ *tug* 'kind of fish trap' + LČ *aj* 'moon, month'.

13. **'big hot month'** (Küä.; Falk):
   13.1 Küä. *uluḡ iziḡ aj* (Radloff I 7 and 1695); LČ *ulug isig aj* 'месяц большой жары' (Dulzon 1952: 119).

   For Küä. *uluḡ* 'big' ~ LČ *ulug* 'id.' see No. 1 and for Küä. *iziḡ* 'hot', LČ *isig* 'id.' see No. 10 above.

   13.2 Čul. *ulu šilgai*[14] 'big hot month', in Falk it is 'большое лето – июль' (cf. 'small hot month' above).

   For Čul. **šilVg* 'hot' see No. 10 above.

14. **'big fish trap month'** (LČ):
   LČ *ulug tug aj* 'месяц больших запоров для ловли рыбы' (Dulzon 1966: 463, Birjukovič 1984: 11, Alekseev 1991: 85).

   For LČ *ulug* 'big' see No. 1 and for LČ *tug* 'kind of fish trap' see No. 12 above.

15. **'(hot) spawn month'** (MČ; Falk?):
   MČ *izig jürgän aj* 'месяц теплой икры' (Dulzon 1952: 119, Dulzon 1966: 463) ~ *isig jurgän aj* 'id. (соотв. июлю)' (Birjukovič 1984: 27) ~ *jurgän aj* 'месяц икры' (ibid. 11) ~ *isägurgaj* 'месяц горячей икры' (Alekseev 1991: 85).

   Cf. MČ *ürgän*[15] 'икра' (Birjukovič 1979: 95) (< **ür-* '**to give birth to' with the semantic development 'to bear, to give birth, to give life' > 'that gives life' > 'spawn') = Kzk. *örkän* 'потомство' (ÈSTJa I 605), Tat.dial. *ürgän* '1. рассада; 2. росток, отросток, побег' (TatRS750), cf. Tuv. *ürgänä* 'икра (рыбья)' (TuvRS 454), cf. also MČ *ürän* 'племя' (Birjukovič 1979: 91) ~ 'поколение' (Birjukovič 1984: 13) ~ 'older tribal-family communy among Chulym Turkic peoples' (Dulzon 1952: 92f.), Küä., Tel., Šr., Sag., Koib., Kač. *ürän* '1. Same, Frucht, Saat, Korn; 2. Nachkommenschaft, Generation' (Radloff I 1827), al-though in this case, the Mo. loan is also taken into account (cf. Clauson 233b, ÈSTJa I 605, VEWT 522a, Rassadin 1980: 49).

   For MČ lexicalisation of participles in *-gan* see Pomorska (2004: 152), espe-cially MČ *tugan* '1. родня, родственник; рожденный; 2. родимое пятно' < **tuggan* < *tug-* 'рожать' (ibid.).

---

[14]   Because of the fricative *-š-* it is probably the MČ form.

[15]   The word *ürgän* 'spawn' has been recorded several times in the source literature but the rise of prosthetic *j* is observed in this name for a month only, cf. No. 27 below.

Falks quotes Čul. *urgai ai* 'длинный месяц – август, так как он продолжался до выпадения снега'. The meaning 'длинный месяц = long month' may suggest a connection with MČ *ūr* 'долго' (Birjukovič 1981: 89) ~ *ur* 'id.' (ibid. 66) ~ *ür* 'id.' (Birjukovič 1979: 132), LČ *ür* 'id.' (Dulzon 1952: 176), Küä., Koib., Sag., Kač. *ür* ~ *ür* 'lange, vor langer Zeit' (Radloff I 1824), Tuv. *ür* 'долгий, долго' (TuvRS 450), Kum. *ür* 'id.' (Baskakov 1972: 264; cf. Clauson 193a), but if this were correct, it would have been difficult to explain the -*gaj* syllable here, so it is more probable that this is the same name as 'spawn month' misprinted for *ürgän*.

15.a **'hot month'** (MČ: Birjukovič 1984, Alekseev):
MČ *isig* 'жаркий месяц' (Birjukovič 1984: 11) ~ *izig* ~ *isigaj* 'id.' (Alekseev 1991: 85).

For MČ *isig* 'hot' see No. 10 above, cf. also No. 27 below.

16. **'harvest month'** (Küä.):
Küä. *oryak aj* (Radloff I 7) ~ 'месяц жатвы – август' (Dulzon 1952: 119).

Cf. Küä. *oryak* '1. Sichel; 2. Ernte' (Radloff I 1061), MČ *orgak* 'серп' (Pomorska 2004: 103) = Sag., Koib., Kač., Kzk. *oryak* '1. Sichel, Ernte' (Radloff I 1061), Tub., Bar. *oryok* 'id.' (ibid.; cf. Clauson 216a-b, ÈSTJa I 468).

17. **'full-grown, ripe bread month'** (MČ: Dulzon 1952, Birjukovič 1979):
17.1 MČ *aš pyštyg aj* 'месяц созревшего хлеба' (Dulzon 1952: 119) ~ *ašpystygaj* 'август' (Birjukovič 1979: 88).

Cf. MČ *aš* ~ *as* 'хлеб; еда' (Birjukovič 1984: 30), LČ *aš* 'хлеб' (Dulzon 1952: 144) ~ 'пища' (ibid. 163), Küä. *aš* 'Speise' (Radloff 1868: 700) ~ 'Nahrung' (ibid. 693) = Tel., Alt., Leb., Šr., Tar., Bar., etc. *aš* 'Nahrung, Speise, Futter' (Radloff I 583), Tr. *aş* 'cooked food; pilaf; soup' (Redhouse 85; cf. Clauson 253b, ÈSTJa I 210ff.).
    Cf. MČ *pyštyg* or *pyštyk*, a hapax legomenon, recorded in this composition only. The sources record only the verb MČ *pyš-* 'поспевать' (Birjukovič 1981: 33) ~ 'созревать; вариться; печься' (Birjukovič 1984: 14) ~ 'варить' (ibid. 56), LČ *pyš-* 'печься' (Dulzon 1952: 175) ~ 'вариться; поспевать' (Dulzon 1966: 458) = Küä., Alt., Tel., Leb., Šr., Kač. *pyš-* '1. weich, mürbe werden, reif werden, reifen, gar werden, gar kochen; kochen, zubereiten; 3. mischen, umrühren, Butter schlagen' (Radloff IV 1321; cf. Clauson 376b-377a, ÈSTJa II 161ff.) and the only possible formation would be the future tense or future participle form in -*lyk* with the assumption of a partial consonant assimilation:[16] *pyšlyk > *pyštyk* and a sonorisation of final -*k* before a subsequent vowel,

---

[16] In fact, only entire consonant assimilation is recorded for MČ, cf. *ättiksiŋ* 'you will do' (Birjukovič 1981: 61), *allyk* 'he will take' (Birjukovič 1979: 24), cf. also Li Yong-Sŏng (2008: 79): „The *l* of -*lIK* is assimilated to the final consonants of the verb stems and thus forms geminate consonants. These geminate consonants become sometimes single consonants".

cf. LČ *pyššyk* 'поспеет, свариться' (Dulzon 1966: 458) with the entire assimilation *š-l* > *š-š*, typical to LČ. The semantics of the entire composition *aš pyštyg aj* would be 'month in which the food will come to ripening'. Another possibility is the nominal stem **pyš*, which has already been assumed for some other languages by Sevortjan (ÈSTJa II 162), and thus the denominal adjective in *-lyg* (cf. Pomorska 2004: 66ff.): *pyš-lyg* > *pyštyg* 'ripe'.

18. **'whitefish (inconnu) month'** (LČ):
LČ *ak pālyk aj* 'месяц белой рыбы (нельмы)' (Birjukovič 1984: 11) ~ *axvalgaj* 'id.' (ibid., Dulzon 1966: 463, Alekseev 1991: 85).

Cf. LČ *ak palyk* 'нельма' (Dulzon 1966: 463) = MČ *ak bālyk* 'нельма' (Birjukovič 1979: 138) ~ *ak pālyk* ~ *akvālyk* 'id.' (Pomorska 2004: 125), Alt. *ak palyk*, *Salmo Lavaretus* (Radloff I 91), Ott. *ak palyk* 'ein Seefisch' (ibid.).

19. **'(cedar) nut month'** (MČ):
MČ *kuzuk aj* 'месяц сбора орехов' (Dulzon 1952: 119, Dulzon 1966: 463) ~ 'месяц орехов (соотв. августу)' (Birjukovič 1984: 27) ~ *kuzug aj* 'id.' (ibid. 11) ~ *kusugaj* ~ *kuʒuxaj* (Cyrillic „кудзухай" (!), misprinted for „кузухай" = *kuʒuxaj*, M.P.) 'ореха месяц' (Alekseev 1991: 85) ~ *kuʒux* (!, misprinted for *kuzux*, M.P.) 'орех поспевает' (Alekseev 1991: 85).

Cf. MČ *kuzuk* 'орех' (Birjukovič 1979: 120), LČ *kuzuk* 'id.' (Dulzon 1952: 166) = Küä., Alt., Leb., Tel., Koib., Kač., Bar., Čag. *kuzuk* 'Cedernüsse' (Radloff II 1019), Šr. *kuzuk* 'Zirbelfichte' (ibid.), Tuba *kuzuk* 'орех' (Baskakov 1966: 131), Kum. *kusuk* 'орех' (Baskakov 1972: 228; cf. ÈSTJa VI 23f.).

20. **'month separating autumn'** (Küä.):
Küä. *küskŭ jarylyš aj* (Radloff I 7).

Cf. Küä. *küskŭ* 'autumn',[17] MČ *küskü* '(an) autumn' (Pomorska 2004: 55 with the examples from many other Turkic languages), LČ *küskü* 'id.' (ibid.), Tuv. *küskü* 'Herbst, dem Herbst eigen' (Ölmez 2007: 212; cf. Clauson 759b, ÈSTJa III 95).
    Cf. Küä. *jarylyš* 'separating'[18] < **jaryl-*,[19] pass. of *jar-* 'zerspalten, zerteilen, auseinanderbringen' (Radloff III 102) = LČ *jar-* 'расщепить' (Dulzon 1952: 152), MČ *čar-* 'рубить' (Birjukovič 1981: 31), Alt., Tel., Leb., etc. *jar-* 'zerspalten, zerteilen, auseinanderbringen' (Radloff III 102), Tr. *yar-* 'to split, rend, cleave, cut through' (Redhouse 1243; cf. ÈSTJa IV 135ff.), for Čul. deverbal derivatives in *-(y)š* see Pomorska (2004: 118ff.).

---

[17] For Küä. the word has been recorded in the names for the months only.

[18] For Küä. the word has been recorded in the names for the months only.

[19] = Tel., Alt. *jaryl-* 'sich trennen' (Radloff III 125), Kom., Kas., Ott., Kar.T *jaryl-* 'Sprünge bekommen, zerplatzen' (ibid.), cf. also MČ *čārьlgan* 'расколотый' (Birjukovič 1979: 105).

21. **'autumn month'** (Küä., MČ: Alekseev):

    21.1 Küä. *küskü aj* (Radloff I 7);

    21.2 MČ *kuskux* (!, M.P.) *aj* 'осенний месяц' (Alekseev 1991: 85).

For Küä. *küskü* ~ MČ *küskü* '(an) autumn' see No. 20 above.

22. **'horse race month'** (LČ, MČ: Birjukovič; Falk):

    22.1 LČ *jaryš aj* 'месяц светлой луны' (Dulzon 1966: 463, Birjukovič 1984: 11) ~ *jaryš* 'осенная светлая луна' (Alekseev 1991: 85) ~ 'месяц конских скачек' (ibid. 61);

    22.2 MČ *čāryš aj* 'месяц светлой луны' (Birjukovič 1984: 11) ~ *čārym* (!, mistakenly for *čāryš*?, M.P.) *aj* 'id.' (ibid. 27);

    22.3 *jariš ai* 'октябрь' (Falk).

Alekseev, in his book on p. 61 explains *jaryš aj* as a month of horse competitions which took place in autumn,[20] cf. MČ *čaryš* 'состязание в беге' (Birjukovič 1984: 72) = Küä., Alt., Tel., Ott. *jaryš* 'Wettrennen' (Radloff III 127), Tuv. *čaryš* 'Wettkampf' (Ölmez 2007: 110), Khak. *čarys* 'бег, состязание в беге; конские скачки' (KhakRS 313), Tr. *yarış* 'race, competition' (Redhouse 1244; cf. Clauson 972a, ÈSTJa IV 148f.).

However, Alekseev also translates LČ *yaryš*, as 'осенная светлая луна = bright / shining autumn moon', the same translation by Dulzon and Birjukovič (↑). The question is, whether this translation is simply incorrect, or it is anyhow justified by the meaning of the Chulym forms. In that case, LČ *jaryš* = MČ *čaryš* should mean 'shining moon'. The verb *jar-* ~ *čar-* is recorded for MČ, cf. MČ *čar-* 'сиять' (Birjukovič 1984: 71) ~ *čāry-* 'ib.' (Pomorska 2004: 109) = Küä. *jar-* in *taŋ jaryp tyr* 'der Morgen brach an', lit. 'dawn has broken' (Radloff 1868: 690), Šr., Sag. *čar-* 'leuchten' (Radloff III 1860), Alt., Tel., Leb., Tar., Kūr. *jar-* 'hell sein, leuchten, Licht ausstrahlen' (ibid. 103; cf. also ÈSTJa IV 134), but in the meaning of the *nomen obiecti* we would rather expect *jaryk* ~ *čaryk*, cf. MČ *jāryk* '1. светло; 2. яркий, ярко' (Pomorska 2004: 109) = Küä., Kom., Leb. *jaryk* '1. hell, leuchtend; 2. Licht, Glanz' (Radloff III 1863; cf. also ÈSTJa IV 135), and not *jaryš ~ *čaryš (for Čul. deverbal nomina in -(y)š see Pomorska 2004: 118), especially that, as far as we know, such a word is not recorded in any other Turkic languages.

Radloff records Šr. *čaryš aj* 'Oktober' (Radloff III 1865) and refers to *jaryš* 'race, competition', cf. also Khak. *čarys ajy* 'уст. месяц бегов и скачек (*октябрь*)' (KhakRS 313), Sag. *čarys aj* (Radloff I 7).

---

[20] „К числу обычаев, связанных происхождением с кочевническим коневодским бытом, следует отнести и обычай устройства скачек на лошадях во время свадьбы, и конные состязания на общедеревенских праздниках осенью. Один из месяцев старинного календаря нижнечулымских тюрков носил название ярыш ай – месяц конских скачек."

23. **'naked leaves month = no leaves month'** (LČ, MČ):

   23.1 LČ *jalac kak aj* 'месяц безлистных (деревьев)' (Dul̇zon 1952: 119, Dul̇zon 1966: 463, Birjukovič 1984: 12, Alekseev 1991: 85);

   23.2 MČ *čalač kak aj* 'гололистный месяц' (Dul̇zon 1952: 119, Dul̇zon 1966: 463) ~ 'безлистный месяц (соотв. примерно октябрю)' (Birjukovič 1984: 27) ~ 'лес голый осенью, листья падают; месяц когда листьев нет и когда все чисто; голый лес' (Alekseev 1991: 85).

   Cf. LČ *jalac* ~ MČ *čalač* [21] ~ MČ *čalāč* 'naked' (Pomorska 2004: 40) = Küä. *jalāc* 'id.' (Radloff 1868: 694).

   Cf. LČ *kak* 'листва' (Birjukovič 1980: 99), MČ *kak* 'лист' (Birjukovič 1984: 37) = Küä., Alt., Tel. *kāk* 'Blatt (eines Baumes)' (Radloff II 57), Tat.dial. *kabak* ~ *kavak* 'leaf' (ÈSTJa V 161), Bar., Kūr. *kavak* 'Blatt (des Baumes)' (Radloff II 50; cf. ÈSTJa V 161, VEWT 215b).

24. **'red leaves month'** (LČ, MČ: Alekseev):

   24.1 LČ *kyzyr* (!, M.P.)[22] *gak aj* 'месяц красных листьев' (Dul̇zon 1966: 463, Alekseev 1991: 85) ~ *kyzyrgak aj* 'id.' (Birjukovič 1984: 12).

   Cf. LČ *kyzyl* 'красный' (Dul̇zon 1952: 166), MČ *kyzyl* 'id.' (Birjukovič 1979a: 53), Küä. *kyzyl* 'rot' (Radloff 1868: 698) = Tu. *kyzyl* 'id.' (Clauson 683b, ÈSTJa VI 194f.).

   24.2 MČ *kyzyl byr* 'красные листья' (Alekseev 1991: 85).

   Cf. MČ *pür* 'листва' (Birjukovič 1979: 16) = Alt., Sag. *pür* 'Baumblatt' (Radloff IV 1397), Tel. *pür* '1. id., 2. Knospe' (ibid.), Krm., Kom. *bür* 'Blatt, Blattknospe' (ibid. 1886), Khak. *pür* 'лист' (KhakRS 168), Tuv. *bürü* 'Blatt' (Ölmez 2007: 103; cf. Clauson 354a).

25. **'month separating winter'** (Küä.):
   Küä. *kyš jarylyš aj* (Radloff I 7).

   Cf. Küä. *kyš* 'Winter' (Radloff II 834), LČ *kyš* 'id.' (Dul̇zon 1952: 153), MČ *kyš* ~ *kys* 'id.' (Dul̇zon 1973: 23) = Tu. *kyš* 'id.' (ÈSTJa VI 253f., Clauson 670a).
   For Küä. *jarylyš* 'separating' see No. 20 above.

26. **'half-winter half-summer'** (MČ):
   MČ *čarym kyš čarym čaj* 'ползимы-полета' (Dul̇zon 1952: 119, Dul̇zon 1966: 463) ~ 'половина зимы, половина лета (соотв. примерно октябрю-ноябрю)'

---

[21] Such forms are recorded in the month names only.
[22] *r* looks strange in this context.

(Birjukovič 1984: 27), MČ *čaža aj*[23] 'половина зимой, половина летом; половина тепла, половина холода' (Alekseev 1991: 85).

Cf. MČ *čarym* ~ *čārym* 'половина' (Birjukovič 1984: 72), LČ *jārъm* 'id.' (Dulzon 1966: 462) ~ *jarym* 'id.' in *jarym gün* 'юг (полдня, полдень)' (ibid. 464) = Küä., Alt., Leb., Kas., Tel., Kom., Kar.L, Kar.T *jarym* 'Hälfte, halb' (Radloff III 128), Šr. *čarym* 'id.' (ibid. 1865), Ott. *jarym* '1. id.; nicht vollständig, unvollständig, unbeendet' (ibid. 128), Tr. *yarım* 'half' (Redhouse 1244), Tuv. *čarym* 'halb; Hälfte' (Ölmez 2007: 110; cf. Clauson 968a-969b, ÈSTJa IV 147).

For MČ *kyš* 'winter' see 25 above.

Cf. MČ *čaj* 'лето' (Dulzon 1952: 130), LČ *jaj* 'id.' (ibid.), Küä., Alt., Tel., Leb., etc. *jaj* 'Sommer' (Radloff III 4), Šr., Sag., Koib. *čaj* 'id.' (ibid. 1825), Tuv. *čaj* 'id.' (Ölmez 2007: 112; cf. Clauson 980a-b, ÈSTJa IV 74).

Special cases

27. MČ *čazyg aj* 'месяц листопада' (Dulzon 1952: 119, Dulzon 1966: 463) ~ 'id. (соотв. сентябрю)' (Birjukovič 1984: 27) ~ *čizyg aj* 'край лета' (Alekseev 1991: 85).

This name for a month is recorded for MČ only, and it seems to have no counterpart in the other Turkic languages. Our sources record no Čul. *čazyg* ~ *čizyg* or *čazyk* ~ *čizyk* in the meaning of 'fallen leaves' ~ 'no leaves', etc., cf. No. 24 above. Assuming *čazyg* ~ *čazyk* as more reliable forms, their first syllable coincides with Turkic *jaz* '1. spring; 2. sommer' = MČ *čas* 'весна' (Birjukovič 1984: 72), LČ *jas* 'id.' (Dulzon 1952: 132), Küä. *jas* 'id.' (Radloff 1868: 701; cf. also ÈSTJa IV 71). If this were so, we would have suggested the derivational suffix *-yg* ~ *-yk* for this. Although Chulym uses the *-(a)k* ~ *-(y)k* deminutive suffix (cf. Pomorska 2004: 59ff.) such a derivative would have no counterpart in any older or newer Turkic languages. Another question is that Čul. *jas* ~ *čas* means 'spring' and not 'summer', and this does not coincide with the place of *čazyg aj* in the lists of Chulym months (i.e. the 9th month in Dulzon's and Birjukovič's lists and the 8th month in Alekseev's list) and commentaries like 'соотв[етствует] сентябрю = a counterpart of September' or 'край лета = the end of summer'.

With the presumption of correctness of Alekseev's *čizyg aj*, we would explain this as a form related to *izig* 'hot', cf. No. 15a above. If this is correct, we should assume the rise of prosthetic *j* in MČ *izig* > *jizig* > *čizig*,[24] cf. also No. 15 above.

If this is the solution for MČ *čazyg*, there still remains the problem of its semantics, i.e. 'hot month' as a counterpart of Semptember and not June–July.

---

[23] This form, if its notation is correct, may be explained as a result of the shortening of **čarym čaj aj*.

[24] For the rise of prosthetic *j* in Turkic languages see Tekin (1994, and 1995: 138ff.).

28. *karakal ai*, по большей части наш сентябрь (Falk).

This name for a month has not been recorded by other authors, and – as far as we know – it has no counterpart in the other Turkic languages. Its notation seems to be anyhow erroneous, since Turkic languages do not have a noun like **karakal*. It is very close to LČ *karagaj* 'сосна' (Dulzon 1952: 166) = Tel., Leb., Šr., etc. *karayaj* 'Tanne' (Radloff II 151; cf. ÈSTJa V 292f.), cf. also MČ *kara kāzy* 'сосна' (Birjukovič 1978: 115) or *karagan*, cf. Tel., Šr. *karayan* '1. robina caragana; 2. Akazienstrauch' (Radloff II 151; cf. ÈSTJa V 293f.).

Such an assumption raises questions, one of them being the fact that no Chulym name for months refers to a name for a tree, especially to an evergreen, fruitless tree like a pine. Thus, 'rowan tree month' or 'acacia tree month' sound more probable but our sources record LČ *kargan* 'смородина = currant' (Dulzon 1952: 160) only.

Conclusions

An analysis of the origin of Chulym month names first of all leads to the conclusion that their year was devided into three main parts: the cold part of the year ('big cold month', 'small cold month'), the hot part of the year ('small hot month', 'big hot month', 'hot month') and something between cold and hot, i.e. autumn part ('month separating autumn', 'autumn month', 'month separating winter', 'half-winter half-summer'). They are closely related to the activities of their users and their main occupations, i.e. fishing ('lean fish month', '(small) fish trap month', 'big fish trap month', 'hot spawn month', 'white fish (inconnu) month'), hunting ('hare month', 'fox month') and collecting forest fruits ['(ceder) nut month', cf. also the names referring to the forest itself like 'naked leaves month', 'red leaves month']. Only two month names refer to the other way of obtaining food, namely land cultivation ('harvest month', 'full-grown, ripe bread month'), both of the names are mentioned by Dulzon and Birjukovič but do not figure in their lists of the month names.

It is worth noting that the number of month names derived from the names of birds is proportionally high ('eagle month', 'crow month', 'cockoo month').

One month name indicates the importance of the horse races among Lower- and Middle-Chulym Turkic peoples.

		Küärik (Radloff)	Lower Chulym	Middle Chulym	Falk
1.	'big cold (month)' ~ 'big month'	+	+	+	–
2.	'small cold (month)' ~ 'small (short) month'	+	+	+	–
3.	'hare month'	–	–	+ (Li Yong-Sŏng)	–

		Küärik (Radloff)	Lower Chulym	Middle Chulym	Falk
4.	'ridge of a year (month)'	–	+	+	+
5.	'small ridge of a year (month)'	+	+	–	–
6.	'fox month'	–	+ (Birjukovič)	+	+
7.	'eagle month'	+	+	+	+
8.	'crow month'	+	+	+	+
9.	'cuckoo month'	+	+	+	+
10.	'small hot month'	+	+ (Dulzon 1952)	–	+
11.	'lean fish month'	–	–	+	–
12.	'riverbank fish trap month'	–	+	–	–
13.	'big hot month'	+	–	–	+
14.	'big fish trap month'	–	+	–	–
15.	'(hot) spawn month'	–	–	+	+ (?)
15.a	'hot month'	–	–	+ (Birjukovič, Alekseev)	–
16.	'harvest month'	+	–	–	–
17.	'full-grown, ripe bread month'	–	–	+ (Dulzon 1952, Birjukovič 1979)	–
18.	'white fish (inconnu) month'	–	+	–	–
19.	'(cedar) nut month'	–	–	+	–
20.	'month separating autumn'	+	–	–	–
21.	'autumn month'	+	–	+ (Alekseev)	–
22.	'horse race month = no leaves month'	–	+	+ (Birjukovič)	+

	Küärik (Radloff)	Lower Chulym	Middle Chulym	Falk
23. 'naked leaves month'	–	+	+	–
24. 'red leaves month'	–	+	+ (Alekseev)	–
25. 'month separating winter'	+	–	–	–
26. 'half-winter half-summer'	–	–	+	–

Abbreviations

Alt. = Altay (= Oyrot), **Bar.** = Baraba, **Čag.** = Chagatay, **Kač.** = Kacha, **Kar.** = Karaim (L = Łuck, T = Troki), **Kas.** = Kasan, **Khak.** = Khakas, **Kirg.** = Kirghiz, **Koib.** = Koybal, **Kom.** = Koman, **Krm.** = Crimean, **Küä.** = Küärik, **Kum.** = Kumandin, **Kūr.** = Kūrdak, **Kzk.** = Kazakh; **LČ** = Lower Chulym, **Leb.** = Lebed, **MČ** = Middle Chulym, **Ott.** = Ottoman Turkish, **Sag.** = Sagay, **Šr.** = Shor, **Tar.** = Taranchi, **Tel.** = Teleut, **Tr.** = Turkish, **Tu.** = Turkic, **Tub.** = Tuba, **Tuv.** = Tuvinian, **Uig.** = Uyghur.

References

Clauson = Clauson G. 1972. *An etymological dictionary of pre-thirteenth-century Turkish.* Oxford.
ÈSTJa I = Sevortjan È.V. 1974. *Ètimologičeskij slovaŕ tjurkskich jazykov.* [vol. I: glasnye]. Moskva.
ÈSTJa II = Sevortjan È.V. 1978. *Ètimologičeskij slovaŕ tjurkskich jazykov.* [vol. II: b]. Moskva.
ÈSTJa III = Sevortjan È.V. 1980. *Ètimilogičeskij slovaŕ tjurkskich jazykov.* [vol. III: v, g, d]. Moskva.
ÈSTJa IV = Sevortjan È.V., Levitskaja L.S. 1989. *Ètimilogičeskij slovaŕ tjurkskich jazykov.* [vol. IV: dž, ž, j]. Moskva.
ÈSTJa V = [Sevortjan È.V.], Levitskaja L.S., Dybo A.V., Rassadin V.I. 1997. *Ètimologičeskij slovaŕ tjurkskich jazykov.* [vol. V: k, k̦]. Moskva.
ÈSTJa VI = [Sevortjan È.V.], Blagova G.F., Levitskaja L.S., Dybo A.V., Rassadin V.I. 2000. *Ètimologičeskij slovaŕ tjurkskich jazykov.* [vol. VI: k (misprinted for: k̦)]. Moskva.
KhakRS = Baskakov N.A., Inkižekova-Grekul A.I. 1953. *Chakassko-russkij slovaŕ.* Moskva.
Radloff I = Radloff W. 1893. *Versuch eines Wörterbuches der Türk-Dialecte.* [vol. I]. Sanktpeterburg.
Radloff II = Radloff W. 1899. *Versuch eines Wörterbuches der Türk-Dialecte.* [vol. II]. Sanktpeterburg.
Radloff III = Radloff W. 1905. *Versuch eines Wörterbuches der Türk-Dialecte.* [vol. III]. Sanktpeterburg.

Radloff IV = Radloff W. 1911. *Versuch eines Wörterbuches der Türk-Dialecte.* [vol. IV]. Sanktpeterburg.

Redhouse = *New Redhouse Turkish-English dictionary.* 1992[(12)]. İstanbul.

ŞorTS = Kurpeşko-Tannageşeva N.N., Akalın Ş.H. 1995. *Şor sözlüğü.* Adana.

TatRS = *Tatarsko-russkij slovaŕ.* 1966. Moskva.

TuvRS = Tenišev È.R. (ed.) 1968. *Tuvinsko-russkij slovaŕ.* Moskva.

VEWT = Räsänen M. 1969. *Versuch eines etymologisches Wörterbuchs der Türksprachen.* Helsinki.

Alekseev V.P. (ed.) 1991. *Tjurki tajeźnegoPričulyḿja. Populjacija i ètnos.* Tomsk.

Anikin A.M. 1997. *Ètimologičeskij slovaŕ russkich dialektov Sibiri. Zaimstvovanija iz uralskich, altajskich i paleoaziatskich jazykov.* Novosibirsk.

Baskakov N.A. 1966. *Severnye dialekty altajskogo (ojrotskogo) jazyka. Dialekt černevych tatar (tuba kiži). Grammatičeskij očerk i slovaŕ.* Moskva.

Baskakov N.A. 1972. *Severnye dialekty altajskogo (ojrotskogo) jazyka. Dialekt kumandincev (kumandy-kiži). Grammatičeskij očerk, teksty, perevody i slovaŕ.* Moskva.

Birjukovič R.M. 1978. K vorposu semantiki čisla v čulymsko-tjurkskom jazyke. – *Jazyki narodov Sibiri. Sbornik statej.* Kemerovo: 115–118.

Birjukovič R.M. 1979. *Zvukovoj stroj čulymsko-tjurkskogo jazyka (metodičeskoe posobie).* Moskva.

Birjukovič R.M. 1979a. *Morfologija čulymsko-tjurkskogo jazyka.* [vol. I: *Kategorija imeni suščestvitelnogo. Učebno-metodičeskie materialy*]. Moskva.

Birjukovič R.M. 1980. K semantičeskomu obosnovaniju kategorii prinadležnosti v tjurkskich jazykach (na materiale čulymsko-tjurkskogo jazyka). – *Voprosy Jazykoznanija* 1980.3: 95–106.

Birjukovič R.M. 1981. *Morfologija čulymsko-tjurkskogo jazyka.* [vol. II]. Saratov.

Birjukovič R.M. 1984. *Leksika čulymsko-tjurkskogo jazyka. Posobie k speckursu.* Saratov.

Dulzon A.P. 1952. Čulymskie tatary i ich jazyk. – *Učenye Zapiski Tomskogo Gosudarstvennogo Pedagogičeskogo Instituta* IX. Tomsk: 76–210.

Dulzon A.P. 1966. Čulymsko-tjurkskij jazyk. – Baskakov N.A. (ed.) *Jazyki Narodov SSSR.* [vol. II]. Moskva: 446–466.

Dulzon A.P. 1973. Dialekty i govory tjurkov Čulyma. – *Sovetskaja Tjurkologija* 1973.2: 16–29.

Erdal M. 1991. *Old Turkic word formation. A functional approach to the lexicon.* [vol. I]. Wiesbaden.

Li Yong-Sŏng 1997. On the origin of *baqa* 'frog, toad, tortoise'. – *Central Asiatic Journal* 41.2: 250–269.

Li Yong-Sŏng et al. (eds.) 2008. *A study of the Middle Chulym dialect of the Chulym language.* Seoul.

Ölmez M. 2007. *Tuwinischer Wortschatz mit alttürkischen und mongolischen Parallelen. Tuvacanın Sözvarlığı. Eski Türkçe ve Moğolca denkleriyle.* Wiesbaden.

Pomorska M. 2000. Consonant alternation in Čulym (1). – *Folia Orientalia* XXXVI: 247–257.

Pomorska M. 2004. *Middle Chulym noun formation.* Kraków.

Pritsak O. 1959. Das Abakan- und Čulymtürkische und das Schorische. – *Philologiae Turcicae Fundamenta.* [vol. I]. Wiesbaden: 598–640.

Radloff W. 1868. *Proben der Volksliteratur der türksichen Stämme Süd-Sibiriens.* [vol. II]. S. Peterburg: 689–705.

Rassadin V.I. 1980. *Mongolo-burjatskie zaimstvovanija v sibirskivh tjurkskich jazykach.* Moskva.

Ščerbak A.M. 1961. Nazvanija domašnich i dikich životnych v tjurkskich jazykach. – *Istoričeskoe razvitie leksiki tjurkskich jazykov.* Moskva: 82–172.
Tekin T. 1994. Türk dillerinde önseste *y*- türemesi. – *Türk Dilleri Araştırmaları* 4: 51–66.
Tekin T. 1995. *Türk dillerinde birincil uzun ünlüler.* Ankara.

Studia Linguistica Universitatis Iagellonicae Cracoviensis
128 (2011)

MAGNÚS SNÆDAL
University of Iceland, Reykjavik

GOTHIC ⟨GGW⟩*

Keywords: historical linguistics, Gothic ponology and phonetics, Holtzmann's Law, 'Verschärfung', *ggw*

Abstract

The paper deals with the orthographic cluster ⟨ggw⟩ in Gothic and the question if it denoted both /ngw/ and /ggw/ or only the former. The paper concludes that internal evidence only points to /ngw/ and that external evidence cannot be used to support double pronunciation of the cluster.

1. Introduction

In Gothic a sound change occurred that is generally called 'Verschärfung' but is sometimes also referred to as 'Holtzmann's Law'. Some scholars believe that this change also occurred in other East-Germanic languages (e.g. Braune 1884:546–547, Streitberg 1943:61), but only Gothic provides reliable examples. A similar change occurred (later?) in Old Norse.

The sound change in question meant that a geminate (or long) semivowel changed into a stop and a semivowel: *-jj-* > Go. *-ddj-*, *-waddjus* 'wall' (OI *-ggj-*, *veggr*, gen. *veggjar*) and *-ww-* > Go. *-ggw-*, *triggws* 'faithful' (OI *-ggv-*, *tryggr*, acc. *tryggvan*). Gothic shows some exceptions to these changes, i.e. they are not found everywhere they might be expected, e.g. Go. *þrije* (gen. of *þreis** 'three') vs. OI *þriggja* (cf. Krause 1968:110). These exceptions are, actually, irrelevant in the present context, as the nature of the 'Verschärfung' is not the issue here. The present paper will concentrate on what is behind (transliterated) orthographic ⟨ggw⟩ although ⟨ddj⟩ will also be treated briefly.

---

* An earlier, Icelandic, version of this paper was presented at the 23rd Rask Conference in Reykjavík, 31 January, 2009.

2. Orthography

It is well known that Gothic orthography followed a Greek model in writing a velar nasal preceding a velar stop with a ‹g›, i.e. the sound combinations [ŋg, ŋk, ŋkʷ] are written ‹gg, gk, gq›. Often a double ‹gg› is used before ‹k› and ‹q›, and ‹ggg› occurs once in Mt 9:15, *atgagggand* '(they) come to', and once in the deed from Arezzo, *killigggans* (for *skilliggans* (acc. pl.) 'solidi'). The nasal quality of the first ‹g› in these clusters is confirmed by scribal errors when it is replaced by an ‹n›. There are five examples in the Codex Argenteus, more precisely in the latter part of Luke. These variants are shown in (1) in comparison with the regular forms:

(1)   **regular forms** : **variant forms**
   briggiþ, briggandans : *bringiþ* (Lk 15:22), *bringandans* (Lk 15:23)
         þagkeiþ : *þankeiþ* (Lk 14:31), *þank* (Lk 17:9)
          igqis : *inqis* (Lk 19:31)

The form *unkjane* (gen. pl. of *unkja** < Lat. *uncia*) in the deed from Arezzo should also be mentioned although it may be considered unreliable as the original no longer exists. Nevertheless, it is interesting in comparison with the form ‹s›*killigggans* found in the same document as mentioned above. Neither should the form *skilligngans* in the last subscription of the deed from Naples be forgotten.

The Gothic praxis in writing the velar nasal deviates from the Greek model in that a final nasal of a prefix is never assimilated to the first consonant of the base. We have *in-g-* (11×), *inn-g-* (27×), *un-g-* (83×). Then, an infixed *þan* 'but, then' does not assimilate to a following velar, *atuhþangaf* 'but then (he) gave' (1×), *atuþþangaggand* 'but then (they) come to' (1×), *biþþangitanda* 'but (we) are also found' (1×), nor does the final ‹n› of the first parts of the following compounds, *þiudangardi* 'kingdom' (69×) and *midjungards** 'inhabited earth' (4×). Here there are 197 occurrences of orthographic ‹ng›, in addition to the two mentioned in (1) above, so this graphic combination is far from unknown. In addition to the occurrences mentioned in (1) we find a further 17 occurrences of ‹nk›, *in-k-* (4×), *un-k-* (13×), and three occurrences of ‹nq›, in *un-q-*. Therefore, in total there are 217+6 examples of an ‹n› written in front of a ‹g›, ‹k›, or ‹q›. This practice in writing the prefixes perhaps influenced the scribe of Luke when he wrote ‹bringiþ›, etc.

2.1 Holtzmann and Scherer

The orthographic cluster ‹ggw› is not confined to words showing Holtzmann's Law, however. It is also found in words such as *aggwus** 'narrow' and *siggwan* 'read, sing'. There is no reason to doubt that in these cases the ‹gg› also denoted [ŋg] so here the cluster stood for [ŋgw] although there is no occurrence of graphic ‹ngw› to confirm it. The question is whether ‹gg› also denoted [ŋg] in the words affected by Holtzmann's Law, i.e. did the Goths write ‹triggws› but pronounce it [triŋgws]? In the oldest Gothic grammars and until ca 1870 it was not doubted that they did.

Holtzmann (1835:862–863) himself was convinced that ‹gg› in the cluster ‹ggw› always stood for a nasal as he was of the opinion that the change later named after him had also occurred in *siggwan* which he compared to OHG *siuwan* 'sew'. Therefore, apparently, he thought that ‹ggw› was always produced by the law. Actually, he also thought that the ‹dd› in ‹ddj› was completely parallel; it represented a palatal or a retroflex nasal ([ɲ] or [ɳ]). Holtzmann was led to this conclusion about ‹ddj› to preserve the consistency between the two changes even though there is nothing in particular pointing to a nasal in that cluster nor that ‹dd› could be used to represent a nasal. Apparently, Holtzmann thought that no stops were in these clusters as he writes:

> Das doppelte *gg* in *ggv* bezeichnet ohne Zweifel einen Nasal, und zwar den gutturalen; auch *dd* in *dd[j]* wird daher einen Nasal ausdrücken sollen, für den Ulfila eine Bezeichnungsart erfinden mufste …

Although the authors of Gothic grammars (after 1835) did not necessarily accept Holtzmann's conclusions about ‹ddj›, they did accept that it represented a new sound combination (presumably [d:j] as it was graphically distinct from both ‹ndj› and ‹dj›) but, on the other hand, that the new ‹ggw› denoted the same sounds as the old one, i.e. [ŋgw]. For example, von der Gabelentz and Löbe (1846:43, 52) do not mention any problem in connection with these clusters and – as their grammar is synchronic rather than historical – they do not mention Holtzmann's Law at all.

Subsequently Scherer (1868:854–855) rediscovered Holtzmann's Law: he appears to be unaware of Holtzmann's paper; at least, he does not mention it at all. Scherer is also the first to insist that Gothic orthographic ‹ggw› had a double pronunciation according to origin, i.e. presumably, an old [ŋgw] and a new [g:w] although he is not particularly specific about the pronunciation. His evidence appears to be that there is no explanation of the nasal in the new combination, or, in Scherer's (1868:855) words: 'Für die Nasalierung, die nach der gangbaren Meinung in den genannten Wörtern eingetreten wäre, wüsste ich absolut keine Erklärung.'

Nevertheless, the explanation of the alleged nasal in *triggws*, etc. could be that the outcome of the change was influenced by a sound combination that already existed in the language, i.e. [ŋgw]. If we look briefly at Old Icelandic, it is of course not certain, despite the spelling, that the stop that resulted from the change in *tryggr*, etc. was necessarily long from the beginning. It is noteworthy that in Old Icelandic there was already a *-gg-* of a different origin but no short *-g-* as a stop (only as a fricative). Therefore, it is not impossible that the result involves an accommodation to what already existed.

3. ‹ddj›

Although not certain, it is generally assumed that in Gothic the phoneme /d/ had two variants: initially and medially after a consonant it was a stop, [d], but medially after a vowel it was a fricative, [ð] (cf. Braune/Heidermanns 2004:75). Then it is assumed that the ‹dd› in ‹ddj› denoted a stop but not necessarily a long one (cf. Braune 1884:546, fn. 3). The difference between *bidja* '(I) pray/ask' and *iddja* '(I) went' then was [bɪðja] vs. [ɪd(ː)ja]. Braune (1884:546) suggested that Gothic *ddj* had developed from original *ggj* (as in Old Norse), i.e. presumably, [jj] > [dʒ] > [dj].

There is no question that the orthographic cluster ‹ggj› had a single value in Gothic. It occurs nine times in the corpus and is confined to two closely related words: *fauragaggi* 'stewardship' and *fauragaggja* 'steward'. Two scribal errors, *fauragagjan* (Lk 16:1) and *fauragagjins* (Lk 8:3), would increase the occurrences to eleven if corrected. Durante (1974:42) assumed that this cluster denoted [ŋgj]. On the other hand ‹ddj› denoted [jj]. It should be noted that the pronunciation [dʒ] is excluded for ‹ddj›. That is shown by the loans *laiktsjo* (beside *laiktio* < Lat. *lectio*) and *kawtsjo** (< Lat. *cautio*). If ‹tsj› here denoted [tsj] or [tʃ] it becomes less likely that ‹ddj› denoted [dzj] or [dʒ], or any other kind of sibilant sound, as then graphic ‹dzj› (or perhaps ‹dsj›) would have been expected. The question remains why it was not possible to use ‹ggj› in both cases as it is likely that the nasal cluster was somewhat palatalised, i.e. [ŋ̩gj] or [ɲjj]. Apparently, a double value of ‹ggj› would not have done more harm than the alleged double value of ‹ggw›.

In the inherited vocabulary of Gothic there was no long or geminated /d/. Holtzmann's Law created a new sound or sound combination denoted in script by ‹ddj›. Only four bases showing this change are attested in the extant Gothic corpus. Of course it is likely that some more forms existed. Thus, Crimean Gothic *ada* 'egg' is sometimes cited as corresponding to Biblical Gothic **addi* (cf. Braune 1884:545, Stearns 1978:127). If this tells us anything it is that ‹ddj› denoted some kind of a /d/. Therefore, ‹ddj› probably denoted [d(ː)j] – although a long fricative, [ð:j], cannot be excluded – and the new sound was tolerated in the language, perhaps because it was somewhat similar to the initial sounds in *diups** 'deep' and *dius** 'animal'. Marchand (1973:89–90) ascribes this to the relative frequency of *iddj-* occurring more than 130 times in the Gothic corpus (mostly in the Gospels). The statistic is shown in (2):

(2) 1   *daddjandeim* (from *daddjan** 'suckle')
   132   *iddj-* (in the pret. of *gaggan* 'go')
    5   *twaddje* (gen. of *twai* 'two')
    11   *-waddj-* (in various forms of *-waddjus* 'wall')

These amount to 149 occurrences and if two scribal errors are added, *atiddedun* (Mk 16:2) and *twadje* (1TimA 5:19), there are 151 occurrences of ‹ddj› in the Gothic corpus. In comparison there are 129 occurrences of ‹ndj›. If the parallel occurrences in the Pauline Epistles are counted once there are 144 ‹ddj› and 101 ‹ndj›. In the Gospels there are 121 occurrences of *iddj-* but only 12 (or seven) in the Epistles.

4. ‹ggw›

It is assumed that in Gothic the phoneme /g/ had similar allophones to /d/, i.e. that it was a stop, [g], initially and medially after a consonant but a fricative, [ɣ], after a vowel (cf. Braune/Heidermanns 2004:71). Therefore, if Holtzmann's Law produced a stop, [gːw], it found no support in Gothic phonology. There is no ⟨gw⟩ initially, and medially it is only found in *bidagwa* 'beggar' (John 9:8). If the form is genuine the pronunciation was presumably [ɣw]. Possibly, it is a scribal error for **bidaga* or **bidaqa* (cf. Lehmann 1986:67, B46). The outcome of the change was, nevertheless, similar enough to one existing cluster, i.e. [ŋgw], and the two coalesced. In fact, this is a kind of analogy (cf. Marchand 1973:89–90), and it is important that within Gothic there is no evidence for a double pronunciation of ⟨ggw⟩. Therefore the pronunciation was formerly assumed to be always the same.

Nevertheless, Scherer's conclusion mentioned above was generally accepted and handbooks postulate double pronunciation (cf. Krause 1968:111). It is grounded primarily in the double origin of ⟨ggw⟩ but some external support is also claimed to exist such as the personal name *Triggua*, *Trigguilla* (believed to be derived from the adj. *triggws*) and the Italian noun *tregua* 'truce' (believed to be a loan from Gothic, i.e. *triggwa* 'covenant'). These will be dealt with in the following subsections. Presumably, this position was held until Marchand (1959:441–442, 1973:60, 77) expressed doubts and stressed that internal evidence pointed to a single pronunciation. This was during the fifties of the last century and it is likely that these doubts entered the handbooks when Ebbinghaus's first revision of Braune's *Gotische Grammatik* was published in 1961 (the sixteenth edition). The traditional view has been restored in the latest (twentieth) edition (Braune/Heidermanns 2004:73).

Marchand (1959:442) mentions three points in support of the opinion that ⟨ggw⟩ was always [ŋgw]. First, the verb *bliggwan** has moved from class II to class III (the class of *siggwan*) as shown by the pret. sg. *blaggw* (instead of the expected **blau*). Second, if there was a difference between /ngw/ and /ggw/ it was easily shown in the orthography with ⟨ngw⟩ and ⟨ggw⟩ respectively. As Wulfila knew Latin he could have followed a Latin model here. Third, the change of geminates to nasal and consonant is widespread enough to be accepted in this case also (here Marchand refers to Schwyzer 1934).

Bennett (1964:22) ignores Marchand's second point but takes up his first and third points. Then he adds that

> … the original /ggw/ was confined to very few words, whereas /ngw/ was many times more frequent and so constituted a well ingrained habit of articulation that would provide the pattern for such a dissimilation.

The statistic for the clusters /ggw/ vs. /ngw/, shown in (3), does not support Bennett's last claim:

(3a) Number of occurrences of /ggw/

14	*bliggw-* 'beat' (incl. *blaggw*, *bluggw-*)
3	*glaggw-* 'accurately'
1	*skuggw-* 'mirror'
44	*triggw-* 'faithful'
62	

(3b) Number of occurrences of /ngw/
   13   *aggw-* 'narrow'
    2   *riggw-* 'tamed' (1TimB 3:3, Cod. A has *rigw-*)
  20   *siggw-* 'recite' (incl. *saggw-*, *suggw-*)
   <u> 1</u>   *swaggw-* 'swey'
  36

Here we have 62 instances of /ggw/ but 36 of /ngw/. If parallel occurrences in the Ambrosian Codices A and B are counted each as one the result is 52 instances of /ggw/ and 29 of /ngw/. Therefore, /ggw/ is almost twice as frequent as /ngw/ but of course the remaining /ng/ could have strengthened the case against /ggw/.

Bennett's points have all been rejected by Voyles (1968:720–721). He concludes that until we have evidence to the contrary, it seems more likely that ‹ggw› represented both /ggw/ and /ngw/. He does not explain why they were not kept distinct in the orthography, but, generally speaking, when our sources use a grapheme or a grapheme cluster consistently for a sound or sound combination that can be shown to be of more than one historical origin, we conclude that coalescence has occurred. We would demand proof for the opposite.

4.1 The case for It. *tregua*

Brosman (1971) tried to provide new evidence for the double pronunciation of ‹ggw›. He asserted that Italian *tregua* 'truce; delay' was really a loan from Gothic *triggwa* 'διαθήκη, covenant'. It is of course not impossible that a word meaning 'covenant, agreement' can change its meaning to 'truce' but there is no particular evidence for such a change of meaning in Go. *triggwa*. Actually, Brosman (1971:171) accepts that it is possible to explain It. *tregua* in a different way – that it is a loan from Franconian or some other Old High German dialect – but he concludes that it is expedient to consider it to be a loan word from Gothic. A simpler explanation, however, emerged.

Pfister (1985:367, 1986:52) points to Lomb. **trewwa-*, in Latinised form *treuua*, that occurs in the Lombard laws with the meaning 'giuramento di non riprendere le ostilità prima del giudizio definitivo del giudice' ('oath not to resume the hostilities before the definitive judgment of the judge'). The meaning development 'time limit, delay' in the It. *tregua* is easily compatible with this. Pfister considers such variant forms as It. *triegua*/*triega* to show an open *ę*, which excludes the Ostrogothic origin of this word. The form *tregua* was in Italy a natural Romanisation of Lat. *treuua* that was a loan from Lomb. **trewwa*. In this case both form and content match, so it cannot be used to support double pronunciation of the Gothic combination ‹ggw›. (That was of course not Pfister's aim; he only wanted to find the origin of It. *tregua*.)

Both Brosman (1971:170) and Pfister (1985:365) consider Spanish *tregua* and similar forms in Provencal (*trega*, *tregua*) and Portuguese (*tregoa*) to be of Visigothic origin, but it is hardly likely that the word is taken as a loan many times from different dialects or languages into different dialects or languages and always has the same meaning. It is more likely that the word was mediated through Latin. The main variants found in Latin are the following, according to Niermeyer (1976:1041, **trewa**): *treua, treoa, triua, tria, traua, tregua, tregia, trega, treva, trevia, treba, trebua.* Apparently, these forms are best explained as originating in a West-Germanic dialect (not affected by Holtzmann's Law) and that the -*g*- is a part of the Romanisation; cf. Meyer-Lübke (1911:678 [nr. 8927 **triuwa**]): "Es ist möglich, daß alle romanischen Formen auf got. *triggwo* [sic] zurückgehen, aber ebensowohl kann das romanische -*g*- aus germ. -*w*- entstanden sein".

The chronology should also be borne in mind as the forms in question are first attested in the eleventh century or later (cf. Pfister 1985:367, 1986:52) and even though they were all originally taken from some kind of Gothic it would be risky to draw from them conclusions about the pronunciation of Biblical Gothic.

4.2 The case for the PN *Triggwa*

Wrede (1891:79) was presumably the first to point to the name *Trigguila, Triggua, Trivvila, Trivva* and its possible connection with the Gothic adj. *triggws* and the ON name *Tryggvi*. The Gothic name is found in six texts and apparently it always refers to the same person (cf. Amory 1997:423–424, Francovich Onesti 2007:99–101) and there is no particular reason to doubt that this person was an Ostrogoth. In (4) the main forms of the name occurring in the data are listed (cf. Reichert 1987:722, 713); first comes the author, then the alleged Gothic nom. sg. form, the normalised, inflectional form in Latin, and the manuscript variants:

(4) Author	nom. sg.	Inflectional form / Manuscript variants
Cassiodorus (III.20; p. 89)	*Triwila**	*Triwilae* (gen. sg.) triuuil(a)e, triullile, triuile, triuiul(a)e, triuule, triuili, gri-
Anon. Valesianus (82; p. 326)	*Triwa**	*Triwane* (abl. sg.) triuuane
Ennodius (ep. 9.21; p. 306)	*Triggwa**	*Triggwa* (abl. sg.) triggua
Boethius (I.4.10; p. 100)	*Triggwila**	*Triggwillam* (acc. sg.) triguillam, trigguilam, tringuillam
Gregor of Tours (III.31; p. 126)	*Traggwila**	*Traggwilanem* (acc. sg.) traguillanem (2), trauuilanem, tranguilanem,
Fredegar (III.43; p. 105)	*Traggwila**	*Traggwila* (nom. sg.), *Traggwilane* (abl. sg.) traquila, traquilani, tranquillani

Wagner (2003) is the last to have discussed this name. He assumes that it was a Gothic name, *Triggwa*, and *Triggwila* with a diminutive suffix. He considers the origin to be clear; the name is derived from the adj. *triggws* and finds a direct match in the Old Norse name *Tryggvi*.[1] Wagner accepts Jellinek's (1926:36) opinion that this is proof that there was no nasal in ⟨ggw⟩ in *triggws*. The double *l* in some of the attested forms is, he thinks, initiated by the Latin diminutive suffix *-ellus*. On the other hand, it is necessary to explain the ⟨g⟩-less forms found in Cassiodorus and the Anonymus Valesianus. Wagner's explanation is that learned men, as they were, understood that there was often a superfluous *-g-* written along with Germanic *-w-* and therefore they, wrongly, dropped the *g* in this case.

This argument should be turned upside down. Cassiodorus and the *Triwila* he mentions were both officials of King Theodoric. The name occurs in a letter Cassiodorus wrote to *Triwila* on behalf of the king. Therefore it is just as likely that Cassiodorus knew *Triwila*, who had the title *saio* (some kind of messenger) and was a *praepositus sacri cubiculi* (Boethius as in (4), Moorhead 1992:73), and that he realised that there was no /g/ in *Triwila's* name and accordingly he did not write a ⟨g⟩. Also, it is likely that Cassiodorus knew literate Goths who were able to help him with the orthography. The situation of the Anonymus Valesianus is somewhat similar.

Where should we look for the origin of this name? Wrede (1891:79) also considers it to derive from the adj. *triggws*. In a footnote he suggests that the forms *Triwa/Triwila* are folk etymologies; an attempt to connect the name with Gothic *triu**, that corresponds etymologically to ModE *tree*. Presumably this means that the 'folk' in question were in need of a new etymology as the relationship of *Triggwa/Triggwila* with the adj. *triggws* was no longer evident. In fact, all this is unnecessary. Probably the forms *Triwa/Triwila* are the original forms and the forms with *-g(g)w-* are the Romanisation of them. The name is simply derived from *triu**, as Wrede found possible. Now, 'tree' is infrequent or even unattested in Early Germanic personal names. Therefore, it is possible that originally this was a nickname. Gothic *triu** as a simplex is only found in the syntagma *miþ hairum jah triwam* (Mk 14:43,48) ʽμετὰ μαχαιρῶν καὶ ξύλον, with swords and clubs'. The base is also found in the compound *weinatriu* ʽἄμπελος, grapevine' and in the derived adj. *triweins* ʽξύλινος, wooden'. Apparently, Go. *triu** meant 'branch, stick, club' whereas the word for 'tree' was *bagms* ʽδένδρον'. Therefore, *Triwa* (and *Triwila* with the diminutive suffix) could have the individualising meaning: 'the one with the club/stick' or, possibly, it referred to the appearance of the name-bearer: 'the one who looks like a club or stick (in some sense)', etc.

5. Conclusions

As a matter of fact we cannot be sure that Go. *triu** had the same meaning in the language of the Ostrogoths in Italy as it had in the Gothic version of the New Testament. The translation was made in the fourth century among the Visigoths in the

---

[1] The name *Tryggvi* is very infrequent in Old Norse sources so one wonders if it was perhaps a nickname originally, not an inherited Proto-Germanic personal name.

Balkan Peninsula and the language must surely have been somewhat different from the language of the Ostrogoths in the sixth century, although they possibly left some marks of their own on the preserved text. The main thing is that we have to live with the fact that there is no reliable evidence that Gothic ‹ggw› was pronounced differently according to origin. Even though we accept that *tregua* and *Trigguila* show that there was no nasal in Gothic *triggwa* we cannot conclude that there was a nasal in *siggwan* for historical reasons. Really, the equation has changed. In that scenario it would be most likely that the combination ‹ggw› was always without a nasal although there was a nasal in the combination ‹gg› in other environments. Brosman (1971:173) admits this but considers the change /ŋgw/ > /ggw/ less likely than /ggw/ > /ŋgw/. Therefore, it should be said once more: there is no internal evidence for double pronunciation of ‹ggw› in Gothic, and the external evidence fails to support it.

References

Anon. Valesianus = Mommsen Th. (ed.) 1892 [reprint 1961]. *Cronica Minora Saec. IV. V. VI. VII. Consvlaria Italica. I. Anonymi Valesiani pars posterior.* Berolini. [Monvmenta Germaniae Historica. Avctorvm antiqvissimorvm IX].

Boethius = Anicii Manlii Torquati Severini Boethii. 1823. *De Consolatione Philosophiæ* libri quinque ex editione Vulpiana […]. Londini.

Cassiodorus = Mommsen Th. (ed.) 1894. *Cassiodori senatoris Variae.* Berolini. [Monvmenta Germaniae Historica. Avctorvm antiqvissimorvm XII].

Ennodius = Vogel F. (ed.) 1885 [reprint 1961]. *Magni Felicis Ennodi Opera.* Berolini. [Monvmenta Germaniae Historica. Avctorvm antiqvissimorvm VII].

Fredegar = Krusch B. (ed.) 1888. *Scriptores Rervm Merovingicarvm.* [vol. II Fredegarii et aliorvm chronica. Vitae Sanctorvm]. Hannoverae. [Monvmenta Germaniae Historica].

Gregor of Tours = Krusch B., Levison W. (eds.) 1951. *Scriptores Rervm Merovingicarvm.* [vol. I.1 Gregorii episcopi Tvronensis libri historiarvm X. 2. ed.] Hannoverae. [Monvmenta Germaniae Historica. Avctorvm antiqvissimorvm VII].

Amory P. 1997. *People and identity in Ostrogothic Italy, 489–554.* Cambridge.

Bennett W.H. 1964. Gothic spellings and phonemes: some current interpretations. – Betz W. et al. (eds.) *Taylor Starck. Festschrift 1964.* The Hague: 19–26.

Braune W. 1884. Gotisch *ddj* und altnordisch *ggj.* – *Beiträge zur Geschichte der deutschen Sprache und Literatur* 9: 545–548.

Braune/Ebbinghaus. 1961. *Gotische Grammatik. Mit Lesestücken und Wörterverzeichnis.* [von W. Braune. 16. Auflage, neu bearbeitet von E.A. Ebbinghaus]. Tübingen.

Braune/Heidermanns. 2004. *Gotische Grammatik. Mit Lesestücken und Wörterverzeichnis.* [von W. Braune. 20. Auflage, neu bearbeitet von F. Heidermanns]. Tübingen.

Brosman P.W. 1971. Romance evidence and Gothic ‹ggw›. – *Indogermanische Forschungen* 76: 165–173.

Durante E. 1974. *Grammatica gotica.* Bologna.

Francovich Onesti N. 2007. *I nomi degli ostrogoti.* Firenze.

von der Gabelentz H.C., Löbe J. 1846. *Ulfilas. Veteris et novi testamenti versionis gothicae fragmenta quae supersunt ad fidem codd. castigata, […]. [vol. II.2 Grammatik der gothischen Sprache].* Leipzig [reprint Hildesheim 1980].

Holtzmann A. (rev.) 1835. Skeireins aivaggeljons thairh Johannen. […] herausgegeben von H.F. Maßmann. […] – *Heidelberger Jahrbücher der Literatur* 28: 854–863.

Jellinek M.H. 1926. *Geschichte der gotischen Sprache.* [Grundriss der germanischen Philologie 1/1]. Berlin, Leipzig.

Krause W. 1968. *Handbuch des Gotischen.* [3., neubearbeitete Auflage]. München.

Lehmann W.P. 1986. *A Gothic etymological dictionary.* [Based on the third edition of *Vergleichendes Wörterbuch der Gotischen Sprache* by Sigmund Feist.] Leiden.

Marchand J.W. 1959. Über *ai au* im Gotischen. – *Beiträge zur Geschichte der deutschen Sprache und Literatur* (H/S) 81: 436–455.

Marchand J.W. 1973. *The sounds and phonemes of Wulfila's Gothic.* The Hague, Paris.

Meyer-Lübke W. 1911. *Romanisches etymologisches Wörterbuch.* Heidelberg.

Moorhead J. 1992. *Theodoric in Italy.* Oxford.

Niermeyer J.F. 1976. *Mediae Latinitatis Lexicon Minus.* Leiden.

Pfister M. 1985. Longob. **baug-, *trewwa, waiß-*. Fonti e metodologia per lo studio del superstrato longobardo. – *Studi linguistici e filologici per Carlo Alberto Mastrelli.* Pisa: 361–371.

Pfister M. 1986. I superstrati germanici nell'italiano. – *Elementi stranieri nei dialetti italiani 1.* [Atti del XIV Convegno dei C.S.D.I., Ivrea 17–19 ottobre 1984; Consiglio Nazionale delle Ricerche, Centro di Studio per la Dialettologia Italiana 17]. Pisa: 37–58.

Reichert H. 1987. *Lexikon der altgermanischen Namen.* [1. Teil: Text]. Wien.

Scherer W. (rev.) 1868. Paradigmen zur deutschen Grammatik […] von Oskar Schade. – *Zeitschrift für die österreichischen Gymnasien* 19: 853–855.

Schwyzer E. 1934. Dissimilatorische Geminatenauflösung als Folge von Übersteigerung, zunächst im Neugriechischen und im Spätaltgriechischen. – *Zeitschrift für vergleichende Sprachforschung auf dem Gebiete der Indogermanischen Sprachen* 61: 222–252.

Stearns MacD. 1978. *Crimean Gothic. Analysis and etymology of the corpus.* [Studia Linguistica et Philologica 6]. Saratoga.

Streitberg W. 1943. *Urgermanische Grammatik.* [Unveränderter Abdruck der 1. Auflage (1896)]. Heidelberg.

Voyles J.B. 1968. Gothic and Germanic. – *Language* 44.4: 720–746.

Wagner N. 2003. *Triggvilla*, Tragvila** und *Triwila*.* Zu *-ggv-* : *-w-* in zwei Ostgotennamen. – *Beiträge zur Namenforschung* 38: 275–279.

Wrede F. 1891. *Über die Sprache der Ostgoten in Italien.* Strassburg.

Studia Linguistica Universitatis Iagellonicae Cracoviensis
128 (2011)

KAMIL STACHOWSKI
Jagiellonian University, Cracow

A NOTE ON LEVENSHTEIN DISTANCE VERSUS HUMAN ANALYSIS

Keywords: Levenshtein distance, loanword adaptation, Dolgan, Russian

Abstract

This paper argues that automatic phonetic comparison will only return true results if the languages in question have similar and comparably lenient phonologies. In the situation where their phonologies are incompatible and / or restrictive, linguistic knowledge of both of them is necessary to obtain results matching human perception. Whilst the case is mainly exemplified by Levenshtein distance and Russian loanwords in Dolgan, the conclusion is also applicable to the approach as a whole.

0. Rationale and introductory notes

In Stachowski (2010), I presented a method of quantifying the phonetic adaptation of loanwords, which heavily depends on prior human analysis. It has been suggested to me that it would be more valuable if the requirement could be removed for an *expert analyst to specify the adaptations ahead of time*. This question leads directly to the problem of how much linguistic knowledge, or knowledge of the languages being analyzed, is necessary for the results of an automatized assay to correlate with human (native speakers') perception.

Levenshtein distance (= edit ~) has more than once been shown to be capable of credible results (see e.g. Heeringa et al. 2006), even for *genetically* and *typologically* quite distant languages, as Kipchak Turkic vs. Iranian in van der Ark et al. (2007). However, it seems that this is much more often applied to *phonologically* quite similar languages such as Dutch, English, German or Norwegian dialects. Moreover, most of these languages are phonotactically relatively rich and therefore lenient, which appears to be key here. This is not at all the case with Dolgan, the Russian loanwords in which I have attempted to analyze. Neither is it the case with a great number of different languages, Turkic and other, to which in theory the method can be applied.

Levenshtein distance has also been criticized for its crudity, resulting in the charge that it *so completely misrepresents the nature of language* (Heggarty 2006: 185). A number of refinements have been proposed, and also a number of other algorithms of varying degrees of advantageousness (see e.g. Heeringa et al. 2006 or Nerbonne, Heeringa 2009, etc.). Nevertheless, I have chosen to use the basic version of the method here for its popularity and simplicity, and because it represents quite well the crucial methodological assumptions common to at least the majority of propositions.

I will: **1.** present the results of contrasting Levenshtein distance with my index of nativization, as applied to Russian loanwords in Dolgan, **2.** provide some further and typologically different examples of the incompatibility of Levenshtein distance with human perception, and **3.** conclude in, hopefully, a positive way.

1. Russian loanwords in Dolgan

In Stachowski (2010), I calculated for each of the 1169 identified Russian loanwords in Dolgan, an index of nativization (= degree of adaptation). It ranges from 0 (not nativized) to 1 (fully nativized). Examples: Russ. *aèropórt* 'airport' > Dolg. *aèroport* id. (index 0), *lódka* 'boat' > *lokka* id. (0.50931), *vétka* '*Siber.* canoe' > *băkkä* id. (1).

The leading assumption of this method is that adaptations which are more common contribute less to the final score than those which are rarer. This entails that adaptations need to be identified ahead of time, and it is here that the first obstacle arises. Some of the adaptations require precisely the knowledge of Dolgan phonology in order to be recognized. For example, the -*dk*- (= [-tk-]) > -*kk*-change observed in *lokka* above, is not merely *an* assimilation but in fact an application of one of Dolgan phonotactic rules which are obligatory in native words across morpheme boundaries. These are also sometimes exercised for loanwords but this is a very rare case (only seven examples in the corpus of 1169 words). Hence the relatively high score of 0.5 although two out of three adaptations have not been applied here – a fully nativized shape would be **luokko* or **lōkko*.

Levenshtein distance is not bothered by the commonness of the given change. It measures the *phonetic* distance between two forms. Naturally, this requires precise phonetic transcriptions of both words in order to return valid results. This is the second obstacle. Detailed recordings are available for Dutch, English, German, Norwegian, etc. but are missing and much more difficult to obtain for lesser known and more distant languages such as Dolgan. What is more, extinct and reconstructed languages have to be automatically excluded, together with any borrowings which occurred from a dialectally mixed society, where the exact pronunciation is often impossible to establish. This happens to be the case with Russian in northeastern Siberia.

If one nevertheless decided to wade on, they would therefore find themselves forced to measure phonological rather than phonetic distance. This allows further investigation but it makes a significant difference.

One difficulty is to decide which phonemes can be treated as corresponding, and which cannot. *V* does not occur in Dolgan but in loanwords. If they were considered Fremdwörter, Dolg. *b* could correlate with both Russ. *b* and *v*. Such a solution might seem to be an exaggeration at first but its fabricated feel quickly wanes away as the number of obstacles of this type grows. This is the reason why I only provide approximate counts of examples below. An exact number would require many methodological decisions and discussing them would be beyond the scope of the current note.

On the other hand, a move to phonology brings the results closer to reality elsewhere. *K* and *ǩ* are allophonic in Russian in some positions, and so they are in Dolgan. In *vétka* 'Siber. canoe', the *k* is not palatalized whereas in *bäǩǩä* id. both *k*'s are, and in both cases this is not phonemic. Adopting a phonological transcription will improve the Levenshtein distance by freeing it from incorporating an irrelevant difference in its result.

I calculated the Levenshtein distance for the entire corpus of Russian loanwords in Dolgan (with *indel = sub = 1*) and contrasted the results with my index. The correlation turned out to be 0.43, and this hardly came as a surprise. First and foremost, the methodological approach is dramatically different. Let us consider a few cases:

* Both measures closely match
  This mostly happens when most of the possible adaptations have not been applied or when very few adaptations are applicable, and they were skipped. Both measures are 0 or draw near to it and thus they match or almost match.
      In the case of Russian loanwords in Dolgan, such examples account for less than a fourth of the total number.
      Examples: Russ. *patrón* 'cartridge' > Dolg. *patruon* id. (index 0.04667), *pártija* 'party' > *pārtija* id. (0.02864), *rabóčij* 'worker' > *rabočaj* id. (0.11023), *žurnál* 'journal' > *žurnāl* id. (0.00828); Russ. *čas* '1. hour; 2. clock', *kak* 'since', *maj* 'May', *šar* 'i.a. balloon' > Dolg. ≡ (indices 0).
      A close match can also happen in other situations, in particular when the adaptations applied exhaust all the possibilities as completely as much they change the phonetic shape.
      However, such examples only account for less than an eleventh of the total number.
      Examples: Russ. *blagosloví* 'may he bless' > Dolg. *lastabi* id. (index 0.78626), *Fëdor* (given name) > *Pädär* id. (0.3666), *vóvse* 'completely' > *buosa* id. (0.44574), *zdoróvʹe* 'health' > *dorōbuja* id. (0.55297).

* The two measures are almost opposite
  This mostly happens when there are very few adaptations possible and they have all been applied but without changing the word's phonetic shape much.

Such cases are very rare and only account for less than a twenty-seventh of the total number.

Examples: Russ. *Ánna* (given name) > Dolg. *Ānna* id., *barán* 'fur jacket' > *barān* id., *pop* 'Orthodox priest' > *puop* id., *ukázka* 'pointer' > *ukāska* id. (all indices 1).

- The two measures diverge randomly
This happens when the degree in which the applied adaptations exhaust all the possibilities, does not coincide with their shape-changing power.

One borderline case of this has already been mentioned above. *-dk-* > *-kk-* in *lódka* 'boat' is phonetically a minor assimilation but in Dolgan, it is a sign of far-reaching nativization. *Óčeredъ* 'order, sequence' > *uočarat* id. (index 0.12155), on the other hand, is phonetically a considerable change but for Dolgan phonology, it is merely a combination of a fairly common substitution of a diphthong for a Russian accented vowel (unsurprisingly, especially often with *ó*), an even more common repair of vowel harmony, and an equally common removal of palatalization from *t́* since such sound does not exist in Dolgan, and *t* does.

This is by far the most common case and it accounts for about two thirds of the total number.

Examples: Russ. *krováth* 'bed' > Dolg. *kyrbat* id. (index 0.99227), *Oksínъja* (given name) > *Oksiäńńä* id. (0.02864), *séjanka* (a kind of meat dish) > *hiäŋki* id. (0.2576), *Vasílъevič* (patronym) > *Bahylajbys* (0.99676).

To conclude, Levenshtein distance applied to Russian loanwords in Dolgan will return a valid and true measurement of phonological difference between the etymon and the loanword – but it will be a purely surface measure which may or may not correlate with actual human perception. More often the latter. The Levenshtein algorithm is quite flexible and probably can be refined so as to take note of those adaptations which are phonotactically trivial but phonetically devastating to the shape of the etymon, such as vowel harmony. Should this prove impossible, another algorithm can be used or a new one can be invented to perhaps achieve a full correlation with human perception. However, the crux is that it will always have to be based on the knowledge of the languages in question. This knowledge can be obscured by using a universal algorithm which itself learns from training data (e.g. Dunning 1994, Sanders, Chin 2009) but this does not change the essential need for such knowledge in general.

2. Other examples

Russian and Dolgan are most definitely not the only pair of languages where phonetic dissimilarity does not necessarily coincide with perception as distant forms.

When a word is borrowed into a language with a phonology considerably more restrictive than that of the donor language, it is prone to be heavily altered, and at the same time, the "new owners" are likely to not even realize that any change has taken place. The Japanese have rendered Engl. *drama* in two ways: [dorama] and [ʒurama] (Polivanov 1968: 237f.). A Polish asked to name a Hungarian author replied that some say [pätɔ·ˈfi] and others say [pätä·fi], without at all being aware of missing the actual pronunciation of [pą̈·tṍfi] by quite a distance. A German, after hearing the names [anja] and [aɲa] repeated many times side by side, was only able to admit that there might perhaps indeed be something like a very slight difference between the two, at the very edge of recognition available to humans.

Stories of this sort will pop up every now and then at any party attended by linguists and they will gather the more applause the more exotic the phonologies in question are when compared to those of the listeners. This is to say, the audience will act much as the Levenshtein algorithm would. However, if they were told to a Japanese, a Polish or a German, chances are that the public would miss the punchline entirely. Knowledge of the relevant phonologies is key here to obtain the desired effect.

There is also the opposite case, when a loanword has not been significantly changed phonetically but in such a way that it raises associations with some other word in the borrowing language. Turkish *okul* 'school' is in fact a neologism and for every Turkish speaker its link to *oku-* 'to learn' is apparent. Polish dialectal *smentarz* 'boneyard' is a result of folk etymology by the dialectal shape *smętek* [-änt-] 'sorrow'. (The literary form is *cmentarz* ≪ Lat. *cœmētērium* id. ≫ Engl. *cemetery*.) French *choucroute* 'sauerkraut' is a loan from Middle German *sūrkrūt* id. despite its shape which resembles more the French words *chou* 'cabbage' and *croûte* 'crust'.

In these cases, the Levenshtein distance is invariably low but actual native speakers' perception is often complicated. They will frequently admit a considerable phonetic similarity but at the same time refuse to connect the two words because lexical and semantic associations with other words they know in their own languages, are too strong.

3. Conclusion

Levenshtein distance, in its basic form and the more so in its highly refined versions, can be a good measure of *phonetic* distance. However, it needs to be remembered that phonetic distance is not necessarily equal to phonological distance, and that neither of them has to be equal to the perceived distance. The results will depart the further, the more and deeper differences there are between the phonological systems from which the compared words are taken. Levenshtein's method can serve as a (very) good approximation for what has been its main domain of implementation so far, i.e. comparison of relatively similar dialects, but it fails when phonologically more distant languages are attempted to be analyzed. Its independence of the knowledge of language is sometimes raised as one of its most important strengths. In many cases, however, this will be the sole feature responsible for its failure.

Leonard Bloomfield is usually credited for the witty saying that *if you want to compare two languages, it helps to know one of them*. He died in 1949 and could not witness or perhaps even foresee the computer revolution of the last decades. But the technological advance does not obsolete his observation. It still helps, and it appears that it always will, if at least one actor of the comparison – be it the algorithm only – knows at least one of the languages being compared.

Abbreviations

Dolg. = Dolgan | **Engl.** = English | **Lat.** = Latin | **Russ.** = Russian

References

van der Ark R., Mennecier P., Nerbonne J., Manni F. 2007. Preliminary identification of language groups and loan words in Central Asia. – Osenova P. et al. (eds.) *Proceedings of the RANLP workshop on computational phonology workshop at the conference Recent Advances in Natural Language Processing*. Borovets: 13–20. [www.let.rug.nl/nerbonne/paper.html, accessed 2010.12.17].

Dunning T. 1994. *Statistical identification of language*. – *Technical Report CRL MCCS* 94-273. New Mexico State University. [ucrel.lancs.ac.uk/papers, accessed 2010.12.18].

Heeringa W., Kleiweg P., Gooskens Ch., Nerbonne J. 2006. Evaluation of string distance algorithms for dialectology. – Nerbonne J., Hinrichs E. (eds.) *Linguistic distances workshop at the joint conference of International Committee on Computational Linguistics and the Association for Computational Linguistics*. Sydney: 51–62. [www.let.rug.nl/nerbonne/paper.html, accessed 2010.12.17].

Heggarty P. 2006. Interdisciplinary indiscipline? Can phylogenetic methods meaningfully be applied to language data — and to dating language? – Renfrew C., Forster P. (eds.) *Phylogenetic methods and the prehistory of languages*. Cambridge: 183–94.

Nerbonne J., Heeringa W. 2009. Measuring dialect differences. – Schmidt J.E., Auer P. (eds.) *Language and space: theories and methods* [= *Handbücher zur Sprach- und Kommunikationswissenschaft* 30.1]. Berlin: 550–67.

Polivanov E.D. 1968. *Statьi po obščemu jazykoznaniju*. Moskva.

Sanders N.C., Chin S.B. 2009. Phonological distance measures. – *Journal of Quantitative Linguistics* 16.1: 96–114. [citeseerx.ist.psu.edu/viewdoc/summary?doi=10.1.1.95.2447, accessed 2010.12.18].

Stachowski K. 2010. Quantifying phonetic adaptations of Russian loanwords in Dolgan. – *Studia Linguistica Universitatis Iagellonicae Cracoviensis* 127: 101–77.

Studia Linguistica Universitatis Iagellonicae Cracoviensis
128 (2011)

MAREK STACHOWSKI
Jagiellonian University, Cracow

GERMAN *IRRWISCH*
'1. WILL-O'-THE-WISP; 2. SCAMP, SCALLYWAG, IMP'
AND POLISH *URWIS* 'SCAMP, SCALLYWAG, IMP'

Keywords: German, Polish, languages in contact, semantics

Abstract

Even if the derivation of the meaning 'scamp, scallywag, imp' < 'will-o'-the-wisp' is generally imaginable (albeit not self-evident) it is assumed here that this change is actually based on addition of a foreign meaning to a German one, rather than on semantic evolution.

The morphological structure of the German word *Irrwisch* causes no problems at all: < *Irr+wisch*, like *Irr+licht* 'will-o'-the-wisp, ghost-lights'. One grows all the more convinced about the correctness of this simple etymology if one realizes that German *Wisch* both etymologically and semantically corresponds to English *wisp* 'bundle of hay, rags, etc. for use as a torch'. The only thing that is somewhat less self-evident here is how the meaning 'scamp etc.' has come into being. The change of 'will-o'-the-wisp' into 'scamp' is admittedly imaginable but far from being natural and granted. Let us put this problem aside for a while and have a look at the other word called in the title of this note.

Polish *urwis* 'scamp etc.' and its older and dialectal variants *urwisz* ~ *urwiś* id. are commonly connected with the verb *urw-ać* 'to tear off'. In S.B. Linde's six-volume dictionary of the Polish language (1807–1814) one can also find (s.v. *urwa*) some other derivatives of this verb explained in Polish and translated into German, e.g. *urw-alec* 'ein Beutelschneider, Betrüger [= cut-purse, fraud]', *urw-aniec* 'ein Galgenvogel, Galgenstrick [= gallows bird]', *urw-ański* 'spitzbübisch, räuberisch [= impish, roguish, brigandish]'. Additionally the variant *urowieś* 'scamp etc.'

is attested there, too, which presumably results from a contamination of *urwiś* id. with *obwieś* 'gallows bird, rogue'.

The semantic connection between 'scamp etc.' and 'to tear off' is readily understood if one considers the German translation 'Beutelschneider' [= English 'cut-purse'] and another Polish word, i.e. *urwipołeć* 'scamp etc.', lit. 'tear off (*urw-i-*) + large cut of meat or fat (*połeć*)', i.e. 'someone who tears off a portion of meat (and runs away)'. Cf. also English *tearaway* 'madcap, reckless person'.

Before we come back to the German *Irrwisch* we should maybe cast a glance at a still other word: German *dalli* 'pronto', *dalli dalli!* 'hurry up!, get a move on!'. It is unanimously reported to have come from Polish *dalej* '1. farther; 2. go ahead!'. This explanation is principally correct; however, the German word-final *-i* clearly points to the Polish dialectal pronunciation: *daléj* (with *é* = narrow [e]) ~ *dalij* ~ *dali* (whereas the double *-ll-* in the German spelling is nothing but an orthographical device signaling the shortness of the preceding vowel). It was certainly Polish maidservants or nursemaids who – when taking care of children in German families – used this word in their Polish dialectal pronunciation that afterwards took root in the German language.

A similar scenario can be conjectured for the word *Irrwisch* as well. In the first phase, its meaning was just 'will-o'-the-wisp'. Then, however, some Polish maidservants might have called the one or another child in a German family *urwisz* or *urwiś* 'scamp etc.'. The variant with *-ś* sounds softer, gentler, tenderer, and this is the form a loving mother or nursemaid can use when speaking a Polish dialect. Anyway, the difference between Polish *-sz* and *-ś* must have been neutralized in the German pronunciation, always resulting in *-sch*,[1] so that both *urwiś* and *urwisz* yielded a German **Urwisch*.

It is quite possible that such a word was auditively associated by German parents with *Irrwisch* 'will-o'-the-wisp',[2] the more so as **Urwisch* would have been understood in German as 'proto-wisp' which makes no sense. A very active child having a lot of energy was sometimes called *Quirl* 'live wire' in German, that is with a noun whose etymological meaning was 'stirring' ~ 'turner', and in this case it is also imaginable that such a child could have been associated with a 'will-o'-the-wisp'. It might have been in this manner that the German word *Irrwisch* has received its second meaning 'scamp, scallywag, imp'.

---

[1] The same is valid for Polish *cz* ~ *ć* > German *tsch*, e.g. Polish *Częstochowa* > German *Tschenstochau*, Polish *Bogucice* [-*ući*-] (a district of Katowice) > German *Bogutschütz*. Interestingly enough, Polish *cz* was sometimes rendered *sch* in German, as in Polish *Czechowice* > German *Schechowitz*, Polish *Czarków* > German *Scharkow*.

[2] Etymologically incorrect associations are of course quite usual in language contacts. Another interesting German-Slavonic example is *Podvihov* (name of a district of the Czech city Opava), that rendered in German *Podwihof*, i.e. with the change of Slavonic *-hov* (< thematic *-h* + suffix *-ov*) into German *Hof* 'yard; courtyard'. – A combination of the Polish *ś* > German *sch* change with a secondary association can also be observed in the name of the Polish village *Sieroty* [śe-] (Silesia) whose German equivalent is *Schieroth*, with German *sch-* for Polish *ś-* and German *roth* 'red'.

Studia Linguistica Universitatis Iagellonicae Cracoviensis
128 (2011)

MAREK STACHOWSKI
Jagiellonian University, Cracow

SIBERIAN LANGUAGES IN CONTACT, 1: COLLECTIVE NUMERALS IN YAKUT, DOLGAN, TUVINIAN, TOFALAR AND SOME OTHER TURKIC LANGUAGES*

Keywords: Turkic languages, Siberian languages, comparative linguistics, areal linguistics, linguistic leagues/areas

Abstract

Morphological categories of Siberian Turkic numerals are particularly complex and therefore deemed to be especially advantageous to areal investigations. The aim of this paper is to see whether (at least some of) the suffixes of collective numerals can readily be used as isogloss connecting Yakut and Dolgan with Tuvinian and Tofalar or, maybe, also some other Turkic languages.

1.

One is sometimes told that Tofalar and probably also Tuvinian are the closest relatives of Yakut and, by the same token, Dolgan that in the course of time evolved from Old Yakut as Icelandic did from Old Norse. (cf. Menges 1955: 122, 131; 1958/59: passim; Schönig 1997: 155; 2001: 86). However, precise arguments have never been formulated and discussed. If this conjecture proves correct the possibility of a new evaluation of the Mongolian ethnonym *Uryangkhay* (earlier used by both Yakuts and Tuvinians as a self-designation) and the earliest history of "Tuvaic" (= Tuvinian + Tofalar) and "Sakhaic" (= Yakut + Dolgan) will probably emerge. Indeed, it is intriguing to learn whether Tuvaic and Sakhaic can be connected into one group

---

[1] This paper was first read at the 4th Polish Conference on Turkology, Poznań, October 7–8, 2010.

(say, an "Uryangkhaic" one), a fact that would allow us to define at least four languages of the region in a somewhat more precise way than on the basis of geography only (like e.g. "Siberian" ~ "North-East" Turkic).

Because the morphological categories of numerals are particularly numerous in Yakut and Dolgan, and since they constitute a rather complex system (see especially the diagram in Stachowski 1997: 337) it seems the most promising course is to examine to what extent this complicated system reflects a joint evolution of Sakhaic and Tuvaic.[1] Both the complexity of the system and the lack of preliminary studies compel us to investigate individual subsystems before more general conclusions can be drawn.

What now follows is, as far as I am aware, the first study concerning the topic of mutual connections between Tuvaic and Sakhaic. It is, for the time being, impossible to decide whether the choice of the collective numerals for the first study is reasonable. Nevertheless, it is good enough to show that these connections are by no means that simple.

2.

The suffix of the collective numerals is +ya ~ +yan in Yakut, but only +yan in Dolgan. The original form of +ya is certainly the Old Turkic suffix +agu (e.g. in OTkc. ikegü 'both; a pair; zu zweit', onagu 'a group of ten' [Erdal 1991: 93; 2004: 225]).

The suffix-final ...n might be interpreted as another collective suffix +(a)n, attested, for instance, in OTkc. oglan 'sons, children' < ogul 'son', eren 'men' < er 'man' (Erdal 1991: 91), and attached to *+agu formations as some type of intensifier, or the like.

The fact, however, that the derivatives with ...n usually have the adverbial meaning 'two at a time, in twos, two by two; zu zweit; вдвоем' in Yakut (cf. JaND 139) suggests that this ...n is a reflex of the instrumental suffix +(u)n rather (Erdal 2004: 175).[2] Now, the development probably was as follows:

(2a)   Proto-Yakut has a reflex of the suffix *+agu.
(2b)   An adverbial collective suffix *+agu+n is invented.[3]

---

[1]   The Dolgan system is not fully identical with the Yakut one. However, for historical reasons its peculiar features evolved only in the 17th century, so that they are inconsequential for the reconstruction of the earliest phases of Proto-Yakut history (and, possibly, also of the cohabitation of Proto-Yakuts and Proto-Tuvinians that must have come to an end after the last Proto-Yakuts had migrated northwards, i.e. in the 16th century at the latest).

[2]   For another example of declensional forms becoming a new morphological category of Turkic numerals cf. the Yakut usage of possessive dative or accusative forms with the meaning of iterative numerals, as in: Yak. ikki 'two' → ikki+s 'second' → ikki+s+iger (dat. 3. sg.) ~ ikki+s+in (acc. 3. sg.) 'for the second time' (Kotwicz 1930: 208), the etymological intervocalic ...s... being pronounced and (apart from Pekarskij's dictionary and some attestations in Sieroszewski's ethnographical study [Stachowski 1991: 308]) also spelt ...h..., i.e. ikkihiger, ikkihin.

[3]   But cf. Menges 1959/60: 105: "[...] -ä(n) < -ä-gi(-n), [...] wahrscheinlich eine verbale Ableitung auf -a/-ä mit dem davon gebildeten nomen verbale auf -γy/-gi/-γu/-gü (mit lativisch-instrumentalischem -n), die noch um ein Suffix -ła/-lä erweitert sein kann – vgl. auch die

(2c)   For some period of time, the division is clear: *+agu* derivatives are used (ad)nominally, *+agu+n* derivatives adverbially.

(2d)   As time goes on, *+agu+n* derivatives start being used (ad)nominally.

(2e)   In the Vilyuy dialect of Old Yakut that was the basis of the future Dolgan language *+agu+n* formations receive the status of the only collective numerals available, whereas the reflex of the suffix *+agu* passes into oblivion.

The lack of old philological sources makes it impossible to decide whether phase (2e) took place still on the Vilyuy (that is, in the first half of the 17th century, at the latest) or rather in Taimyr (that is, in the second half of the 17th century, at the earliest).

3.

The Tuvaic functional counterparts of the Yakut suffix *+ya(n)* are as follows:

(3a)   Tuv. *+älä(n)*, *+aldyrzy*;
(3b)   Tdž.[4] *+ān*;
(3c)   Tof. *+ālyn*, *+ān*.

Some facts can be easily observed here:

(3d)   The final *...n* can emerge and disappear in Tuv. *+älä(n)* as is also the case with Yak. *+ya(n)* but the initial parts of these suffixes differ rather considerably.

(3e)   Tuv. *+älä(n)* and Tof. *+ālyn* are probably one and the same suffix.

(3f)   Differences concerning the vowel quantity are not self-evident.

(3g)   An *...l...* can be observed in some variants; its function and origin are unclear.

(3h)   The suffixes without *...l...* (in Yakut, Tuvinian and Todža) probably constitute a separate group.

(3i)   The initial syllable in Tuv. *+aldyrzy* is reminiscent of the initial syllable in Tuv. *+älä(n)* and Tof. *+ālyn* but the subsequent syllables are strikingly different from each other.

The crucial question is now whether the Tuvinian, Todža and Tofalar suffixes are closer to those in Yakut and Dolgan than their counterparts in other Turkic languages are, to the extent that one could even draw an isogloss entitled "Collective numerals" separating the languages forming a "Tuvaic-Sakhaic Language Community", if there was such a thing, from all the other Turkic languages.

---

mongolischen num. collectiva auf *-yuła/-gülä*". – This suggestion seems to have never been accepted in Turkology.

4   Tdž. = Todža ~ Tožа, a north-eastern dialect of Tuvinian (Sat 1997: 384).

4.

If a modern morpheme (or a part of one) is a regular reflex of a protolanguage morpheme (or a part of one) it cannot be considered a regional-specific feature (unless it has perished in all the other regions). This is why we have first to reconstruct the situation in the protolanguage, and then to exclude the ordinary heritage in order to find what elements and constructions are regional innovations.

Also the Tuvinian suffix +aldyrzy in (3a) can be readily excluded from further considerations here, being a morpheme that does not, on the one hand, reflect the PTkc. *+agu, and, on the other, is restricted to Tuvinian only which means that it can neither throw new light on the Proto-Turkic collective suffix nor create an areal isogloss.[5]

The long vowel in the first syllable of the suffix +ālā(n) seems to be original, i.e. +alā(n) < +ālā(n) because this change occurs more frequently than the opposite (which is easily understandable since the ā – ā > a – ā change reduces the articulatory effort) and, besides, this vowel is always long in Tofalar (the position before a syllable with a high vowel will probably have supported the original vowel length since this is a general tendency in the Siberian Turkic languages).

Now, the suffixes in (3a–c) may, apart from +aldyrzy, be divided into two groups:

(4a)   those with ...l..., i.e. Tuv. +ālā(n), Tof. +ālyn;
(4b)   those without ...l..., i.e. Tof. Tdž. +ān.

One of the imaginable explanations of this situation is that both groups are genetically connected with each other, and (4b) < (4a). Another possibility is that both groups of suffixes are genetically not connected to each other at all and their phonetic similarity is fully accidental. Yet another solution is that some parts of the suffixes are genetically identical whereas the rest are accidentally similar. Even if this last possibility looks the most complex and least probable it presumably best expresses the morphological and genetic reality.

The explanation of Tdž. and Tuv. +ān is relatively easy: < PTkc. *+agu (collective numerals) + *+(u)n (instrumental case), and nothing prevents us from assuming that the suffixes +ālā(n) and +ālyn possibly include the same instrumental marker, as well.

Three etymologies of the Tuvinian suffix +ālā(n) have been suggested so far:

The first possibility is that gerunds in -yp were shortened, e.g. PTkc. *üč+egü 'three at a time' > *üč+egü+len- 'to become a group of three persons' > *üč+egü+len-ip 'having become a group of three persons' > Tuv. üžēlēn 'three together, (as) a group of three persons, three at a time' (F.G. Ischakov, cited after MTof. 122 sq.). – The semantic and

---

[5]   Additionally, its morphological structure is not quite clear. Even if one understands al... in +aldyrzy as an element other than āl... in +ālā(n) one will not readily accept the explanation of this suffix as a composition of *+al- (verb formation) + *-dyr- (causative) + *+y+zy (double possessive suffix), as GTuv. 211 sq. puts it, because, firstly, there seems to be no need for reconstructing a *double* possessive suffix, and, secondly, a possessive suffix cannot be attached directly to a verbal stem.

categorial change is well known in the Siberian and the Kipchak Turkic languages.[6] Nevertheless, some objections should be raised here. Apocope of the gerund -*p* can often be observed in Khakass and in Shor; it sometimes occurs in Tuvinian, too, but it is unknown from the other Turkic languages. Meanwhile, the forms in ...*lan* are attested also in some other areals, e.g. Old Uzb. +*ala(n)*, Uyg. +*i(j)len*, Kar. and KBalk. +*awlan*, and so on (MTof. 123). Besides, Ischakov's interpretation leaves the moveable ...*n* unexplained.

Ischakov's and Pal'mbach's other etymology connects the final ...*n* with the participle suffix -*gan* (GTuv. 211), i.e. +*ālān* < *+*agu*+*lā-gan*. – Here, too, the moveable character of the final ...*n* remains unclear, and their comment that *onālā* is apparently a «truncated form» ("по-видимому [sic!], является усеченной формой") cannot be called an explanation at all. Nevertheless, the very existence of formations with the compound suffix *+*agu*+*lā-gan* seems quite sure in view of attestations like Nog. *onawlagan* 'ten at a time' (GTuv. 211). Furthermore, formations like Nog. *onlagan*, Kzk. *ondagan* id. show that the suffix *+*lā-gan* could have also been attached to cardinal numbers.[7] But then, how did the forms without ...*n* (like Tuv. *onālā* id.) emerge?

A different interpretation again comes from V. I. Rassadin: If the element ...*l*... is an old marker of collectivity,[8] then: +*ālān* < *+*agu* (coll.) + *+*l* (coll.) + *+*(u)n* (instr.) (MTof. 123). – In this case, however, the vowel preceding the *+*n* causes problems because it is both long and low whereas the vowel of the Turkic instrumental is short and high: *+*un*. A merging like *+*lā* + *+*un* > *+*lān* is also out of the question because, first, it is usually the final vowel of the preceding syllable that is dropped in the Turkic languages and, besides, no nominal suffix *+*lā* is known.

In this situation, I am rather inclined to suggest a morphologically somewhat more complex structure, yet one that can explain forms both with and without ...*n*.

In view of Nog. *onlagan*, Kzk. *ondagan* 'ten at a time' the existence of the verb *ōn*+*lā*- may be considered certain (although its – transitive? – meaning cannot; 'to act ten at a time'?). In view of Nog. *onawlagan* id. the verb *ōn*+*agu*+*lā*-, too,

---

[6] Cf. Tuv. *orusta*- 'to speak Russian' > *orustap* 'in Russian; по-русски'; Chul. *čaŋy* 'new' > *čaŋy-la-p* 'having made anew' > *čaŋlap* > *čallap* 'again' (Pomorska 2004: 150).

[7] Some additional new questions can be posed in this context: If *+*lā-gan* formations can be accepted as certain do they also make possible the existence of hypothetical +*lan*- verbs from which Ischakov's and Pal'mbach's *+*lan-yp* gerunds could be derived? What was the semantic difference between: (a) *+*lā*- and *+*lan*- derivatives from numerals?; (b) *+*lā-gan* derivatives from collective and those from cardinal numbers?

Besides, if ...*dyr*... in Tuv. +*aldyrzy* (see (3a) above) really is a causative suffix (GTuv. 211 sq.) [which does not, however, sound very convincing in view of the following syllable ...*zy*, allegedly being a possessive suffix (GTuv. 211 sq.) – attached to a verbal stem?; with ...*z*... after the stem-final consonant?] and the preceding syllable al... is the verbal suffix +*al*- (as in *saryg* 'yellow' > *sarg*+*al*- 'to turn yellow') the whole construction *+*al-dyr*- forms transitive verbs which is more or less astonishing from the viewpoint of collective numbers with their meaning 'being / having become (so and so many persons at a time)'. On the other hand, +*lā*- verbs (whose existence cannot be denied because of Nog. *on(aw)lagan*, see above) also display transitive senses.

[8] For this interpretation of the consonant *l* in +*lar* (plural), +*lyg* (adjectives of possession) and +*lӳn* (Yakut comitative case) see Kotwicz 1936: 30. The idea was first suggested in Böhtlingk 1848.

should be regarded as sure. Now, the Tuvinian form *onālān* might be accepted as a Tuvinian phonetic reflex of **ōn+agu+lā-gan* (> Nog. *onawlagan*), as was suggested by Ischakov and Pal'mbach (GTuv. 211). Then, however, the form *onālā* remains unexplained.

That is why I would rather start with *onālā* which can be explained as an old substantive in **-g*, i.e. Tuv. *onālā* < *ōn 'ten' + **+agu* (coll.) + **+lā-* (verb) + **-g* (deverbal substantive). Thus, its morphological meaning was roughly 'a group of those (**-g*) who became/acted (**+lā-*) all together (**+agu*) (in groups of / a group of) ten (*ōn)', i.e. ≈ 'a group of ten acting together'.

For Tuv. *onālān* 'ten at a time' two explanations are possible: either one suggested by Ischakov and Pal'mbach (< **ōn+agu+lā-gan*) or one based on instrumental derivation from *onālā*, i.e. **ōn+agu+lā-g* (> Tuv. *onālā*) + **+un* (instr.) > Tuv. *onālān*.

In none of the cases above can *onālā* be viewed as a «truncated form». Moreover, this derivation avoids the collective element ...*l*... whose precise meaning and very existence in Proto-Turkic are highly debatable even today.

5.

Let us move on now to conclusions concerning areal connections:

(5a)   The basic idea of a morphological category of collective numerals exists in most of the Turkic languages. Consequently, it can be accepted for the Proto-Turkic language, too. Its marker was the suffix **+agu* whose direct modern reflexes are: Yak. *+ya*, Oyr. *+ū* ~ *+u*,[9] Kirg. *+ō*, Tat. *+aw*, Kar. KBalk. Uzb. *+ow*. In other words, the consistency among these data results from their common protolanguage starting point and, for this reason, does not yield any information concerning areal connections and later morphological innovations in individual Turkic languages.

(5b)   Reflexes of the instrumental suffix **+(u)n* attached to the collective suffix **+agu* can only be found in Yakut and Dolgan (*+yan*) on the one hand, as well as in Todža and Tofalar (*+ān*) on the other. Indeed, this cannot be but a regional innovation, missing everywhere else and, by the same token, suggesting that this combination (**+agu+n* (adv.) 'such and such a number of persons at a time') forms an isogloss connecting Yakut and Dolgan with Tofalar and Tuvinian (represented in this context, however, by one dialect only).

(5c)   Rassadin's cautious conjecture that the Kipchak suffix *+ālyn* might have been created under the influence of Uyg. *+(j)lan* (MTof. 123 sq.) – whether correct or not – cannot be automatically extended to Tuvaic and Sakhaic, i.e. the languages that attach the instrumental suffix directly to the nominal **+agu* stem

---

[9]   For Oyrot, only a short vowel suffix *+u* is adduced in GOjr. 84, whereas MTof. 122 has only *+ū*. The fact that the literary Oyrot adjective suffix is *+lu* ~ *+lū* (its North Oyrot dialectal correspondence being *+lyg*, cf. e.g. North Oyr. *tattyg* 'sweet' = liter. Oyr. *tattu* ~ *tattū* id., GOjr. 25) makes it possible to accept a parallel alternation for the collective suffix.

and therefore have modern reflexes without the consonant ...*l*... which would point to a verbal derivational base.

(5d) The idea that the verb based suffixes with ...*l*... and the noun based ones without ...*l*... were created everywhere in the Turkic linguistic world in exactly the same period does not sound convincing. Rather, the noun based suffixes without ...*l*... but with the instrumental *+*(u)n* (Yakut, Dolgan, Todža, Tofalar) came into being first. It can even be imagined that a reflex of *+agu+n* originally covered the whole Tuvinian territory but was, over time, replaced by a newer construction with *+agu+lā-g(+un)* that expanded from west to east. What ensued was an asymmetrical distribution: the older form +*ān* is now limited to Todža only, that is, to the north-eastern edge of the Tuvinian linguistic community (and preserved in still more northern languages like Tofalar, Yakut and Dolgan) whereas the newer construction +*ālā(n)* has dominated all the rest of the Tuvinian territory.

(5e) As was suggested in (5d) above, the Tuvinian (Todža)-Tofalar-Yakut-Dolgan *+agu+n* isogloss is, as a matter of fact, not just an areal innovation, but, rather, an areal preservation of an archaism that arose originally as an areal innovation.

References

GOjr. = Dyrenkova N.P. 1940. *Grammatika ojrotskogo jazyka*. Moskva, Leningrad.
GTuv. = Ischakov F.G., Pal'mbach A.A. 1961. *Grammatika tuvinskogo jazyka. Fonetika i morfologija*. Moskva.
JaND = Ubrjatova E.I. 1985. *Jazyk noril'skich dolgan*. Novosibirsk.
MTof. = Rassadin V.I. 1978. *Morfologija tofalarskogo jayzka v sravnitel'nom osveščenii*. Moskva.

Böhtlingk O. 1848. Kritische Bemerkungen zur zweiten Ausgabe von Kasem-beks türkisch-tatarischer Grammatik. – *Bulletin de la classe des sciences historiques, philologiques et politiques de l'Académie Impériale des Sciences de St. Pétersbourg* 117.V: 312–336.
Erdal M. 1991. *Old Turkic word formation. A functional approach to the lexicon*. [vol. 1]. Wiesbaden.
Erdal M. 2004. *A grammar of Old Turkic*. Leiden, Boston.
Kotwicz W. 1930. Contributions aux études altaïques. – *Rocznik Orjentalistyczny* 7: 130–234.
Kotwicz W. 1936. *Les pronoms dans les langues altaïques*. Kraków.
Menges K.H. 1955. The South Siberian Turkic languages. I: General characteristics of their phonology. – *Central Asiatic Journal* 1: 107–136.
Menges K.H. 1958/59. Die türkischen Sprachen Süd-Sibiriens, III: Tuba (Sojoŋ und Karaγas), 1. Zur Charakteristik einer einzelnen sibirisch-türkischen Gruppe. – *Central Asiatic Journal* 4: 90–129.
Menges K.H. 1959/60. Die türkischen Sprachen Süd-Sibiriens, III: Tuba (Sojoŋ und Karaγas), 2. Zur Charakteristik einer einzelnen sibirisch-türkischen Gruppe. – *Central Asiatic Journal* 5: 97–150.
Pomorska M. 2004. *Middle Chulym noun formation*. Kraków.

Sat Š.Č. 1997. Tuvinskij jazyk. – Tenišev È.R. et al. (eds.) *Jazyki mira – Tjurkskie jazyki*. Moskva: 384–393.

Schönig C. 1997. Wie entstand das Südsibirische Türkisch? – Kellner-Heinkele B., Zieme P. (eds.) *Studia Ottomanica*. [FS Gy. Hazai]. Wiesbaden: 147–163.

Schönig C. 2001. Some basic remarks on South Siberian Turkic and its position within North East Turkic and the Turkic language family. – *Dilbilim Araştırmaları* 2001: 63–95.

Stachowski M. 1991. Über jakutische Glossen im Werk von W. Sieroszewski. – Brendemoen B. (ed.) *Altaica Osloensia*. Oslo: 301–315.

Stachowski M. 1997. Bemerkungen zu Zahlwörtern sowie Datums- und Altersangaben im Dolganischen und Jakutischen. – Berta Á., Horváth E. (eds.) *Historical and linguistic interaction between Inner-Asia and Europe*. Szeged: 317–339.

Studia Linguistica Universitatis Iagellonicae Cracoviensis
128 (2011)

GRZEGORZ SZPILA
Jagiellonian University, Cracow

LITERARY PAREMIC LOCI
IN SALMAN RUSHDIE'S NOVELS

Keywords: proverbs, paremiostylistics, paremic loci, novels, Salman Rushdie

Abstract

The paper deals with the identification of proverbs in a literary text, which is believed to be the initial stage in the analysis of paremias in literary context and part and parcel of any paremiostylitic analysis. Proverbs manifest themselves in what the author calls a paremic locus. Paremias are present in a text on the formal level, where a particular proverb is signalled by its structure, either canonical or modified. Proverbs can be identified as well on the semantic plane, although in this case their presence is impossible to ascertain in objective terms. The author analyses the ten novels by Salman Rushdie, which all provide ample evidence of paremic loci.

An analysis of paremias in any written or spoken material must involve the stage of proverb identification. In fact, the identification of proverbs is a *sina qua non* for further analysis to take place. It is the initial requirement for any kind of paremic investigation, equally so for paremiostylistics, which I use to refer to an analysis of proverbs in literary texts (Szpila 2007, 2008a).[1] Only after all the proverbs have been registered, that is identified, can the next steps be taken by paremiologists and paremiostylisticians. We may of course wonder if there is an earlier stage in the analysis of proverbs in a literary text for example and indeed we could say perhaps that the process of identification may be eased as well as influenced by the specific characteristics of a literary genre, an author and his literary output as such. All such literary characteristics may make an analyst more sensitive to the paremiological or paremiostylistic character of the text he is studying. The list of proverbs established

---

[1]   In its broader sense paremiostylistics is an investigation of proverbs in all kinds of discourse.

for a particular text, a fragment of a text or indeed a collection of texts (by the same writer, for instance) is a result of what I call a paremic or phraseological reading of text, that is such reading which focuses on the identification and interpretation of all the potential phraseological and paremiological loci therein (cf. Szpila 2009a). In fact, only such a list provides the ultimate evidence of the phraseological / paremic character of the material studied. On the other hand, however, the overall metaphorical character of a text, which may be to a lesser or greater extent due to phraseological metaphors, can easily make the identification of proverbs a more difficult process as some seemingly paremic metaphors can simply not be meant to be proverbial at all and should perchance be treated as novel metaphors instead.

In this article I would like to focus exclusively on the process of the identification of proverbs in literature, with the novels by Salman Rushdie serving as illustrations. Rushdie's books are extremely useful as they provide not an inconsiderable number of examples of paremic as well as phraseological loci. I consider Rushdie to be a phraseological writer as he makes use of many a phraseological unit, which represent all possible phraseological categories, as well as many proverbs (my corpus comprises over 100 proverbs – paremic types – and over 200 actualizations – paremic tokens – in all his ten novels so far).[2]

To start with I would like to define a paremic locus, whose identification I would like to address in the subsequent paragraphs. A paremic locus is a narrative space (any text space) which can be matched with a proverb. A paremic locus is not necessarily to be associated with a proverb's form: a paremic locus can be a proverb in its canonical form, which is the prototypical paremic locus, but it may be any stretch of text which delineates the boundaries of a proverb's presence and manifestation. Neither is the paremic locus to be identified as a narrative space which is within a proverb's referential scope. A paremic locus is where we see a signal, either semantic or formal or both, of a proverb, which then is analysed as applying to various elements of the text, so it is a question of the proverbs' function with reference to a novel's plot and its interpretable semantics. This physical anchoring of a proverb may be then scrutinized against the semantics of the text and described in terms of the proverb's micro- and macrofunctions as well as hyper- and metafunctions (cf. Szpila 2009b).

As paremic loci are not necessarily proverbs in their canonical forms, not all of them can be identified without difficulty. It may happen of course that an analysed text comprises proverbs in their unmodified standard – canonical – forms and no other proverbs are found in less obvious paremic loci. Rushdie's novels do not fall into this category and therefore they are a valuable source of information concerning the ways in which proverbs may manifest their presence in literary texts. As might be expected, examples of paremic loci which can be matched with proverbs are found in his novels, for example: *Easier said than done* (SV 401), *Patience is a virtue* (H 97),

---

[2]   A detailed analysis of the forms and functions of proverbs in Salman Rushdie's novels can be found in Szpila (2008a).

Every cloud has a silver lining (MC 425), *If the cap fits, wear it* (G 179), *Practice makes perfect* (G 166). These proverbs are used in the respective novels in their unaltered forms. It may happen of course that within one literary corpus (all Rushdie's novels, for example), a proverb is used in more ways than one and its manifestations need to be described and classified differently. It is interesting to note at this point that in the analysed corpus about 70% of the proverbs are modified and only 30% are used by the novelist in their unaltered forms (cf. Szpila 2008a). So only the latter figure accounts for the most prototypical occurrences, with the remaining 70% manifesting their semantics through a variety of semantic and formal textual actualizations. When saying that a proverb is used prototypically in its unaltered form, I do not mean that this is how proverbs in general are used and that only in literature are they actualized differently. It would go against the intuitive as well as research-based observations to say that proverbs are not employed in innumerable ways in everyday communication, a fact which is reflected in literary texts. Obviously, literary language permits greater freedom in the creative manipulation of both the form and semantics of proverbs, but the differences are perhaps only in the quantity, not the quality of deployment.

On the strength of the above we can say that the identification of proverbs used in their unaltered forms is the easiest task of all and therefore I treat them here as prototypical uses as well as a starting point for any investigation. This applies as well to foreign proverbs which may be cited in their original form, for example: *Noblesse oblige* (*MLS* 333). If there is a likelihood of the proverb remaining unidentified the writer may resort to signalling the proverbial status of a structure via various textual markers of this genre. The most obvious is to simply name a locus proverbial by referring to the fixed expression in an appropriate way, by means of metatextual elements (cf., for instance, Barkema 1996: 145, Lüger 1996: 94), as in, for example, *EF* (169), the paremia *The end justifies the means* is called "a profound principle" and the proverb *Never look a gift horse in the mouth* in *EF* (269) is simply called a proverb. The quotational status of proverbs, their echoic status (Sperber and Wilson 1986: 238–239), is signalled in "He moves in mysterious ways: men say" (*SV* 95) or even by punctuation as in "I would like to say only this: that charity begins at home" (*GBHF* 134).

By the same token, the writer may refer to familiarity as a feature of all fixed expressions, for example: "Where there's a will, etc., I couldn't help thinking" (*GBHF* 189) and "don't look a gift horse andsoforth" (*SV* 39), with the markers of familiarity serving to activate the mental lexicon and steer our attention towards the stock of memorized items. Even in "Because a cat may look at a queen" (*GBHF* 385) the subordinator serves as a marker of familiarity as it refers to proverbs since a reservoir of familiar arguments.

These different references to the genre of proverb structure employed help to classify paremias easily even if a given proverb itself is not used in its canonical form(s) (cf. *GBHF* 385, *EF* 269). Indeed, it seems that by signalling their status among other expressions a writer is no longer interested in playing with their form and semantics, so the unmistaken evocation of the proverbs in the reader's mind comes to the fore. The function of such markers is to match a particular proverb with a particular text space.

Both canonical forms of proverbs and proverbiality markers of all types are not that frequent in the analysed novels. Consequently the identification of the remaining paremias may present various degrees of difficulty. The difficulty increases with the extent to which a given proverb in modified, that is when the canonical form has to be established, most importantly for the purpose of reference, through an intricate process of interpreting the modified form and matching it with its standard form. The difficulty is even greater when the semantics of a locus is not immediately apparent to the reader. Such cases cover all manner of textual operations on both the form and semantics of paremias, however, it is not my aim to analyse all of them. Let me just provide certain examples to illustrate my point: "WHERE THERE'S A WILL. The realization of his own power, of Virgil Jones' meaning, dawned on him" (*G* 72), "No accounting for tastes, that's all" (*SV* 7), "Nothing to it but organization; old Army habit, dies darn hard" (*MC* 311), "Love does not conquer all, except in the Bombay talkies; rip tear crunch will not be defeated by a mere ceremony; and optimism is a disease" (*MC* 444), "Violence was violence, murder was murder, two wrongs did not make a right: these are truths of which I was fully cognisant" (*MLS* 365), "Did you not see the everyday live-and-let-live miracles thronging its overcrowded streets?" (*MLS* 351). These examples show operations of subtraction, addition, as well as grammatical modifications and syntactic function shift. They are only a fraction of all the operations Rushdie uses to contextualize his proverbs (cf. Szpila 2008a). I would claim, however, that the identification of the corresponding proverbs is not significantly hindered. The subtraction of a proverb's elements, for example, is as frequent as the quoting proverbs in their complete forms and nowise is it difficult to establish a paremic locus (cf. Hewings, Hewings 2005: 96). However, we must not treat all alterations as insignificant in this respect as some may without doubt obscure the paremic picture. Paremic loci are occasionally marked by the significant lexical items of a proverb which serve as allusive devices (cf. Szpila 2008b). The allusive use of proverbs is a further strategy of proverb deployment, with the identification of the proverb alluded to is not difficult as the allusive loci contain characteristic elements of the proverbs. Identification is also necessary to interpret the intended meanings, cf. "Wasn't that a flying pig" (*GBHF* 293), "The old problem of ends and means" (*F* 227), "Pot and kettle, replied the voice. Mote and beam." (*G* 91), "'Talk about pot and kettle,' he said. Question of mote and beam" (*SV* 278). These examples contain unmistaken reference to the respective proverbs and cannot be analysed without direct reference to them. Sometimes proverbial allusion may not be so obvious as the proverbial elements in question may be interpreted metaphorically without any reference to the semantics of the corresponding proverb. However, it is worth pondering to what extent the interpretation of such loci is determined by the reader's paremic knowledge and to what extent, on the other hand, we can construe the intended meaning without direct access to the proverb. And also, to what extent did Rushdie manipulate the proverb structure, did he simply apply the individual meanings to the elements without ever thinking of the proverb in question or did he intend to put the reader in mind of the proverb regardless of the ease with which the latter (reader) might interpret the fragment non-paremically?

The most interesting cases which have inspired me to focus on the recognition stage in a paremio-stylistic analysis are what I call, broadly speaking, and for lack of a better term, proverbial paraphrases. These are loci which semantically correspond to particular proverbs and function pragmatically as the latter, but which express the proverbial sense in totally different or alternative ways. The pragmatic context and the similarity to the proverbial images make us consider such loci as paremic in nature. Let us take the following as illustrative examples: "Mr Gibreel Farishta on the railway train to London was once again seized as who would not be by the fear that God had decided to punish him for his loss of faith by driving him insane" (*SV* 189) and "'God chooses many means', Ayesha rejoiced, 'many roads by which the doubtful may be brought into his certainty.'" (*SV* 240). To me the former example corresponds to *Whom the gods would destroy they first make mad* and the latter to *God moves in mysterious ways* (cf. *SV* 95). Probably, it is impossible to give a precise definition of a paremic paraphrase, or how similar or how different it should be from the corresponding proverb. Is, for example, the following: "the cover is not the best guide to the book" (*SV* 257) a paraphrase of *You can't tell a book by its cover* or not?

Sometimes, even a large stretch of narrative may feel to the reader as an extended version of a particular proverb. This could be illustrated by the following paragraph from *The satanic verses* (134), which could perhaps be matched with the proverb *An Englishman's home is his castle*:

> Usually she was implacable in defence of her beloved fragment of the coast, and when summer weekenders strayed above the high tide line she descended upon them *like a wolf on the fold*, her phrase for it, to explain and to demand: – This is my garden, do you see. – And if they grew brazen, – getoutofitsillyoldmoo, itsthesoddingbeach, – she would return home to bring out a long green garden hose and turn it remorselessly upon their tartan blankets and plastic cricket bats and bottles of sun-tan lotion, she would smash their children's sandcastles and soak their liver-sausages, smiling sweetly all the while: *You won't mind if I just water my lawn?*

But it is probably pushing his luck on the reader's part to consider this as a paremic locus in which the proverb remains unspoken while the narrative begs to be summarized in the precious few words of the proverb. Such type of the semantic presence of a proverb is arguably the most elusive to prove, as the matching is a subjective operation on the part of the reader.

Yet another class of doubtful paremic loci is the following: proverbs that correspond to idioms which are treated as their allusions (Moon 1998: 29, 113) such as **Forbidden fruit** *is sweet* (*GBHF* 84, 129), *It is* **the last straw** *that breaks the camel's back* (*GBHF* 351), and **The rotten apple** *injures its neighbours* (*SC* 373). They are systemic allusions unlike novel textual ones and they can be omitted if we treat them as idioms only. In my approach to proverbs and idioms, however, I treat such fixed expressions as paremias but due to their unquestionable relationship to idioms I consider them as peripheral, as also they are infrequent.

Last but not least, when identifying proverbs in a literary text such as a novel we may encounter apparently paremic loci but it is questionable which proverb they contain or refer to as there may be two or even more proverbs that can be matched with them. A case in point would undoubtedly be a contamination of two or more proverbs which may occur, however, to the best of my knowledge there is no example of paremic contamination in Rushdie's novels unlike idiomatic contamination which are found therein. I have found one example of a paremic locus which may illustrate this point, namely: "Once divided, always divided" (*MLS* 49). This paremic locus can be matched with *A house divided against itself cannot stand*. This matching is made possible not only due to the similarity of the lexical content of the quote with the proverbial content but also due to the proverb being used in the novel three more times (1, 34, 99), and where all of the actualizations are semantically co-referential with reference to the theme of the novel. The reference to the proverb is reinforced as if by one of the frequent proverbial structures: *Once ... (sth), always ... (sth)*. The example then is a contamination of a concrete paremia and a paremic structure which carries the logico-semantic value of the proverbs which have this particular surface form. Moreover, not all expressions which share this or similar structures with established paremias can be legitimately defined as paremic loci. The justification should be sought in the semantics and functions they perform in the text *vis à vis* paremic senses and roles.

Apart from this type of contamination many paremic loci in Rushdie's novels have to be matched with the same or similar proverbial structural skeletons and the textually bound formations may be treated as either referring to a particular proverb or rather its formal syntactic schemata. For instance: "One betrayal often deserves another" (*EF* 292), "Once a scam man, always a ditto" (*SV* 262), "One boy's Paradise could be another fellow's Hell" (*SV* 203), "Surprise is the best policy" (*SV* 156) and "Murder breeds death" (*MC* 271). Here again we may be tempted to refer these loci to the proverbs *One good turn deserves another, Once a thief, always a thief, One man's meat is another man's poison, Honesty is the best policy* and *Familiarity breeds contempt*. Nevertheless, it remains out of the realm of possibility to decide if Rushdie uses these proverbs as structural templates only or has intended to play with their form and semantics. It has to be stated that the novel expressions do not modify the meanings of the quoted proverbs but they drink deep of the logical relations established by them which can be used to express other truths, however personal, subjective and situation-bound as they may be. I am tempted to treat such paremic locis as border line cases again occupying a position between the reference to particular proverbs on the one hand and the reflection of the polyfunctionality of some proverbial structures on the other.

And last and perhaps not least again, peripherally located are "new proverbs" or "pseudo-proverbs", original formulations of a principle, or truth aspiring to the status of paremia as being universally applicable. We can find such examples in Rushdie's novels and although such loci cannot be matched with any existing proverbs, we can say that they are proverbial in nature, viz. they are categorically matched with proverbs as a category of signs. A case in point might be: "Proper sowing ensures a good harvest" (*S* 153) or "A compulsory ocean sounds worse than a forbidden well" (*SV* 240).

I have essayed to highlight only a few ways in which proverbs can manifest themselves in a literary text and some problems which arise at the level of paremic recognition in texts. Although Rushdie's novels serve as good examples of paremic actualizations, due to the frequency of their occurrence as well as the multifaceted character of their actualization, this description cannot be treated as exhaustive. I hope I have managed to show yet again some of the difficulties which await a paremiostylistician at a very early stage of a paremic analysis of a literary text. Further studies of literature and proverbs deployed therein in all likelihood will reveal further problems as regards the recognition stage of paremic presences in literary texts as well as some ways of solving them.

References

Barkema H. 1996. Idiomaticity and terminology: A multi-dimensional descriptive model. – *Studia Linguistica* 50.2: 125–160.

Hewings A., Hewings M. 2005. *Grammar and context*. London, New York.

Lüger H.-H. 1996. Satzwertige Phraseologismen im Text. Elemente eines Mehrebenen-modells. – *Beiträge zur Fremdsprachenvermittlung* 30: 76–103.

Moon R. 1998. *Fixed expressions and idioms in English*. Oxford.

Sperber D., Wilson D. 1986. *Relevance. Communication and cognition*. Oxford.

Szpila G. 2007. Paremiologia a stylistyka. – *Stylistyka* XVI: 613–632.

Szpila G. 2008a. Paremic verses: proverbial, meanings in Salman Rushdie's novels. – *Journal of Literary Semantics* 72: 97–127.

Szpila G. 2008b. Paremic allusions in Salman Rushdie's novels. – *Proverbium* 25: 379–397.

Szpila G. 2009a. In search of phraseo-sense: Salman Rushdie's idiomatic meanings. – Chrzanowska-Kluczewska E., Szpila G. (eds.) *In search of (non)sense*. Newcastle upon Tyne: 88–99.

Szpila G. 2009b. Physical anchoring and referential scope of idioms and proverbs in literature. – Fedulenkova T. (ed.) *Cross-linguistic and cross-cultural approaches to phraseology*. Arkhangelsk, Aarhus: 171–181.

Salman Rushdie's novels

EF = Rushdie S. 2008. *The enchantress of Florence*. London.

F = Rushdie S. 2001. *Fury*. New York.

G = Rushdie S. 1996. *Grimus*. London.

GBHF = Rushdie S. 1999. *The ground beneath her feet*. New York.

H = Rushdie S. 1991. *Haroun and the sea of stories*. London.

MC = Rushdie S. 1995. *Midnight's children*. London.

MLS = Rushdie S. 1996. *The Moor's last sigh*. London.

S = Rushdie S. 1995. *Shame*. London.

SC = Rushdie S. 2005. *Shalimar the clown*. London.

SV = Rushdie S. 1998. *The satanic verses*. London.

Studia Linguistica Universitatis Iagellonicae Cracoviensis
128 (2011)

ANNA TERESZKIEWICZ
Jagiellonian University, Cracow

RHETORICAL STRATEGIES ON WWW.IREPORT.COM

Keywords: user-generated content online, participatory websites, discourse analysis

Abstract

The study concentrates on the phenomenon of user-generated content on the internet. The article presents an introductory analysis of various rhetorical strategies used by the authors of commentaries on one of the popular user-contributory sites, i.e. www.iReport.com. The analysis of this site shows that there exists a range of diverse means of expression used by the enthusiasts of broadcasting online, involving the submission of written articles, live video commentaries, audio files and cartoons. The study shows that users shape the features of the content in different manners and resort to the use of a variety of rhetorical devices. To the main properties of discourse belong personalization, interactivity, use of figurative and vivid language.

As the title suggests, the study aims to review the rhetorical strategies used in online commentaries on www.iReport.com, a user-generated website. The research focuses on examples of user-created content on the web specifically, because it is in this medium that the phenomenon has seen a dynamic increase.

My aim was to examine the means which amateur commentators use in order to present the news, opinions and commentaries and also the degree to which they exploit the affordances of the internet. I hypothesized that the lack of editorial insight and also the technological possibilities should encourage the contribution of uninhibited, unrestrained and deeply varied content.

I. User-generated content

The phenomenon of user-participation in the creation of online content has developed significantly during the last few years, due to the affordances of internet technologies. The advent of Web 2.0 technologies, which contributed to the wide-spread use of easy publishing tools and mobile devices, has played a special role in the spread of this phenomenon. Web 2.0, in contrast to its predecessor, Web 1.0, places more emphasis on the content produced by users, on their active participation in information exchange and their contribution of various data to websites (cf. Cormode and Krishnamurthy 2008, Harrison and Barthel 2009). In this way, the online audience has turned into an active participant in the process of producing online content and publishing commentaries and other type of data (Bowman and Willis 2003: 7). The Web 2.0 applications include video-sharing web sites, such as YouTube, networking sites, such as Facebook, MySpace, collaborative knowledge portals and encyclopedias, such as Knol or H2G2.

II. iReport.com

For the following study, I chose one of the popular user-contributory sites, i.e. iReport.com. The headline of the site – "Unedited. Unfiltered. News" – describes the basic characteristics of the project. The content of the site is generated by users and is not moderated by the editors before its publication. Moderation of the news can be performed after the message has been published on the website, as the community has the right to block a message if it is vulgar or defamatory. The basic and most conspicuous characteristic of the site is semiotic intertextuality, as it presents both textual, audio and video content. Still images dominate on the site, especially live commentaries and graphic representations. (Fig. 1.)

What follows is an introductory content analysis of the project in question. The material for the following analysis comprises 243 messages which achieved the status of the most viewed and most commented in August and September 2009. To the most frequent channels of expression belong video files, graphic messages and textual commentaries. Due to a heterogeneous shape of the site, the study required the application of different methods of analysis of the content. In the following research, we present the most conspicuous properties of each of the types of the comments, presenting content analysis of the page, with special focus on the linguistic properties of the messages, i.e. their discourse properties, syntactic and lexical features. This description should be treated as an introductory presentation of the research area in question, as each of the channels of expression calls for a more profound study of their shape.

The first look at the collection of the messages proves that it is considerably varied, ranging from plain, commonplace messages to very sophisticated commentaries and complex video files. The posts are characterized by ingenuity and daring, which is a direct consequence of the freedom of publication on the site. Since the authors are not constrained and influenced by editors or gatekeepers, they can enjoy a significantly greater autonomy in the choice of the subject and shape of the message. A review of the messages allows us to observe that the authors resort to the use of different rhetorical devices to present their point of view and to influence the audience.

1. Video files (56%, 136 messages)

As mentioned above, video files belong to the most frequent channels exploited by the authors. On average, every 2 minutes a new movie is added to the site, which is a sign of the dynamic activity of the community of users. The messages transmitted in the movies as well as the behaviour of the users deserve closer attention as they exhibit interesting properties. The most conspicuous features of the language of video messages are personalization, interactivity, as well as figurative and vivid style.

1.1 Personalization

The first feature worth noting is the personalization of the posts. The commentaries have a strong personal touch. The authors quote stories of their own life and present their personal experiences. This feature, characteristic of the majority of the posts in the material analyzed, can be illustrated in the movie posted by a user named OCGirl, presenting a commentary on the celebration of Mother's Day. (Fig. 2.)

> Hey everybody
> I am not only a super mom but I'm a cool mom as well. And the reason I say that is that ever since my boys were small I have never ever grounded them. And the reason I have never believed in grounding my boys is that when you just ground somebody and send them to a room or have them stand in the corner your are not really teaching them to resolve issues so whenever my boys get into a fight or argue with each other I literally have them talk it out like in a presidential debate. That's what I do is because I think that the earlier we can start communication with kids at a younger age the more it can help them for the rest of their lives.

The author of this message concentrates on herself, quotes her personal experiences with raising children and cites her methods of educating them. Personalization is visible in the frequent references to the self, in the use of 1st person pronouns (*I'm a super mom, I teach them, my boys*). She tries to convince the viewer that she is right in her approach and encourages him/her to follow her methods. This may be also observed in the opposition between *I* and *you*, which she introduces (*when you ground somebody…*), in order to prove that what *you* do is wrong. A further point is the use of inclusive *we* (*the earlier we can start communication…*), which stands for the group of parents or caretakers who are all encouraged to act in the manner proposed by the speaker.

1.2 Interactivity

The aforementioned references to viewers signal a further characteristic of the messages apart from personalization, that is their profoundly dialogical and interactive nature. The authors in the messages posted on the site frequently provoke the audience and invite the readers to enter into a discussion and to exchange opinions. The dialogical character of the messages is manifested in direct references to viewers, in questions directed at listeners, in the use of the 1st and 2nd person plural pronouns (e.g. *we, you*). All these means enhance the contact of the authors with the receivers and mark solidarity with them.

1.3 Figurative style

The authors, in order to make their expressions more vivid, frequently resort to the use of figurative language – incorporating analogies, metaphors or similes. For instance, the user identified as Adriana presented a video in which she expresses just one sentence – *the pig is already in the air and has already landed*. Though the commentary is short, it is meaningful and rich in content, and can be seen as an example of a double metaphor. In this statement, the user refers to two important events which were hotly discussed on the internet, i.e. the flight of the President's airplane above Manhattan and the spread of the so-called swine flu at the end of April. In this short and simple message she expressed her negative attitude towards the flight of the plane, which terrified many people and brought back the events of 9/11. At the same time though, she has passed on the news about the first instance of the virus confirmed in the USA (the pig has landed, i.e. the virus has come).

This particular tendency towards figurativeness of description and also exemplification of certain phenomena can be seen in the following movie, in which the author describes the state of American economic situation by comparing it to an airplane. (Fig. 3.)

> You know our nation, is really nothing more than a big fancy airliner flying in the sky. It has a number of things that make it work. It has two wings – a right wing and a left wing, it has a tail which is a kind of centre of things. And most important it has a pilot who controls. Our nation and this airplane is on a diet now caused by a failing economy. The airplane is beginning to spin and fall towards the earth. Now it's a time that all the various parts must stay intact and connected to the airplane. And the pilot, whoever that person is, we have to trust that he knows what he's doing. People from the back of the plane should be deterred from rushing up and grabbing the controls. More than one person on the controls can lead to serious problem of confusion. At a very critical time this nation must pull together, because if the airplane doesn't stay together the chances of pulling it out of the dark are rather remote my friend.

As the author states – America, just like an airplane, has two wings (political parties), the centre, and the pilot (the President) who controls the flight. Due to the economic crisis, American industry is deteriorating – that is the plane has started to go down. The speaker uses the extended simile, which has certain features of allegory as well, to make the message more evocative to viewers and thus to encourage cooperation in the nation and trust in the President in order to go through the difficult period. The user resorts as well to non-verbal means of expression. The message he wants to transmit is enhanced by his appearance, as he is wearing a pilot's cap.

1.4 Vivid style

The user quoted above, who calls himself Dimmit, is especially creative. In his live comments, he often applies additional, non-verbal strategies to supplement and intensify his message. This can be seen in the following post where he presents his opinion on gun control in America, holding a gun in his hand and wearing another characteristic cap. (Fig. 4.)

There's nothing that makes me feel more secure than my gun. I feel manly when I hold it. It's an AKC 40 caliber Mauser Revolver. And I've even taken lessons on how to shoot it, I went to one of those safety classes. I hear people talking of gun control. I didn't like to idea of gun control, but then many years ago one man climbed up a tower of one of the prestigious universities and started shooting people with a long gun and I said, My God, we need to control these bloody things, so I've given a though all over the years and the reality is this, we cannot control the gun. It's been invented, the same as the computer has been invented. It's really hard to uninvent something, once it is, so if anybody could present a plan of gun control that would really work, then I might be for it. But the reality is there's no way to control the guns. We just control the guns of the honest people, not the bad guys – they'll always get the guns, and there's nothing worse than to be in a situation when the other guy's got a gun and is shooting at you and you don't have a gun. It's just a bad position to be in. So, I won't support gun control, unless somebody comes with a plan that really works.

Due to the non-verbal means used, the message is presented with exceptional vividness, which is additionally enhanced by the deeply rhetorical nature of the expression. The tone of the message is intensely persuasive – with the very first sentence, which is a strong assertion about the importance of the gun in his life, the user tries to convince the viewer of the advantages of possessing a gun. Similarly, the next sentence, though simple and short, expresses a close association between the possession of a weapon and masculinity. The user also resorts to straightforward statements of truth, such as *the reality is this, we cannot control the gun, there's no way to control the guns*, etc. These strong affirmations are to convince the addressee that no other solution to the problem is possible. In addition, persuasive tone of the message is achieved by the exemplification of the message with real-life situations, where the user quotes both authentic events (gunfire at university) and fictitious, yet probable, situations. Rhetorical nature of this post is combined with orality and informality, which are manifested in the presence of interjections, the use of colloquialisms and contractions.

This video also illustrates the above-mentioned personalization – the user quotes his own feelings and experiences associated with the possession of a gun (the use of personal pronouns *I, my, me*). There are also elements of interactivity to be found – when he refers to the viewers directly (*the other guy is shooting at you and you don't have a gun*).

In both cases, the non-verbal strategies support the textual message, highlight and enhance the point being made and make it more effective. The introduction of unexpected effects at the end (i.e. the user is lighting a cigarette and suddenly the "smoke police" knock on the door, at which point he chooses to use his gun) aim at achieving maximum appeal and originality of the message.

The use of figurative and vivid language, and the use of non-verbal means of expression make the messages more expressive, eye-catching and appealing, but also easier to digest by the users, and bring the message closer to their concrete experience. They help convince listeners and persuade them towards accepting the viewpoint of the author. Thus, they enhance the expressive function of the message, as well as its impressive and aesthetic functions. Their role is to influence the viewers' opinions, to amaze and / or surprise them and to affect their imagination.

These videos illustrate different approaches toward the form of the presentations. On the one side, we have the presentations recorded in plain rooms and halls without much care devoted to the background or to the appearance of the speaker. On the other side, the rooms are carefully designed, perhaps recording studios, with well-thought out scenography and ornamentation of the message. These examples show that the introduction of video commentary allows the authors to achieve a more credible and direct experience than would be possible with text messages alone.

2. Graphic representations (23%, 55 posts)

In addition to live commentaries, users present their opinions and comments in graphic form, i.e. with a cartoon or a drawing. Although such forms are also present in traditional media, the online drawings deserve mentioning due to their great variation and the creativity of their authors. The lack of the above mentioned editorial restraints allows users not to be constrained by standard conventions or rules of political correctness.

In designing their pictures, the authors utilize a variety of means of expression, among which, the following are the most frequent:

1. The use of cultural symbols, characters and book heroes
    The first frequent means of expression is by reference to common film and book heroes, e.g.:
    a. famous movie doctors – the author of the collage uses popular doctor-characters from movies and cartoons (e.g. Dr Quinn, Dr House, Dr Hibbert), suggesting that their help could be sought in the face of swine-flu. (Fig. 5.)
    b. Star Trek – the author refers to the characters of Star Trek to describe the activities of the Democrats. He compares the party to the Borg (i.e. an integrated collective formed through forced assimilation; they do not exhibit a desire for negotiation or reason). (Fig. 6.)
    c. Hulk – comparing President Barack Obama to the Incredible Hulk, as a reaction to the overuse of the word *outrage* by the President. (Fig. 7.)

2. Usage of cultural symbols in word plays
    Users as well refer to cultural symbols, as in the following picture, where the title *Encyclopedia Baracobama* can be seen as a blend of the proper name *Barack Obama* and the noun *Americana*, thus being a clear reference to the *Encyclopedia Americana*. (Fig. 8.)

3. Drawings describing recent events
    A further frequent method of expressing one's opinion via an image is the use of drawings. In Fig. 9, the user shows a negative attitude to the extensive coverage

of the news concerning the spread of swine flu, which is broadcast at the expense of the discussion of other problems.

Graphic representations frequently have the role of supplementing textual messages, which constitute the last type of files.

3. Textual messages (21%, 52 messages)

These messages comprise only textual content. As such they exhibit similar characteristics to the posts which can be found on discussion forums. The basic characteristics of these posts are their informality and a high degree of emotiveness and expressiveness.

As far as the content of these posts is concerned, we may distinguish two main content areas – i.e. personal experiences and current world affairs.

1. Messages concentrating on the self – personal experiences (54%, 28 posts)
    This group of messages concentrates on the presentation of personal experiences; the authors concentrate on the self and on the revelation of subjective feelings, e.g.:[1]

    > My mother was an aspiring actress in Hollywood. She gave up when she got married to my Dad. If she were still here I would ask her why she gave up because it would be fun to tell people my mother is an actress. :)

    > i love Pontiacs! I've always liked them since I was 4 years old & my dad had a '69 firebird. I also drove a '74 pontiac grand prix when I was 13. I've had 2 bonne's, grand prix, trans-am, & gto. Loved every single one of 'em!

    > When I was growing up, I had a fascination with the stars and astronomy.My Grandpa bought me about the constellations and taught me to identify Orion, the Big and Little Dippers and find the North Star.

    These messages illustrate the above-mentioned personalization of the posts. Clearly, the posts represent the authors' strong need for self-expression.

2. Messages directed at particular addressees (46%, 24 messages)
    Very often the posts take the format of a message or a letter, directed at a specific person. These messages contain statements of opinion and raise questions concerning current affairs. Obviously, the questions are rhetorical in nature and their function is solely expressive. They also contribute to creating an illusion of a dialogical and interactive situation, e.g.:

    > Dear President
    > My name is Zeeshan Usmani, and I have a quick question to ask. Why can't we solve the problem we have created for ourselves? and why we have to beg to USA everytime anything goes wrong in Pakistan?I appreciate your time, Thank You

---

[1]   All the messages are quoted in their original form, keeping the errors made by the authors.

Hi Larry.
I just have a few questions all related. I know you have time restraints and all but when you ask your guests a question on your show, why don't you let them answer before you interupt them, you do this all the time. Oprah does the same thing and it really bothers me. Do you think they are either boring answers or long winded? Why is this done so often?

I didn't vote for you but I do appreciate that you are the right person at the right time for what must be the ugliest job in the world right now. Heck, I'd even forgive you if you took up smoking again.

The rhetorical nature of the messages is confirmed by the following passage which exemplifies the features presented above, i.e. the personalization and dialogical character of the text:

May I ask you when you will stop this genocide, women and kids are paying the price of your actions, your Nation is being hurt daily, what about your own family and your own daughters, would you ever imagined you would have been born a woman, what would be your position if you were born a woman, why do you let your own people kill and treat women like less than an animal,
I am asking too much,
to respect your own people and specially kids and women,
what will you do next,
what will be your agreement with the leaders of the world,
what are you waiting to change your position re this crazy war, and what is your position re Pakistan, well that is an obvious one,
what is exactly what you want to get with this non stop violence, haven't you see or you don't care the way you're people are suffering...................
yes politics and rulling a Country can be very dirty,
but I really would like to know how do you feel as a human being,
I bet you don't feel,
because if you were a true religious man,
you wouldn't be doing what you are doing to your people and to your brothers in faith......................................

This user, in contrast to Dimmit, who tried to present rational arguments for his opinions, resorts solely to emotional persuasion. The message, deeply emotional in tone, takes the form of a stream of consciousness, presenting an unsegmented flow of thoughts. Basically, it delineates the complaints associated with the social situation in Pakistan in the form of an accumulation of questions and accusations directed at the President of the country. The questions have a different character, being both deliberative and persuasive. They range from direct questions concerning particular problems (*what will be your agreement with the leaders of the world*), to conditional questions regarding unreal situations (*what would be your position if you were born a woman*). In three places, the list of questions is interrupted by ironic acknowledgments of truth and an ostensible agreement (*well, that is an obvious one, yes politics and ruling a country can be very dirty*). These suspension points help leave certain things unsaid and achieve the effect of reticence. In the message we can see the elements of doubt, rejection, and evaluation. The user refers to common moral values, focusing on an emotional, not rational evaluation of reality.

As far as the form of these posts is concerned, their major characteristics include the following:

a. high frequency of 1st person pronouns, e.g.:

> I became an avid Sci Fi fan early on and joined the Science Fiction Book Club when I was in 7th grade.

> I never thought I would ever say this but I think Adam is the first guy I have ever seen that looks good in makeup. I think he could open the door for more men to wear it.

> 100 days in office, you have done so well. Africans will go on singing your victory.

> In Africa you are my Kenyan Brother, President Barack Obama and My beautiful sister, The First Lady Michelle Obama.

b. contractions, as signals of casual, colloquial style, e.g.:

> haven't you see or you don't care the way you're people are suffering...................

> I don't feel the makeup made him look feminine at all.

c. exclamatory sentences, emphatic repetitiveness, use of different rhetorical devices, such "the list of three", e.g.:

> Great job President Obama!! Thank you, thank you, thank you!!

> WELL, SORT OF... AND I REALLY LOVE MY CITY!!!

d. rhetorical questions, e.g.:

> Could the picture not have been made using photoshop and exising images????
> Why waste millions in tax payer money???

e. emphasis, expressed by means of capital letters, e.g.:

> YOU HAVE BOTH BECOME THE ROLE MODEL FOR OUR AFRICAN CHILDREN AND OUR AFRICAN LEADS.

f. wordplay, e.g.:

> The best way to end the mess we are in is to start by making NOBAMA and his freak followers the NOBAMAITES as long as this MISERABLE FAILURE is in office we are bound for disaster.

where *NOBAMA* and *NOBAMAITES* may be seen as instances of blending, while the *MISERABLE FAILURE* is a further example of emphasis described above.

All these features point to the deeply informal and also the emotional nature of the posts. The expressive nature of these statements is emphasized by an excessive use of punctuation marks (suspension points, exclamation marks, question marks) and capital letters. These examples show that textual commentaries, similar to video files, are subjective, emotional and exhibit a deeply dialogical character. Worth noting are frequent grammatical and spelling mistakes.

4. Conclusions

Taken together, interactivity and personalization are the most important features characteristic of the posts. The interactive nature can be seen in direct reference to listeners, in the usage of 1st and 2nd person plural pronouns (*we, you*), which are used to highlight common experiences and create a sense of comradery with the receivers. In addition, worth noting is the frequent use of questions of different types, such as deliberative questions, expressing the dilemmas of the speaker, persuasive questions and finally, rhetorical questions, by means of which users express their judgments. All these aim at influencing the user, and their interactive and dialogical formulas constitute an attractive means of expressing personal evaluations in a covert way.

The material analysed lets us see that iReport commentaries present a deeply personalized view. In the majority of the messages, the authors focus on the presentation of the self and the description of personal experiences. It seems that participatory sites are treated as the perfect place for satisfying the need for self-expression, for turning to a wider audience and becoming known in the media.

Interestingly, there is a frequent lack of matter-of-fact argumentation and of rational judgments. The majority of the posts rely solely on emotional persuasion that aims to influence the emotional attitudes of the receivers. The use of colloquial language predominates in the messages, making the commentaries easier to follow.

It seems, though, that the personal and emotional side actually decides about the popularity of such collaborative projects. Viewers seem to appreciate the originality of the posts and the human texture permeating through the messages.

Yet, it is not only personalization and interactivity that decide the popularity of the site. Its value is additionally enhanced by its multimedia character and the multitude of the channels of expression available. The site is a symbiosis of textual, audio and visual media and it constitutes a clear confirmation of the popularity of visual culture. The written word is here dominated by images, which are downloaded to the website every few minutes. The users seem to appreciate the array of the multimedia available, which are visible in the form of their messages. The majority of the users want to stand out from other authors and strive for maximum appeal of their messages. This focus on attractiveness is especially noticeable in the video files. Here, the authors present live shows. These posts assume the character of an interactive performance.

The freedom to publish anything enhances creativity. It contributes to a greater diversity of content and enables a more intensive exchange of opinions. Naturally, this freedom can have a different, negative side. The lack of control creates favourable conditions for the publication of defamatory and inappropriate messages, which frequently appear on the site. Additionally, it needs to be acknowledged that the site is rich in useless and meaningless content. This contributes to the growing trivialization of the online content. The discovery of a valuable contribution often constitutes a real challenge.

References

Bowman S., Willis C. 2003. *We media. How audiences are shaping the future of news and information*. Retrieved from: www.hypergene.net/wemedia on 18th March 2009.

Brown G., Yule G. 1983. *Discourse analysis*. Cambridge.

Cormode G., Krishnamurthy B. 2008. Key differences between Web 1.0 and Web 2.0. – *First Monday* 13.2. Retrieved from: http://firstmonday.org/htbin/cgiwrap/bin/ojs/index.php/fm/article/view/2125/1972 on 21st May 2009.

Ferenc T., Olechnicki K. (eds.) 2008. *Obrazy w sieci. Socjologia i antropologia ikonosfery Internetu*. Toruń.

Gumperz J. 1982. *Discourse strategies*. Cambridge.

Harrison T., Barthel B. 2009. Wielding new media in Web 2.0: exploring the history of engagement with the collaborative construction of media products. – *New Media and Society*, 12.1–2: 155–178.

Jones S. 1998. *Doing internet research*. Chicago.

Korolko M. 1990. *Sztuka retoryki. Przewodnik encyklopedyczny*. Warszawa.

Ong W. 2002. *Orality and literacy*. London.

Ziomek J. 1990. *Retoryka opisowa*. Wrocław.

Fig. 1. iReport home page (www.iReport.com, 20th September 2009)

Fig. 2. OCGirl's commentary (www.iReport.com/docs/DOC-236314, 22nd September 2009)

Fig. 3. Dimmit's commentary (www.iReport.com/docs/DOC-219776, 15th September 2009)

Fig. 4. Dimmit's commentary (www.iReport.com/docs/DOC-240815, 15th September 2009)

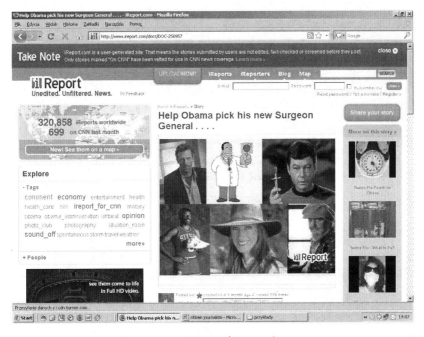

Fig. 5. www.iReport.com/docs/DOC-250957, 27th September 2009

Fig. 6. www.iReport.com/docs/DOC-255639, 28th September 2009

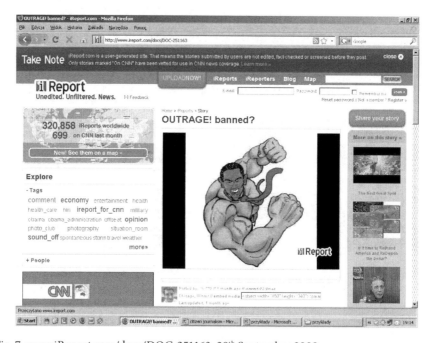

Fig. 7. www.iReport.com/docs/DOC-251163, 28th September 2009

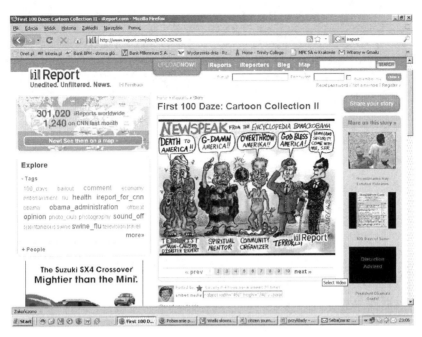

Fig.8. www.iReport.com/docs/DOC-252425, 29th September 2009

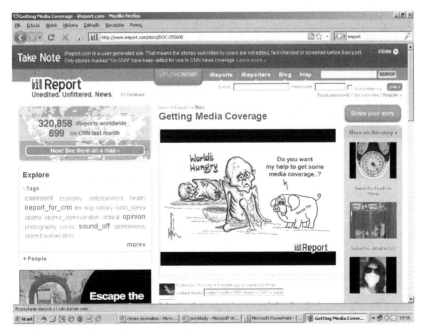

Fig. 9. www.iReport.com/docs/DOC-255608, 27th September 2009

Studia Linguistica Universitatis Iagellonicae Cracoviensis
128 (2011)

DEIRDRE WILSON
University College, London

PARALLELS AND DIFFERENCES
IN THE TREATMENT OF METAPHOR
IN RELEVANCE THEORY AND COGNITIVE LINGUISTICS*

Keywords: metaphor, lexical pragmatics, communication, inference

Abstract

Both cognitive linguists and relevance theorists are developing original approaches to metaphor. Both shed new light on old debates and suggest fruitful directions for research. Although there has so far been little interaction between the two approaches, Raymond Gibbs and Markus Tendahl (2006, 2008) have recently begun to compare them and consider how they might be combined. This paper is intended as a contribution to that debate. After outlining some parallels and differences between the two approaches, I will discuss how they might fit together to give a fuller picture of the role of metaphor in language and thought.

1. Introduction

In the last twenty-five years, traditional approaches to metaphor (in classical rhetoric or Gricean pragmatics, for instance) have been increasingly questioned on both theoretical and experimental grounds. Where traditional approaches treat metaphor

---

* A version of this paper was presented at the Institute of Philology, Jagiellonian University, in June 2010. I would like to thank the Director of the Institute, Dr. hab. Elżbieta Chrzanowska-Kluczewska and her colleagues for wonderful hospitality during my visit there. I would also like to thank Prof. Dr. Hab. Elżbieta Mańczak-Wohlfeld for inviting me to publish my paper in this journal. I am particularly grateful to Dr. Maria Jodlowiec for her warmth and generosity throughout my time in Krakow, and for valuable discussion and comments. The research was supported by CSMN (University of Oslo) and the Norway Research Council.

as a departure from a maxim, norm or convention of literal truthfulness, there is a growing consensus that the Romantic critics of classical rhetoric were right to see metaphor as entirely normal, natural and pervasive in language. Where traditional approaches treat metaphor as a purely decorative device with little or no cognitive significance, it is increasingly recognised that most metaphors cannot be paraphrased in literal terms without loss to the meaning. Relevance theorists and cognitive linguists, who have both explicitly distanced themselves from traditional approaches to metaphor, are part of this growing consensus.

However, relevance theorists and cognitive linguists see metaphor as entirely normal and natural for rather different reasons. Cognitive linguists have argued that metaphor is pervasive in language because it is pervasive in thought.[1] As Lakoff and Johnson (1980: 153) put it, "Metaphor is primarily a matter of thought and action and only derivatively a matter of language." On this approach, linguistic metaphors are treated as surface reflections of underlying conceptual mappings between different cognitive domains (e.g. the domains of love affairs and journeys, theories and buildings, arguments and fights), and have their roots in cognition rather than communication. Relevance theorists, on the other hand, have argued that metaphor arises naturally in linguistic communication, as language is loosely used in an attempt to convey complex thoughts which may be vague, but need not themselves be metaphorical. On this approach, there is a continuum of cases between literal talk, loose talk, hyperbole and metaphor, none of which is necessarily a surface reflection of any pre-existing conceptual mapping. As Sperber and Wilson (2008: 84) put it,

> We see metaphors as simply a range of cases at one end of a continuum that includes literal, loose and hyperbolic interpretations. In our view, metaphorical interpretations are arrived at in exactly the same way as these other interpretations. There is no mechanism specific to metaphor, no interesting generalisation that applies only to them.

Until recently, relevance theorists and cognitive linguists have been more concerned with developing and applying their own approaches than comparing them with those of others. A notable exception has been Raymond Gibbs, whose pioneering experimental work draws on elements of both cognitive linguistics and relevance theory, and has had an important influence on both. In two recent papers, Gibbs and Markus Tendahl (2006, 2008) suggest that, despite some fundamental differences, relevance theory and cognitive linguistics may be seen as providing complementary rather than contradictory approaches to metaphor, and have begun to consider how they might be combined:

> Many metaphor scholars ... see these alternative theories as being radically different. After all, cognitive linguistics and relevance theory adhere to very different goals

---

[1]   For cognitive linguistics approaches to metaphor, see Lakoff & Johnson (1980, 2003), Grady (1997), Gibbs (1998), Fauconnier & Turner (2002, 2008), Ruiz de Mendoza & Perez Hernandez (2003), Hampe (2005) and Müller (2008); see also McGlone (2001).

and methodological assumptions… These different goals and working assumptions are so great, in fact, that few metaphor scholars have tried to systematically
compare these two theories to understand how and why they differ. Yet there is also
a small underground movement, as we have personally noted at various metaphor
conferences, to begin thinking about ways that cognitive linguistics and relevance
theory perspectives on metaphor may be complementary. These discussions arise
as metaphor scholars … struggle with the deficiencies of each theory and begin to
understand that both perspectives have something very important to contribute
toward a comprehensive, cognitive theory of metaphor. (Tendahl & Gibbs 2008: 1824)

In this paper, I would like to take up Gibbs and Tendahl's challenge and suggest
some ways in which the two approaches to metaphor might combine.

One way of reconciling the apparently incompatible views of relevance theorists
and cognitive linguists about the origin of metaphors would be to look for evidence
that some metaphors arise in language use and others in thought. As Gibbs and
Tendahl point out, relevance theorists and cognitive linguists tend to focus on metaphors of rather different types. Whereas relevance theorists offer many analyses
of standard examples such as (1a)–(1c), which are familiar from classical rhetoric,
cognitive linguists have been more concerned with examples such as (2a)–(2c), which
they see as reflecting conceptual mappings across cognitive domains:

(1) a. Robert is a *computer.*
    b. Susan is a *wild rose.*
    c. Sally is an *angel.*

(2) a. Bill's marriage is *on the rocks.*   (LOVE IS A JOURNEY)
    b. He *destroyed my defences.*   (ARGUMENTS ARE FIGHTS)
    c. Your theory is *falling apart.*   (THEORIES ARE BUILDINGS)

For anyone attempting a unitary account of metaphor, the challenge would be to
show how both types of example can be analysed in the same way. In fact, relevance
theorists have consistently argued that terms such as *metaphor* and *irony* pick out
a variety of loosely related phenomena which do not necessarily all work in the
same way: in other words, they have consistently argued that metaphor and irony
are not *natural kinds.* There is thus a genuine question about whether the examples
in (1) and (2) exploit the same cognitive and communicative mechanisms, and if
so, whether they fit better with the relevance theory or the cognitive linguistics
approach.

A further way of exploring the possible interrelations between the relevance
theory and cognitive linguistic treatments of metaphor would be to look at the
central role of concepts in both approaches. According to relevance theory, hearers understand linguistic metaphors by using linguistic and contextual clues to
create new 'ad hoc' (occasion-specific) concepts, which are typically not identical
to any of the concepts linguistically encoded by the metaphorically-used word
or phrase, although they inherit some of their inferential properties from those

concepts. It might then be reasonable to assume that the repeated use of linguistic metaphors linking items from distinct cognitive domains might set up patterns of conceptual activation similar to those that cognitive linguists see as characteristic of conceptual metaphor. To take just one illustration, many cultures have a set of flower metaphors (e.g. *daisy, lily, violet, rose*) which are typically applied to women. From a cognitive linguistics perspective, these linguistic metaphors might be seen as surface reflections of an underlying conceptual metaphor WOMEN ARE FLOWERS, based on systematic correspondences between the domains of women and flowers. From a relevance theory perspective, these linguistic metaphors would be seen as originating in creative uses of language for opportunistic communicative purposes, which, if repeated often enough, might result in the setting up of systematic correspondences between the domains of women and flowers. Here again, there is a genuine question about whether, and to what extent, conceptual cross-domain mappings originate in language use, and are therefore to be explained at least partly in pragmatic terms.

My aim in this paper is to argue that relevance theory offers a genuine alternative to cognitive linguistic approaches to metaphor, and can complement these approaches in at least two ways: first, by showing how some metaphors can arise as creative loose uses of language, and second, by showing how the idea that linguistic metaphors create new 'ad hoc' concepts has interesting implications for the cognitive linguistics treatment of metaphor. I hope the resulting picture will provide a basis for future discussion and stimulate further research on the possible interrelations between the two approaches.

2. Metaphor and lexical pragmatics – How word meanings are modified in use

The aim of a pragmatic account of metaphor is to explain how hearers recognise the intended meaning of a metaphorical utterance in context. According to relevance theory, linguistic metaphors originate as loose uses of language, in which a word or phrase is used to communicate a novel 'ad hoc' concept which is broader (more general) than the encoded lexical meaning. In the metaphor *Robert is a computer*, for instance, the sentence uttered is (3a), and the encoded lexical meaning of the word *computer* is the concept COMPUTER, which denotes a certain type of machine used for processing information:

(3) a. **Sentence uttered**: Robert is a *computer*
    b. **Lexical meaning of 'computer'**: COMPUTER (i.e. a type of machine)

What the speaker communicates by use of the word *computer* in (3a), however, is not the lexical meaning COMPUTER but an 'ad hoc' concept with a broader denotation, which is constructed in the course of interpreting (3a), and which applies not only to actual computers but also to people who share some of the encyclopaedic properties of computers (for instance, they process information accurately, lack common sense, intuition, human feelings, and so on). Thus, what might be communicated by uttering (3a) on a particular occasion could be represented as in (4), where COMPUTER* is a broader, 'ad hoc' concept whose denotation includes both computers and some humans:

(4) a. *Speaker's explicit meaning*: Robert is a COMPUTER*
    b. *Implicatures*: Robert lacks feelings, processes information well (etc.)

Relevance theory's treatment of metaphor is part of a more general approach to lexical pragmatics which is based on the following assumptions. First, the lexical meaning of a word is merely a clue to the speaker's meaning, and the concept communicated by use of a word typically differs from the lexical meaning. Second, metaphor is just one of many ways in which lexical meanings can be modified in use. The concept communicated by use of a word may be narrower (more specific) or broader (more general) than the lexical meaning (or it may be narrower in some respects and broader in others, as is often the case in metaphor). Third, there is a continuum of cases of broadening, ranging from strictly literal use, through various shades of approximation to hyperbole and metaphor, with no sharp cut-off point between them. Fourth, all these cases are interpreted in the same way: there are no special pragmatic principles or mechanisms that apply only to metaphors. And fifth, contrary to what is generally assumed in Gricean pragmatics and philosophy of language, the concept communicated by use of a word contributes to what the speaker is taken to have asserted (i.e. the truth-conditional content of the utterance), and not only to what is implicated (Wilson & Carston 2007; Sperber & Wilson 2008). Since metaphorical uses of language – just like strictly literal uses – contribute to truth-conditional content and fall within the scope of logical connectives, they cannot be dismissed as marginal to the concerns of linguistics proper.[2]

The case of lexical narrowing can be illustrated using an example from Fauconnier & Turner (2002: 27). As Fauconnier and Turner point out, the phrase *red pencil* is semantically very vague: the concept RED PENCIL applies to any pencil that stands in some relation to the colour red, e.g. pencils which are painted red, pencils that write in red, pencils smeared with lipstick, pencils used to record the activities of a team dressed in red, and so on. Still, when a teacher marking an essay says "I need a red pencil", she will certainly have some specific sub-type of red pencil in mind, and in order to understand her, the hearer must infer what particular type of red pencil this is. In other words, the teacher must be understood as asking not simply for a RED PENCIL, but for a RED PENCIL*, where RED PENCIL* denotes the particular sub-type of pencil she has in mind. The interpretation of virtually any utterance involves some such form of lexical narrowing, and one of the goals of lexical pragmatics is to explain how it is achieved.

---

[2]   For recent relevance-theoretic treatments of metaphor, see e.g. Carston (2002), Higashimori (2002), Wilson & Sperber (2002), Vega Moreno (2007), Wilson & Carston (2007, 2008), Sperber & Wilson (2008).

Similarly, the interpretation of virtually any utterance involves some form of lexical broadening, in which the concept communicated by use of a word is more general than the lexical meaning. The broadening can be almost imperceptible, as in the following cases of approximation:

(5) a. The play starts at 7.00.
   b. Jane's hair is *straight*.

The speaker of (5a) would generally be understood as communicating that the play starts, not at 7.00 on the dot, but at approximately 7.00 (i.e. 7.00*), and the speaker of (5b) would generally be understood as communicating that Jane's hair is, not straight in the strict geometric sense, but merely straight in an approximate sense appropriate to human hair (i.e. STRAIGHT*). The interpretation of virtually any utterance involves similar types of approximation, where a term with a strict meaning is loosely applied to what Lasersohn (1999) calls a "penumbra" of cases which fall just outside the linguistically-specified denotation.

According to relevance theory, approximation shades off imperceptibly into hyperbole. Consider the utterances in (6):

(6) a. The lecture hall was empty.
   b. The water is freezing.

Let's suppose that *empty* in (6a) is narrowed to mean (roughly) 'empty of people' (as opposed, say, to 'empty of furniture').[3] Then the utterance would traditionally count as an approximation if the speaker is taken to mean that there were only a very few people present. In this case, use of the word *empty* would be understood as intended to convey a concept EMPTY*, meaning 'close enough to EMPTY for the differences to be inconsequential'. By contrast, the same utterance would traditionally count as a hyperbole if the speaker is taken to mean that, although many people were present, there were more empty seats than might have been expected or desired. In this case, use of the word *empty* would be understood as intended to convey a broader concept EMPTY**, meaning 'closer to EMPTY than expected or desired'. Here, it is easy to see there is a whole continuum of intermediate cases, with no sharp cut-off point between approximation and hyperbole. For relevance theorists, this is not a matter for concern, since they claim that the distinction between approximation and hyperbole has no theoretical significance: an utterance does not have to be recognised as an approximation or hyperbole to be understood, no special interpretive mechanisms are needed in either case, and both are understood in the same way. However, for theories which draw a sharp distinction between literal and

---

[3]   A more precise formulation would take account of the fact that narrowing and broadening apply at the level of the *denotation* of a concept rather than its *meaning*, so that the 'ad hoc' concept obtained by narrowing *empty* in (6a) is not EMPTY OF PEOPLE, but simply a concept EMPTY* that is satisfied only by rooms EMPTY OF PEOPLE (and so on for other examples). For ease of exposition, I will ignore this issue here (see Sperber & Wilson 1998).

figurative uses of language, or which treat approximation and hyperbole as involving different interpretive mechanisms, the fact that there is no clear cut-off point between them should be a serious matter for concern. Similar points apply to (6b), where there is a continuum of cases between the use of *freezing* to mean 'actually FREEZING', 'almost FREEZING' and 'closer to FREEZING than expected or desired'.

Although metaphor has received a great deal of attention in cognitive linguistics, and in philosophy and psychology more generally, hyperbole has received much less attention. According to relevance theory, there is no clear dividing line between hyperbole and metaphor, and an adequate account of metaphor should therefore apply to hyperbole in the same way. To illustrate, consider the utterances in (7):

(7) a. John is a giant.
　　b. John is as tall as the Eiffel Tower.
　　c. John is incredibly tall.

One possible way of distinguishing hyperbole from metaphor would be to treat hyperbole as involving an increase in quantity along a single dimension (e.g. height), while metaphor would involve a qualitative change (so that the speaker in metaphorical uses of (7) would be understood as attributing to John properties not directly linked to height). According to this criterion, (7a) would count as a hyperbole if taken to mean that John is very tall for a human, and as a metaphor if taken to mean that John stands out for other reasons than simply his height. However, again there is a gradient between the two types of case, with increases in quantity along a single dimension ultimately leading to a qualitative change. For instance, all three utterances in (7) activate thoughts of John's height as being not merely human but superhuman, and these carry implications for other properties than simply his height. Thus, hyperbole shades off imperceptibly into metaphor, and is not reducible to an ornamental device with little or no cognitive significance. From a cognitive linguistics perspective, if metaphor is analysed in terms of cross-domain mapping, it follows that hyperbole must be analysed in a similar way. But while hyperboles such as (7a) or (7b) might conceivably be analysed in terms of such mappings (e.g. between the domains of people and superhumans, or people and buildings), others, such as (7c), have no obvious analysis in conceptual metaphor terms.

The relevance theory approach to lexical pragmatics suggests that it should be possible to find a single utterance which can be intended and understood literally, loosely, hyperbolically or metaphorically on different occasions. Here is an illustration:

(8) The audience slept through the lecture.

In certain circumstances, an utterance of (8) might be intended and understood as making the very strong claim that the audience was literally asleep throughout the lecture. In other circumstances, it might be intended and understood as making the slightly weaker claim that the audience was, if not literally asleep, at least on the point of falling asleep during the lecture: in traditional terms, it would then count as an approximation. In different circumstances, (8) might be intended and understood as claiming, still more weakly, that the audience was, if not asleep or on the point of sleep, at least in a physical state of drowsiness during the lecture: in traditional terms, it would then count as a hyperbole. Finally, in many circumstance, (8) might be intended and understood as making a weaker claim still: that the audience, if not literally asleep, on the point of sleep or even feeling physically drowsy, was at least extremely bored and unresponsive during the lecture: in traditional terms, it would then count as a metaphor. This example illustrates two central features of relevance theory's approach to lexical pragmatics: that there is a continuum of cases between literal use, approximation, hyperbole and metaphor, and that the choice between different possible interpretations is heavily context dependent.

The flexibility and context-dependence of lexical-pragmatic interpretation presents a challenge for both relevance theory and cognitive linguistics. The goal of pragmatics is to explain how hearers infer the speaker's intended meaning from clues provided by the utterance and the context. But if utterance interpretation typically involves the narrowing or broadening of lexical meaning, as relevance theory claims, how do hearers *ever* recognise the speaker's intended meaning? What factors trigger the narrowing or broadening process? What determines the direction it takes, and when it stops? Similarly, if utterance interpretation typically involves the use of conceptual metaphors, blending, domain mapping, and so on, as cognitive linguistics claims, how do hearers *ever* recognise the speaker's intended meaning? What factors trigger the mapping / blending process? What determines the direction it takes, and when it stops? Here, relevance theory has a concrete proposal to make, which may be of interest to cognitive linguists attempting to answer parallel questions about how linguistic metaphors are used and understood. In the next section, I will briefly outline the basic features of the relevance theory approach and illustrate its application to metaphorical examples such as those in (1) and (2) above.

3. Relevance theory and metaphor interpretation

The goal of lexical pragmatics is to explain how lexical meanings are adjusted in the course of communication. The explanation suggested by relevance theory is that lexical meanings are adjusted in order to satisfy *expectations of relevance*. In a nutshell, the theory claims that utterances addressed to one raise expectations of relevance not raised by other stimuli, and that hearers are entitled to treat the encoded linguistic meaning as a clue to the speaker's meaning, and to follow a path of least effort in adjusting this encoded meaning to a point where it yields an overall interpretation that satisfies those expectations.

In more technical terms, relevance is defined as a property of inputs to cognitive processes (whether external stimuli, which can be perceived and attended to, or internal representations, which can be stored, recalled, or used as premises in inference). An input is relevant to an individual when it connects with available contextual assumptions to yield positive cognitive effects (for instance, true contextual implications, warranted strengthenings or revisions of existing assumptions). For present purposes, the most important type of cognitive effect is a contextual implication: an implication deducible from input and available contextual assumptions together, but from neither input nor contextual assumptions alone. Other things being equal, the more implications derived, and the smaller the mental effort required to represent the input, access an appropriate set of contextual assumptions and derive these implications, the greater the relevance of the input to the individual at that time.[4]

Relevance theory is based on two general claims about the role of relevance in cognition and communication:

Cognitive Principle of Relevance:
Human cognition tends to be geared to the maximisation of relevance.

Communicative Principle of Relevance:
Every act of overt intentional communication conveys a presumption of its own optimal relevance.

The Cognitive Principle of Relevance yields a variety of predictions about human cognitive processes. It predicts that the human cognitive system has evolved in such a way that our perceptual mechanisms tend spontaneously to pick out potentially relevant stimuli, our memory retrieval mechanisms tend spontaneously to activate potentially relevant assumptions, and our inferential mechanisms tend spontaneously to process them in the most productive way. This principle has essential implications for human communication. In order to communicate, the communicator needs her audience's attention. If attention tends to go automatically to what seems most relevant at the time, then the success of communication depends on the audience taking the utterance to be relevant enough to be worthy of attention. Wanting her communication to succeed, the communicator, by the very act of communicating, indicates that she wants the audience to see her utterance as relevant, and this is what the Communicative Principle of Relevance states.

According to relevance theory, the presumption of optimal relevance conveyed by every utterance is precise enough to ground a specific comprehension heuristic that hearers can use in interpreting the speaker's meaning:

Presumption of optimal relevance
a. The utterance is relevant enough to be worth processing.
b. It is the most relevant one compatible with the communicator's abilities and preferences.

---

[4]　For fuller exposition of relevance theory, and comparison with alternative approaches, see Sperber & Wilson (1995), Carston (2002) and Wilson & Sperber (2004).

Relevance-guided comprehension heuristic

a. Follow a path of least effort in constructing an interpretation of the utterance (e.g. in resolving ambiguities and referential indeterminacies, adjusting lexical meaning, supplying contextual assumptions, deriving implications, etc.).

b. Stop when your expectations of relevance are satisfied.

A hearer using this heuristic during online comprehension should proceed in the following way. The aim is to find an overall interpretation that satisfies the presumption of optimal relevance. To achieve this aim, he must enrich the decoded sentence meaning at the explicit level, and complement it at the implicit level by supplying contextual assumptions which will combine with it to yield enough implications to make the utterance relevant in the expected way. What route should he follow in disambiguating, assigning reference, adjusting lexical meaning, constructing a context, deriving conclusions, etc.? According to the relevance-theoretic comprehension heuristic, he should follow a path of least effort in looking for implications, and stop when the resulting overall interpretation yields enough implications to satisfy his expectations of relevance.

As noted above, the goal of lexical pragmatics is to explain what triggers pragmatic adjustment processes such as lexical narrowing and broadening, what direction they take, and when they stop. Relevance theory suggests the following answers to these questions. First, lexical adjustments are triggered by the search for an interpretation that yields enough implications to satisfy the expectations of relevance raised by the utterance. Second, they follow a path of least effort, starting with the most accessible contextual assumptions, the most accessible narrowings or broadenings, the most accessible implications. Third, they involve mutually adjusting tentative hypotheses about contextual assumptions, explicit content (including adjusted 'ad hoc' concepts) and implications so that the resulting overall interpretation satisfies the expectations of relevance raised by the utterance. And finally, the adjustment process stops when the expectations of relevance raised by the utterance are satisfied (or abandoned). I will shortly illustrate how this is done.

As noted above, an important ingredient of this account is the idea that lexical comprehension typically involves the construction of an 'ad hoc' concept, or occasion-specific sense, which may be broader or narrower than the encoded lexical meaning. Use of the term *ad hoc concept* in this connection is often traced to the psychologist Lawrence Barsalou (1987, 1993), whose work on categorisation showed that prototypical narrowing (i.e. the interpretation of a general term as picking out the subset of prototypical category members) was much more flexible and context-dependent than had previously been assumed. In later work by the psycholinguist Sam Glucksberg and colleagues (2001), and by relevance theorists (e.g. Carston 2002; Wilson & Sperber 2002), it was suggested that the outcome of the 'ad hoc' concept construction process could also be a broadening of the encoded lexical meaning. This opened up the possibility of a unified account on which lexical narrowing and broadening (or a combination of the two) are the outcomes of a single interpretive process which fine-tunes the interpretation of almost every word.

A second important ingredient of this approach to lexical pragmatics is the assumption that lexical concepts (e.g. COMPUTER, GIANT) provide access to an ordered array of encyclopaedic information about items falling under the concept. This encyclopaedic information is not seen as part of the semantic content of the concept, but as providing a reservoir of potential contextual assumptions which, when added to the context, can contribute to relevance by yielding contextual implications. A given encyclopaedic assumption will be more or less accessible on different occasions, and will yield different potential implications depending on what else is present in the utterance and the discourse context. It will therefore make different contributions to relevance on both the processing effort and cognitive effect sides. Thus, a speaker who intends her utterance to be understood in a certain way should make sure that the appropriate encyclopaedic assumptions are accessible enough to be selected, added to the context and used to derive the intended implications by a hearer using the relevance-theoretic comprehension heuristic.

To illustrate how this account might apply in a case of lexical narrowing, consider how the utterance in (9) might be understood by a hearer using the relevance-theoretic comprehension heuristic:

(9) *Teacher, carrying a pile of essays*: I need a red pencil.

As noted above, the concept RED PENCIL is semantically vague: its denotation includes any pencil that stands in some relation to the colour red, and it will provide access to a huge array of encyclopaedic information about such pencils and their uses. Still, according to relevance theory, the utterance of (9) creates a presumption of relevance which entitles the addressee to follow a path of least effort in constructing an overall interpretation on which the utterance yields enough implications to make it relevant in the expected way. According to spreading activation models of memory, the most accessible assumptions in the encyclopaedic entry for RED PENCIL at any given point will be those simultaneously activated by several features of the utterance and the discourse context. With (9), the fact that the speaker needs a RED PENCIL should activate encyclopaedic information about the *uses* to which RED PENCILS can be put. The fact that the speaker is a teacher will add an extra layer of activation to information about the uses of RED PENCILS *by teachers*, and this will include the information that teachers use pencils *that write in red when marking essays*. The fact that the teacher is carrying a pile of essays will add a further layer of activation to this same encyclopaedic assumption that teachers use pencils that write in red when marking essays, which should therefore be the most accessible assumption in the encyclopaedic entry for RED PENCIL during the interpretation of the utterance in (9). By assuming that the phrase *red pencil* was intended to convey not the very general encoded concept RED PENCIL but the narrower concept RED PENCIL* (i.e. 'pencil used to write in red'), the hearer can thus arrive at an overall interpretation which satisfies his expectation of relevance by implying that the teacher wants him to help her find a RED PENCIL*. According to the relevance-theoretic comprehension heuristic, he is justified in making this assumption, because it is the least effort-demanding way of finding an overall interpretation that yields enough implications to make the utterance relevant in the expected way.

To illustrate how the same account might apply in a case of lexical broadening, consider how the utterance in (8) above (repeated below for convenience) might be understood by a hearer using the relevance-theoretic comprehension heuristic:

(8) The audience slept through the lecture.

On a Gricean account, (8) should have four distinct interpretations: as a literal assertion, an approximation, a hyperbole or a metaphor. Of these, the hearer should test the literal interpretation first, and consider a figurative interpretation only if the literal interpretation blatantly violates the maxim of truthfulness. However, the fact that there is both experimental and introspective evidence against the Gricean account when construed as a model of utterance comprehension (e.g. Gibbs 1994; Glucksberg 2001; Wilson & Sperber 2002) justifies the search for an alternative analysis of (8). According to relevance theory, there is no presumption that literal interpretations are the first to be tested. The encoded concept SLEEP is merely a point of access to an ordered array of encyclopaedic assumptions from which the hearer is expected to choose in constructing an overall interpretation that satisfies his expectations of relevance. Here, the encyclopaedic entry for SLEEP might give access to the following type of assumptions:

Encyclopaedic entry for sleep:
a. become mentally disengaged
b. lose interest in one's surroundings
c. become motionless and unresponsive
d. gradually lose consciousness
e. undergo physical changes (snoring, slowed heart-rate, deep breathing, etc.)

In different discourse contexts, different members of this set will be more or less accessible, and depending on which of them are chosen, the result will be a relatively narrower or broader interpretation of the word *slept*. Here, a literal interpretation will result only if assumption (e) is added to the context. However, since it is extremely rare for the audience actually to lose consciousness at a lecture, this assumption is unlikely to be strongly activated in that particular discourse context. By contrast, the mention of an audience at a lecture is quite likely to activate assumptions such as (a)–(c), having to do with loss of interest, unresponsiveness and mental disengagement. These assumptions, if added to the context, would contribute to relevance by providing access not only to information about the state of the audience but also to further implications about the quality of the lecture or of the lecturer. The resulting interpretation (which would be traditionally classified as hyperbolic or metaphorical) would be likely to satisfy the expectations of relevance raised by the utterance. Only if this interpretation fails to satisfy those expectations would the hearer be justified in accessing further contextual assumptions and moving towards a more literal interpretation.

One consequence of this approach to lexical pragmatics is its prediction that, typically, a loose interpretation, based on a few highly accessible encyclopaedic properties, will satisfy the hearer's expectation of relevance without a more literal interpretation ever being considered. To illustrate this point further, consider a recent attested example in which the word *giant* was metaphorically used. When the novelist John Updike died in January 2009, many obituaries contained comments such as the following:

(10) Updike was a *giant.*

The question is, how should this utterance be understood? The encyclopaedic entry for GIANT might provide access to information of the following sort: that giants have extraordinary height, imposing presence, powers beyond those of ordinary humans, stand out from the crowd, and so on. What is interesting about this example is that, even though the word *giant* is very often used hyperbolically to mean 'unusually tall' (as in (7a) above), the utterance of (10) in this particular discourse context would intuitively not be taken to implicate that Updike was very tall. This is so even though giants are stereotypically associated with unusual height, and, moreover, despite the fact that Updike himself happened to be unusually tall. The relevance-theoretic account sheds some light on how this utterance would be understood. In the first place, the expectations of relevance raised by an obituary of a public figure would lead the audience to look for implications having more to do with lifetime achievements than with physical properties. In this case, processing (10) in the context of easily accessible encyclopaedic information about Updike's status as a novelist should yield enough implications to satisfy the audience's expectations of relevance without information about his physical stature being considered at all. As a result, an obituarist who did want to draw attention to Updike's height as well as his achievements as a novelist would have to rephrase (10) in such a way as to encourage them to look for further implications. One way of doing this would be as in (11):

(11) Updike was a giant, in every sense of the word.

This reformulation calls for extra processing effort, and according to the relevance-theoretic comprehension heuristic, it should thus encourage a search for extra implications. An alternative strategy used by several of Updike's obituarists was to describe him not simply as a *giant,* but as a *literary giant,* or a *giant of American literature,* again calling for more processing effort but creating more precise expectations of relevance which exclude the possibility of considering Updike's physical stature at all.

　　Returning now to the examples in (1) and (2), I will briefly illustrate how this approach might apply in a case of each type. Consider, first, how the metaphor *Robert is a computer* might be understood in the following two exchanges:

(12) a. *Peter*: Is Robert a good accountant?
　　 b. *Mary*: Robert is a computer.

(13) a. *Peter*: How good a friend is Robert?
 b. *Mary*: Robert is a computer.

In each case, the encoded sense of *computer* activates some encyclopaedic features of computers that they may share with some humans. Like the best accountants, computers can process large amounts of numerical information and never make mistakes, and so on. Unlike good friends, computers lack emotions, intuitions, common sense, concern for others, and so on. In each case, in interpreting Mary's utterance, Peter constructs an 'ad hoc' concept COMPUTER* which is indicated, though not encoded, by the word *computer*, such that Robert's falling under this concept has implications that answer the question in (12a) or (13a). Notice that Mary need not have a very precise idea of the implications that Peter will derive, as long as her utterance encourages him to derive the kind of implications that answer his question in the intended way. So the Romantics were right to argue that the figurative meaning of a linguistic metaphor cannot be properly paraphrased. However, this is not because the meaning consists of some non-truth-conditional set of associations or "connotations", as the Romantics believed, but because it involves an 'ad hoc' concept which is characterised by its inferential role rather than by a definition, and, moreover, because this inferential role – to a much greater extent than in the case of mere approximations – is left to the hearer to elaborate. In relevance-theoretic terms, metaphorical communication is relatively weak communication (on the notion of weak communication, see Wilson & Sperber 2004; Sperber & Wilson 2008).

Finally, consider how the metaphorical utterance in (2a) above (repeated below for convenience) might be analysed on this approach:

(2) a. Bill's marriage is *on the rocks*.

Let's suppose that this metaphor is being encountered for the first time by someone whose encyclopaedic information about marriage contains no conceptual metaphors of the type MARRIAGES ARE JOURNEYS. In this discourse context, the hearer would be entitled to expect (2a) to achieve relevance by carrying implications about the state of Bill's marriage, and the most highly activated assumptions in his encyclopaedic entry for the concept ON THE ROCKS would be those that apply not only to voyages but also to (some) marriages. For instance, both voyages and marriages have a shorter or longer duration, and may end in more or less desirable or unexpected ways. Both voyages and marriages have participants who may experience various degrees of fear or distress and need various forms of help or comfort if they end in undesirable or unexpected ways. Given this, it should be possible to construct an 'ad hoc' concept ON THE ROCKS*, which is indicated, though not encoded, by the phrase *on the rocks*, and which is such that the claim that Bill's marriage falls under this concept carries implications about the state of his marriage that make the utterance relevant in the expected way. Similar implications would be carried by a wide range of linguistic metaphors unconnected with the conceptual metaphor MARRIAGES ARE JOURNEYS.

For instance, descriptions of Bill's marriage as *down the drain, down the plughole, out of the window, up in flames, on its last legs, on its deathbed,* and so on, would achieve relevance in broadly similar ways (but with subtle differences in the types of implications they activate, which would make the choice between them more than a purely arbitrary affair).

This analysis shows how the linguistic meaning of the phrase *on the rocks* might be spontaneously adjusted in constructing an interpretation that is relevant in the expected way, even by someone with no previous experience of metaphorical uses linking love affairs to journeys. But of course, many of the examples used in both relevance theory and cognitive linguistics contain metaphorical expressions whose interpretation is more or less a matter of routine. Moreover, cognitive linguists have made valuable contributions to our understanding of how linguistic metaphors often cluster around a central theme, so that a marriage may be described, for instance, not only as *on the rocks,* but in other terms related to voyages: e.g. *in the doldrums, stormy, tempestuous* or *becalmed.* I will end this section by considering how the repeated use of linguistic metaphors may lead to the setting up of systematic conceptual correspondences of the type that cognitive linguists have so fruitfully studied.

According to relevance theory, the lexical meaning of virtually every word in an utterance is contextually adjusted in order to satisfy expectations of relevance. The adjustment process may be a spontaneous, one-off affair, involving the construction of an 'ad hoc' concept which is used once and then forgotten; or it may be regularly and frequently followed, by a few people or a group, until, over time, the resulting 'ad hoc' concept may stabilise in a community and give rise to an extra lexicalised sense (Sperber & Wilson 1998; Vega Moreno 2007; Wilson & Carston 2007). As Vega Moreno (2007) shows, routinisation affects the amount of processing effort needed to understand an utterance: the more a word is broadened or narrowed in a particular way, the less effort it will cost to follow the same route in the future, and hence the more likely it is to be followed by hearers using the relevance-theoretic comprehension heuristic.

Repeated encounters with linguistic metaphors linking two conceptual domains (e.g. the domains of marriage and voyages, or women and flowers) may lead to the setting up of systematic cross-domain correspondences of the type familiar from cognitive linguistics, so that thoughts of marriage may automatically activate aspects of our encyclopaedic information about journeys, and thoughts of women may automatically activate aspects of our encyclopaedic knowledge of flowers, just as cognitive linguists predict. These cross-domain correspondences would in turn facilitate the production and interpretation of new linguistic metaphors based on the same conceptual activation patterns, resulting in thematically-related clusters of linguistic metaphors, just as cognitive linguists predict. On relevance theory's account, these patterns of activation would ultimately derive from the repeated use of linguistic metaphors, and thus arise for communicative rather than purely cognitive reasons.

4. Broader implications

As Tendahl and Gibbs (2008: 1824) point out, relevance theory and cognitive linguistics differ in some of their goals and working assumptions. These differences
have often obscured the broader parallels in their approaches to metaphor, and to
lexical meaning in general. Having drawn attention to some of these parallels and
argued that in many respects the two approaches are complementary rather than
contradictory, I will end by outlining some of the differences between them and
considering how they might be resolved.

As noted above, a central difference is that cognitive linguists see linguistic
metaphors as depending on pre-existing cross-domain mappings, whereas relevance
theory suggests that cross-domain conceptual mappings may result from repeated
use of linguistic metaphors, but are not essential to either the production or the
interpretation of metaphors. More generally, relevance theorists see metaphors as
arising primarily in linguistic communication, whereas cognitive linguists see them
as arising primarily in thought. I have suggested that the two approaches could be
reconciled by finding evidence that some cross-domain mappings arise in language
and others in thought.

However, these differences in the treatment of metaphor can be traced to a more
fundamental difference in the relative priority that the two approaches assign to
the study of communication (as opposed to cognition). Both relevance theory and
cognitive linguistics reject the Conduit metaphor (i.e. the code model of communication) as inadequate, and both advocate an inferential approach to communication. But while cognitive linguists tend to assume that understanding utterances
is simply a matter of applying general-purpose cognitive and linguistic abilities to
the communicative domain, relevance theorists have argued that understanding
utterances involves special-purpose inferential procedures that apply only in the
communicative domain. According to relevance theory, utterance comprehension
involves not merely drawing common-sense inferences, but drawing inferences
about the *communicator's meaning*, which is a complex mental state consisting
of both an informative and a communicative intention. Inferring this meaning
therefore crucially involves an ability to "mindread" (i.e. to infer the mental states
of others on the basis of their behaviour), and there is a growing body of evidence
that "mindreading" is a special-purpose inferential ability with its own specific patterns of development and breakdown.[5] In fact, relevance theorists have gone even
further, and argued that the ability to infer communicators' meanings involves
more specialised inferential procedures attuned to regularities that exist only in
the communicative domain (Sperber & Wilson 2002).[6] These regularities include
the fact described in the Communicative Principle of Relevance, that utterances
(and other acts of overt communication) raise expectations of relevance not raised

---

[5]   See Astington et al. (1988), Wellman et al. (2001), Sodian (2004), Matsui et al. (2006, 2009).

[6]   Further evidence that communication is a special-purpose ability is provided in Southgate
     et al. (2007), Liszkowski et al. (2008), Southgate et al. (2009), and Wilson (2009, forthcoming).

by ordinary actions, and underpin the relevance-theoretic comprehension heuristic, a special-purpose inferential procedure which yields valid results only when applied to overt communicative acts. These differences in the treatment of overt communication in relevance theory and cognitive linguistics could be resolved by further developmental or neuropsychological evidence.

It is worth pointing out that while waiting for this issue to be resolved, cognitive linguistics still stands to benefit from relevance theory in two important ways. In the first place, cognitive linguists face a major challenge in explaining how hearers not only understand most metaphorical utterances, but typically understand them in the way the speaker intended. A pragmatic approach such as relevance theory, which fits well with many of the assumptions of cognitive linguistics, suggests a natural way of explaining how the inferences hearers draw in communicative situations might be suitably constrained. In the second place, although cognitive linguists and relevance theorists have both emphasised the importance of inference in metaphor interpretation, cognitive linguists face a major challenge in explaining how the inferences that hearers draw in the course of utterance comprehension are properly warranted. Lakoff and Johnson (2003: 246) see the key to their approach to conceptual metaphor as lying in the fact that "we systematically use inference patterns from one conceptual domain to reason about another." But as both conceptual metaphor theorists and blending theorists recognise, not all the inferential patterns from one conceptual domain are valid when carried over to the other. What is needed is some way of distinguishing mere conceptual associations or co-activations from valid inferences. Here again, relevance theory suggests a possible way out. What makes it valid to draw a particular inference in interpreting a given utterance is that, unless this inference were valid, the utterance would not yield enough implications to be relevant in the expected way. Thus, a speaker who formulates her utterance in such a way as to encourage her hearer to derive a certain inference is largely responsible for its validity. Thus, here again, a pragmatic account of metaphor of the type proposed by relevance theory might have worthwhile implications for cognitive linguistics.

References

Astington J. et al. (eds.) 1988. *Developing theories of mind*. Cambridge, New York.

Barsalou L. 1987. The instability of graded structure in concepts. – Neisser B. (ed.) *Concepts and conceptual development*. Cambridge, New York: 101–140.

Barsalou L. 1993. Flexibility, structure and linguistic vagary in concepts. – Collins A. et al. (eds.) *Theories of memory*. Hove: 29–101.

Carston R. 2002. *Thoughts and utterances: The pragmatics of explicit communication*. Oxford.

Fauconnier G., Turner M. 2002. *The way we think: Conceptual blending and the mind's hidden complexities*. New York.

Fauconnier G., Turner M. 2008. Rethinking metaphor. – Gibbs R. (ed.) *The Cambridge handbook of metaphor and thought*. Cambridge: 53–66.

Gibbs R. 1994. *The Poetics of Mind: Figurative Thought, Language and Understanding*. Cambridge.

Gibbs R. 1998. The fight over metaphor in thought and language. – Katz N. et al. (eds.) *Figurative language and thought*. New York, Oxford: 88–118.

Gibbs R., Tendahl M. 2006. Cognitive effort and effects in metaphor comprehension: Relevance theory and psycholinguistics. – *Mind & Language* 21: 379–403.

Glucksberg S. 2001. *Understanding figurative language: From metaphors to idioms*. Oxford.

Grady J.E. 1997. THEORIES ARE BUILDINGS revisited. – *Cognitive Linguistics* 8: 267–290.

Hampe B. 2005. On the role of iconic motivation in conceptual metaphor: Has metaphor theory come full circle? – Maeder C. et al. (eds.) *Outside in, inside-out. Iconicity in language and literature*. [vol. 4]. Amsterdam: 39–66.

Higashimori I. 2002. Metaphor understanding in relevance theory: From loan concept metaphor to TIME is SPACE metaphor. – *Translation and Meaning* [Part 6].

Lakoff G., Johnson M. 1980. *Metaphors we live by*. Chicago. [2nd edition 2003].

Lasersohn P. 1999. Pragmatic halos. – *Language* 75: 522–551.

Liszkowski U. et al. 2008. Twelve-month-olds communicate helpfully and appropriately for knowledgeable and ignorant partners. – *Cognition* 108: 732–739.

McGlone M. 2001. Concepts as metaphors. – Glucksberg S. *Understanding figurative language: From metaphors to idioms*. Oxford: 90–115.

Matsui T. et al. 2006. On the role of language in children's early understanding of others as epistemic beings. – *Cognitive Development* 21: 158–173.

Matsui T. et al. 2009. Understanding of speaker certainty and false-belief reasoning: A comparison of Japanese and German preschoolers. – *Developmental Science* 12: 602–13.

Müller C. 2008. *Metaphors dead and alive, sleeping and waking: A dynamic view*. Chicago.

Ruiz de Mendoza Ibáñez F., Perez Hernandez L. 2003. Cognitive operations and pragmatic implication. – Panther K.-U., Thornburg L. (eds.) *Metonymy and pragmatic inferencing*. Amsterdam: 23–49.

Sodian B. 2004. Theory of mind: The case for conceptual development. – Schneider W. et al. (eds.) *Young children's cognitive development*. London: 95–130.

Southgate V. et al. 2007. Infant pointing: Communication to cooperate or communication to learn? – *Child Development* 78: 735–740.

Southgate V. et al. 2009. Sensitivity to communicative relevance tells young children what to imitate. – *Developmental Science*: 1013–1019.

Sperber D., Wilson D. 1995. *Relevance: Communication and cognition*. [2nd edition]. Oxford.

Sperber D., Wilson D. 1998. The mapping between the mental and the public lexicon. – Carruthers P., Boucher J. (eds.) *Language and thought*. Cambridge: 184–200.

Sperber D., Wilson D. 2002. Pragmatics, modularity and mindreading. – *Mind & Language* 17: 3–23.

Sperber D., Wilson D. 2008. A deflationary account of metaphors. – Gibbs R. (ed.) *The Cambridge handbook of metaphor and thought*. Cambridge: 84–105.

Tendahl M., Gibbs R. 2008. Complementary perspectives on metaphor: Cognitive linguistics and relevance theory. – *Journal of Pragmatics* 40: 1823–1864.

Vega Moreno R. 2007. *Creativity and convention: The pragmatics of everyday figurative speech*. Amsterdam.

Wellman H. et al. 2001. Meta-analysis of theory of mind development: The truth about false belief. – *Child Development* 72: 655–684.

Wilson D. 2009. Irony and metarepresentation. *UCL Working Papers in Linguistics* 21: 183–226.

Wilson D. [forthcoming]. Pragmatic processes and metarepresentational abilities: The case of verbal irony. – Matsui T. (ed.) *Pragmatics and theory of mind*. Amsterdam.

Wilson D., Carston R. 2007. A unitary approach to lexical pragmatics: Relevance, inference and ad hoc concepts. – Burton-Roberts R. (ed.) *Pragmatics*. Basingstoke: 230–259.

Wilson D., Carston R. 2008. Metaphor and the 'Emergent Property' problem: A relevance-theoretic approach. – *The Baltic International Yearbook of Cognition, Logic and Communication* 3 (2007). Online: http://www.thebalticyearbook.org/.

Wilson D., Sperber D. 2002. Truthfulness and relevance. – *Mind* 111: 583–632.

Wilson D., Sperber D. 2004. Relevance theory. – Horn L., Ward G. (eds.) *The Handbook of pragmatics*. Oxford: 607–632.

Studia Linguistica Universitatis Iagellonicae Cracoviensis
128 (2011)

GRZEGORZ SZPILA
Jagiellonian University, Cracow

Teresa Zofia Orłoś et al. (eds.). *Wielki czesko-polski słownik frazeologiczny / Velký česko-polský frazeologický slovník*. Kraków 2009

Wielki czesko-polski słownik frazeologiczny is an ambitious enterprise: not only is it the most sizeable dictionary of Czech and Polish phraseology to date but also and, more importantly, it is a well executed lexicographical task. The dictionary, published in 2009 shortly after the death of the editor-in-chief, Professor Teresa Zofia Orłoś, is as broad in scope as it is clear and consistent in presenting the collected phraseological material.

The dictionary comprises seven sections in all: the introductions written in Polish and Czech (vii–xx) by Orłoś, the bibliography (xxi–xxii) containing both the literature the editor makes reference to in her introductions as well as the dictionaries and sources from which in large part the dictionary material comes, the list of abbreviations and symbols used in the lexicon (xxiii–xxiv), the list of abbreviations employed in the Czech examples (xxv–xxvi), the dictionary itself (1–668), and the index of Polish-Czech phraseological units (669–775).

The introduction to the dictionary is more than just the obligatory tour through the macro- and microstructure of the lexicon. In this part Professor Orłoś addresses several aspects of the language contact between Czechs and Poles, which in one way or another have been translated into the creation of this dictionary. The editor starts with the importance of the political and cultural relationship between the two neighbouring countries, in which the role of the Czech language surfaces on more than one occasion. Apart from the obvious contact between the two European (and European Union) countries, Orłoś claims that interest in the Czech language is evinced by the fact that many young people take up courses in the language at Polish universities and elsewhere. In the Czech Republic Polish courses are also run at university level, with the presence of both languages in the media of the respective countries as well as academic, cultural and political exchange between Poland and the Czech Republic. The dictionary is thus addressed to all those wishing to keep and strengthen these contacts via their improved knowledge of the Czech language: students, translators, interpreters amongst others.

In the introduction the dictionary is presented against a background of Czech-Polish lexicography. This which includes a few dictionaries of phraseological units, as well as the Czech dictionaries, both general and those of phraseologisms, which served the Polish team as the source of the entries.

The adjective in the title *frazeologiczny* ('phraseological') is used in its broad sense, that is the dictionary registers combinations of at least two words with more or less opaque meaning (VIII). However, it needs to be said that in the dictionary we can find expressions which can be classified as collocations, with meanings that are semantically transparent, for instance: *holá/očividná/pustá/vyložená lež, očitý svědek, skryté/tajné přání*. The lexicon can by any standard be understood as a dictionary of idioms *par excellence* as it includes winged words, sayings and proverbs as well. The majority of the examples come from the dictionaries mentioned in the introduction. However, as the editor says (IX), some entries represent phraseological units which have not been yet registered in Czech dictionaries. The latter came from TV programmes and the Internet as well as personal contacts between the editorial team and their Czech friends and acquaintances. The lexicon contains circa 5000 phraseological units. This is an impressive number even if we can find some gaps in the collected material (cf. the lack of *ani za živého boha – za Chiny Ludowe, boj o koryto – wyścig szczurów, být bit jako žito – dostać lanie, být blahem bez sebe – być w siódmym niebie*), which is not so much a criticism as an acknowledgment of the fact that the work of lexicographers is always plagued by the issue of choosing some lexical material over other possible candidates.

In the Polish component of the lexicon, that is the Polish equivalents, the authors used some Polish phraseological sources, amongst which Müldner-Nieckowski's *Wielki słownik frazeologiczny języka polskiego* (2003) seems to be the major authority in establishing the counterparts of the Czech phraseological units.

The macrostructure of the lexicon is arranged around the key words of the phraseological units. That means that each registered phraseologism is placed according to the alphabetical position of the key lexical element. The key words are in the main nouns, although on some occasions the key elements are verbs or adjectives, for example: *někomu spadla čelist* can be found under the key element *čelist*, *jiná písnička* under *písnička*; *říkat si o to* under *říkat*, *vzít to z(v)ostra* under *vzít*, *mlčet jako zarytý* under *zarytý*, *přísně utajený* under *utajený*. In some cases the key word does not belong to any open class of words, such as *sám a sám*, which is located under the lexeme *sám*. This arrangement of phraseological units is, according to the authors, easier to manage than the thematic arrangement found in Müldner-Nieckowski's dictionary. In case of uncertainty, the user is advised to take advantage of the Polish-Czech index of phraseologisms, which refers him to the given entry of a Czech expression.

Many phraseological units in the dictionary have more than one variant, although there are also many phraseological units represented by one form only, for example: *fata morgána, stavět na písku, zdravý nemocný*. The lexicon does not fail to list possible grammatical and lexical variations either, for instance: *bít se / bojovat / bránit se jako lev, mít dobrou hubu / mít hubu pěkně proříznutou, ježkovy oči/voči/zraky*.

In this case the phraseological unit is listed under the first variant keyword, as in *jít na flám/tah*, which has to be looked up at *flam*. Nevertheless, some expressions are not accompanied by all their variants, for instance, the phraseological unit *sbíhají se mu sliny v ústech* has another variant *sbíhají se někomu v puse sliny* and for *dělat/ udělat brajgl* we can cite one more verb: *ztropit* (neither is listed in the dictionary).

The microstructural information in each entry contains register and style labels, such as pot. 'colloquial' (which for some reason is not listed in the abbreviations section of the lexicon), iron. 'ironic', wulg. 'vulgar', pol. 'political', publ. 'journalistic' and many others. The authors are also right in stating that certain labels assigned by dictionaries do not always correspond to the users' actual usage of the phraseologisms.

Semantically speaking, each entry is provided with information of two types. Firstly, the meaning of a Czech phraseologism is non-phraseologically paraphrased in the Polish language. This semantic explanation of the sense enables the user to comprehend the semantics of the Czech expression. The explication of the sense of a Czech phraseologism is at the same time a paraphrastic clarification of the corresponding Polish equivalent, be it a phraseologism or a free syntagma or a lexeme. Thus Czech users can simultaneously make sure that the sense of a Czech expression covers the meaning of the Polish counterpart.

The most important part of the dictionary is nevertheless the selection of suitable equivalents. The authors distinguish three types of Polish counterparts. Firstly, in cases when the Czech expression has a Polish phraseological equivalent, the authors opt in the first place for that which contains the same key word as the Czech phraseologism, for instance: *utopit/otrávit červa – zalać/zalewać robaka, přejít od slov/řeči k činům – przejść od słów do czynów, morální políček – być dla kogoś policzkiem*. Secondly, in very many cases the Czech phraseological units have formal and semantic equivalents in the Polish language, which the dictionary duly registers, cf. *desátá múza – dziesiąta muza, duševní pokarm/strava – strawa duchowa, psí život – pieskie życie*. In other cases the lexicon records Polish counterparts that are only semantically equivalent: *vykročit/vkročit do života/světa – stanąć na własnych nogach, mít špičku – być na rauszu, řádit jako tajfun – iść jak burza, noční sůva – nocny marek*. Even culture-bound expressions are matched with Polish equivalents, for instance the Czech phraseologism *lhát jajo baron Prášil* has the following Polish equivalent *kłamać jak z nut*.

Thirdly, if there is a lack of suitable Polish equivalents, the dictionary cites Polish phraseologisms with related senses: *špivané řemeslo – brudne interesy, mokra/ brudna robota, být/pocházet z malých poměrů; vyrůsat v malých poměrach – być/ żyć w trudnych warunkach, (musieć) zaciskać pasa; wywodzić się / pochodzić z prostej rodziny / nizin społecznych, být v pohybu – (zmieniać się) z dnia na dzień, być w ciągłym ruchu.*

If a Polish equivalent has the same key word the dictionary registers possible variants as well, for instance: *kam ho sem čerti nosou? – gdzie kogoś diabli niosą, że też go diabli przynieśli/nadali, sbíhají se mu sliny v ústech – ślinka leci/cieknie/ napływa/płynie komuś do ust, (být) bledý / zblednout jako plátno – (stać się) biały/*

blady jak płótno/kreda/opłatek. It must be mentioned that some variants of the Polish equivalents were not listed, for instance: *bít (moc) do očí/voči* vs. *rzucać się w oczy* and *uderzać w oczy*.

Each entry is accompanied with examples extracted from the Czech National Corpus, the Internet version of *Lidové noviny* and other sites, as well as various Czech dictionaries. In some cases the phraseologisms are illustrated with examples of the authors' making. Each example is translated into Polish, which shows the contextual – translational – equivalents of the Czech phraseological units. The final element of the entry is a reference to synonymous phraseologisms registered in the dictionary, which allows the user to compare and contrast the given expressions, for example: *vzácný pták = velké zvíře, chopit se díla = jít na věc, mít buňky na/pro něco = mít něco od pánaboha.*

Concluding, it must be stressed that the dictionary in question is an exceptionally valuable lexicographic achievement. It focuses not only on nominal, verbal, adjectival and adverbial phraseological units, but it also describes propositional phraseologisms, such as sayings, proverbs and winged words, and quantitatively its scope exceeds all the other Czech-Polish phraseological dictionaries. The presentation of the material is executed with clarity and precision, providing the potential reader with all the necessary information regarding phraseological meanings, actual usage, style and register as well as helping him to establish the best Polish equivalents possible. It is undoubtedly as inestimably useful a reference book for students of Czech in Poland as well as Czechs learning Polish as it is an ideal point of reference for lexicographers compiling dictionaries of other languages. In its final form the dictionary is a perfect tribute to the work and legacy of the late Professor Teresa Zofia Orłoś, a fact of which Henryk Wróbel in a short postlude makes suitable mention.

GUIDELINES FOR AUTHORS

Contents

Articles should be written in English, and contain a short abstract in English and a list of keywords.

Non-English speakers are required to have their manuscripts read by a native speaker before submission. Manuscripts should be checked with regard to consistency of spelling, punctuation and use of abbreviations. National colloquialisms should be avoided, and gender neutral language used.

Format

The electronic copy of the manuscript should be in one of the following formats: OpenDocument (odt), Microsoft® Word 97/2000/XP/2003 (doc) or LaTeX (tex). The body of the text should be typed in Times New Roman, 12 points, and with 1.5 line spacing.

The text should be encoded in Unicode. Symbols thus unavailable should be changed to unequivocal escape sequences (e.g. #V/ for 'capital letter V with acute'). In such case, a list of all escape sequences used is required, together with an explicit clarification.

Graphs, charts, etc. should be attached separately in one of the following formats: Portable Document Format (pdf), Encapsulated PostScript (eps), Scalable Vector Graphics (svg), LaTeX (tex), Portable Network Graphics (png), JPEG (jpg), Graphics Interchange Format (gif), Tagged Image File Format (tiff), GIMP XCF Image (xcf), or clear freehand.

Citations and abbreviations

We ask the Authors to compile their bibliography in keeping with the following guidelines:
- In the description of a publication the basic separation sign is a dot. Use a comma when enumerating names, places of publication, or information placed in square brackets; write page numbers after a colon, and separate the collective publication from its fragment with a dash.
- Information concerning authors / editors
  Place the initial of the first name followed by a dot after the author's surname; do not separate the initials of names of the same author / editor with a space;

separate two authors/editors with a comma. Additional information concerning the authors is placed after the surname(s); if there are more than two authors/ editors, provide only the name of the first one and use the abbreviation *et al.*; the author of a review obtains the abbreviation (*rev.*); the editor(s) is/are marked with the abbreviation (*ed./eds.*)

- Typeface
  Write the title of the primary item (a book or a journal) in italics; the remaining titles (of an article, chapter, entry in a collective publication) are left in the Roman type.
- Additional information concerning a journal
  Numerical data supplementing the title of the journal are written with Arabic digits and separated with a dot.
- Additional information concerning a book
  All the additional information concerning a book is placed after the title, in square brackets, written with Roman numerals and with the use of the following abbreviations: *vol.* (volume, fascicle), *ed.* (edition), *transl.* (translated by), *reprint.*
- Place of publication
  Write names of the places of publication in the language of the original; several places of publication are separated with a comma; the name of the country or state specifying the place of publication is placed in brackets after the name of the city.
- Explanation of abbreviations
  The explanation of abbreviations should be provided at the beginning of the bibliographical information, before other items.
- Footnotes should not contain references to bibliographical information – this should be inserted in the continuous text, e.g. Puzynina (1997), (Puzynina 1997: 22).

Examples:

Dahl = Даль В. 1978–1980. *Толковый словарь живого великорусского языка.* [vol. I–IV]. Москва.

ÈSTJa I = Sevortjan È.V. 1974. *Ètimologičeskij slovaŕ tjurkskich jazykov.* [vol. I *glasnye*]. Moskva.

ÈSTJa III = Sevortjan È.V., Levitskaja, L.S. 1989. *Ètimologičeskij slovaŕ tjurkskich jazykov.* [vol. III *dž, ž, j*]. Moskva.

EWU = Benkő L. (ed.) 1993–1994. *Etymologisches Wörterbuch des Ungarischen.* Budapest.

Campbell L. 1990. Syntactic reconstruction and Finno-Ugrian. – Andersen H., Koerner K. (eds.) *Historical linguistics 1987.* Amsterdam (Philadelphia): 51–94.

DeCock S. et al. 1998. An automated approach to the phrasicon of EFL learners. – Granger S. (ed.) *Learner English on computer.* London, New York: 67–79.

Georg S. (rev.) 1999–2000. Werner 1997b. – *Ural-Altaische Jahrbücher. Neue Folge* 16: 304–309.

Hughes A., Lascaratou C. 1982. Competing criteria for error gravity. – *English Language Teaching Journal* 36.3: 175–182.

Krapels A.R. 1990. An overview of second language writing process research. – Kroll B. (ed.) *Second language writing.* Cambridge: 37–56.

Laurence S., Margolis E. 2005. Number and natural language. – Carruthers P. et al. (eds.) *The innate mind: structure and contents.* Oxford: 216–235.

Milewski T. 1948. *Zarys językoznawstwa ogólnego*. [pars II *Rozmieszczenie języków*, vol. II *Atlas*]. Lublin, Kraków.

Serbat G. 1996. *Grammaire fondamentale du latin*. [vol. VI *L'emploi des cas en latin*, vol. I *Nominatif, Vocatif, Accusatif, Génitif, Datif*]. Louvain, Paris.

Slobin D. 1996. From 'thought and language' to 'thinking for speaking'. – Gumerz J., Levinson S. (eds.) *Rethinking linguistic relativity*. Cambridge (UK): 70–96.

Werner H. 1997a. *Die ketische Sprache*. Wiesbaden.

Werner H. 1997b. *Abriß der kottischen Grammatik*. Wiesbaden.

Submission

Altogether, three copies of the manuscript are required. One hard copy should be sent to:

Barbara Podolak
Institute of Oriental Studies
al. Mickiewicza 9/11
31-120 Cracow, Poland

and two electronic copies, a pdf and an odt/doc/tex, should be sent to:

barbara.podolak@uj.edu.pl.

Authors are asked to state their affiliation in the manuscript or the accompanying letter.

Marta Dąbrowska   md_doc@interia.pl
Marcin Jaroszek   marcin.jaroszek@uj.edu.pl
Michael Knüppel   MichaelKnueppel@gmx.net
Janina Labocha   janina.labocha@uj.edu.pl
Michał Németh   michal.nemeth@uj.edu.pl
Dariusz Piwowarczyk   dariusz_piwowarczyk@yahoo.com
Marzanna Pomorska   marzanna.pomorska@uj.edu.pl
Magnús Snædal   hreinn@hi.is
Kamil Stachowski   kamil.stachowski@gmail.com
Marek Stachowski   stachowski.marek@gmail.com
Grzegorz Szpila   grzegorz.szpila@uj.edu.pl
Anna Tereszkiewicz   anna.tereszkiewicz@interia.pl
Deirdre Wilson   deirdre.wilson@ucl.ac.uk